The King

The King

A Life of King Juan Carlos of Spain

José Luis de Vilallonga

Translated by Anthea Bell

WEIDENFELD & NICOLSON

London

First published in Great Britain in 1994 by
Weidenfeld & Nicolson, an imprint of
the Orion Publishing Group Limited,
5 Upper St Martin's Lane, London WC2H 9EA

Originally published as *Le Roi*

A catalogue record for this book is available
from the British Library

ISBN 0 297 81358 7

Typeset by Create Publishing
Services Ltd, Bath, Avon
Printed and bound in Great Britain by
Butler & Tanner Ltd, Frome and London

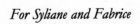

For Syliane and Fabrice

Contents

What is Spain? An eddy of dust on the road of history after a great people has passed at the gallop.

José Ortega y Gasset

We, who are as worthy as you, swear allegiance to you who are no worthier than us and accept you as our sovereign, so long as you will respect our laws and our liberties.

(Oath of allegiance sworn to the kings of Aragon
by their subjects at the ceremony of investiture)

Family Tree of the
Spanish Royal Family

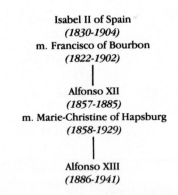

Isabel II of Spain
(1830-1904)
m. Francisco of Bourbon
(1822-1902)

Alfonso XII
(1857-1885)
m. Marie-Christine of Hapsburg
(1858-1929)

Alfonso XIII
(1886-1941)   m

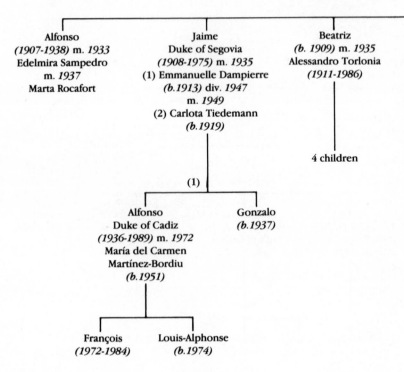

Alfonso	Jaime	Beatriz
(1907-1938) m. *1933*	Duke of Segovia	*(b. 1909)* m. *1935*
Edelmira Sampedro	*(1908-1975)* m. *1935*	Alessandro Torlonia
m. *1937*	(1) Emmanuelle Dampierre	*(1911-1986)*
Marta Rocafort	*(b.1913)* div. *1947*	
	m. *1949*	
	(2) Carlota Tiedemann	
	(b.1919)	

4 children

(1)

Alfonso	Gonzalo
Duke of Cadiz	*(b.1937)*
(1936-1989) m. *1972*	
María del Carmen	
Martínez-Bordiu	
(b.1951)	

François	Louis-Alphonse
(1972-1984)	*(b.1974)*

Victoria of Great Britain
(1819-1901)
m. Albert of Saxe-Coburg Gotha
(1819-1861)

Beatrice
(1857-1944)
m. Prince Henry of Battenberg
(1858-1896)

Victoria Eugenia of Battenberg
(1887-1969)

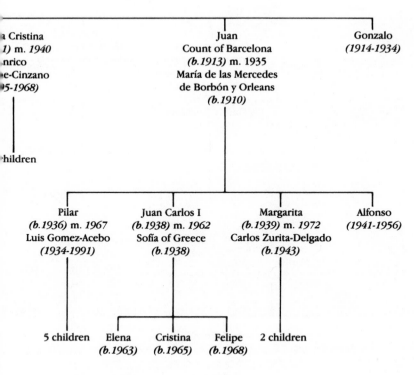

a Cristina
1) m. *1940*
nrico
e-Cinzano
5-1968)

Juan
Count of Barcelona
(b.1913) m. 1935
María de las Mercedes
de Borbón y Orleans
(b.1910)

Gonzalo
(1914-1934)

hildren

Pilar
(b.1936) m. *1967*
Luis Gomez-Acebo
(1934-1991)

Juan Carlos I
(b.1938) m. *1962*
Sofía of Greece
(b.1938)

Margarita
(b.1939) m. *1972*
Carlos Zurita-Delgado
(b.1943)

Alfonso
(1941-1956)

5 children

Elena
(b.1963)

Cristina
(b.1965)

Felipe
(b.1968)

2 children

Chronology

14 April 1931: proclamation of the Republic in Madrid. King Alfonso XIII goes into exile in Rome.

16 February 1936: victory of the Popular Front.

17 July 1936: beginning of the Spanish Civil War.

3 January 1938: birth of the Infante Juan Carlos in Rome.

15 January 1941: Alfonso XIII abdicates in favour of his third son Don Juan, who takes the title of Count of Barcelona.

28 February 1941: death of Alfonso XIII in Rome.

March *1942*: the royal family leaves Fascist Rome and joins Queen Victoria Eugenia in Lausanne.

2 February 1946: Franco promulgates the Fundamental Laws making Spain a kingdom without a king.

25 August 1948: meeting between the Count of Barcelona and Franco off La Coruña. They settle Juan Carlos's future.

8 November 1948: Juan Carlos goes to Spain to pursue his studies there.

29 December 1954: meeting between the Count of Barcelona and Franco in Spain to decide on the subsequent course of Juan Carlos's studies.

January *1955 – December 1959*: Juan Carlos attends the three military academies.

18 July 1957: Franco officially announces that after him Spain will have a Catholic king, without specifying a name.

1960: Juan Carlos enters the independent university of Madrid.

14 May 1962: the marriage in Athens of Juan Carlos of Spain and Sofía of Greece.

14 December 1966: referendum on the Organic Law of the kingdom. 95% of the votes are in favour of the Spanish monarchy.

17 July 1969: Franco announces that Juan Carlos is to be his successor. On 22 July 1969 he submits his successor's name to the Cortes. Next day the new Prince of Spain takes an oath of loyalty to Franco.

20 December 1973: assassination of Admiral Luis Carrero Blanco, vice-president of the government.

19 July 1974: Franco is hospitalized. Juan Carlos temporarily assumes power.

31 October 1975: Juan Carlos again becomes temporary head of state.

2 November 1975: Juan Carlos goes to El Aaiún during the Spanish Sahara crisis.

20 November 1975: death of Franco.

22 November 1975: Juan Carlos takes the oath as King of Spain.

***July** 1976*: Juan Carlos appoints Adolfo Suárez prime minister.

16 November 1976: political amnesty. Reform of the political institutions on 15 December. Legalization of the Spanish Communist Party on 9 April 1977 and of the trades unions on 29 April.

14 March 1977: the Count of Barcelona renounces his dynastic rights in favour of his son.

15 June 1977: victory of Adolfo Suárez's UCD (Democratic Centre Party) in the elections to the parliamentary Cortes, the first elections held under a system of universal suffrage.

27 December 1977: the new constitution.

23 February 1981: attempted *coup d'état* in which Lieutenant-Colonel Tejero seizes the Cortes.

28 October 1982: Felipe González and the socialists win the parliamentary elections.

1 January 1986: Spain enters the EEC.

12 April 1992: the king opens the World Exhibition in Seville.

Introduction

When we began the conversations of which this book is the outcome, Don Juan Carlos asked me, 'Do you think there was any monarchist feeling in Spain when I became king on 22 November 1975?'

I was taken aback, and hesitated for a few seconds before replying. I knew from my father, who had spent part of his life in the service of Don Alfonso XIII,[1] how dangerous it can be to tell kings the unvarnished truth. On the other hand the truth, of all things, can hardly be improved upon without the risk of making it a half-truth, and I was particularly anxious to be sincere with this man who always looked me straight in the eye and had made me the royal gift of trusting me.

'No, Señor,' I replied, 'there was no monarchist feeling when you came to the throne except among a few nostalgically minded people who remembered your grandfather's reign.'

Don Juan Carlos kept his eyes on me, and I added, 'But a "Juancarlist" feeling very soon arose.'

I could tell he did not care for this comment, and we changed the subject.

Some years earlier, in September 1982, during the weeks running up to the parliamentary elections which gave an absolute majority to the PSOE (the *Partido Socialista Obrero Español,* the Spanish Socialist Party), I had a long conversation with Felipe González in his unpretentious flat

---

[1] King of Spain, reigned until 14 April 1931, when the republic was proclaimed.

in the La Estrella quarter of Madrid. We were in a tiny sitting room furnished with a few armchairs upholstered in black leather and a low table on which I noticed several boxes of cigars, the latest disc of Camarón de la Isla,[1] and a collection of poems by Miguel Hernández. Felipe, following the direction of my gaze, asked me, 'Did you know that when they brought Miguel Hernández's execution warrant to Franco for his signature, he said crossly, "Another Lorca? No, certainly not!", and commuted the death sentence to a term of imprisonment, which poor Miguel was never to complete. Hernández seemed pre-destined to meet a violent death; Valentín González, the famous "Campesino", nearly had him shot during the Civil War when he discovered that his political commissioner in the 5th Regiment was reciting poetry to the militiamen in the trenches.'

Carmen Romero, married to the young secretary-general of the PSOE and lovely in the style of those Andalusian women whose innate beauty shines through the irony lurking in their eyes, gave us coffee and cognac. During the interview which followed, I asked Felipe the same question Don Juan Carlos was to ask me several years later: 'Was there any monarchist feeling in Spain at the time of Franco's death?'

Felipe's long, brown hands made an airy gesture. 'None at all.'

'Is there today?'

He thought for a moment before replying. 'What we have today, at the national level, is a feeling of deep respect and admiration for the way the King of Spain does his job. I think that's the fundamental point. It is also the reason why, when people discuss the importance of the monarchy as an institution compared with the importance of the person of the king, I can't see any real basis for such a discussion. I can never go along with the argument put forward by some monarchists – there aren't many of them, luckily – who claim that the monarchy is the real substance and democracy is only a by-product. Personally, I believe that the real substance of the monarchical system is in fact the deep need felt by the Spanish people for liberty and peaceful coexistence in a democracy. That's what really matters. It is not a question of putting the institution before the person of the king, or vice versa. Don Juan Carlos is a man whom the Spanish people respect, and that man embodies the

[1] Famous gypsy flamenco singer who died in July 1992.

institution. Because let us be under no illusion, it was not the institution in itself which won the Spaniards over but the king.'

Felipe González lit one of the long Havana cigars which Fidel Castro sends him regularly by diplomatic bag, and murmured, 'Fortunately for this monarchy, there is no monarchist party to "defend" it. Monarchists are always the people who undermine monarchies.'

I then asked if he thought it possible that the old question of monarchy versus republic would resurface once the socialists were in power. Felipe González answered with a categorical 'No.' And as Carmen Romero listened, amusement in her eyes, he told me, 'Before my first interview with Don Juan Carlos, whom I'd never met before, I had talked to the members of the party management about the possibility that I might have to discuss that subject. Personally I didn't think that the king, as head of state, would broach it. So I was extremely surprised when Don Juan Carlos, sitting opposite me, asked in a disconcertingly casual way, "Tell me, why are you socialists republicans?" I explained that the PSOE had never yet supported the monarchy because the monarchy had always been anti-socialist.'

'I'm not a politician,' I said, 'only a writer with a fair number of contacts in the political world, but I think I can guess what was in the king's mind.'

Felipe looked at me with curiosity. 'Perhaps our guesses are the same,' he replied.

'My own belief is that Don Juan Carlos looks forward to the day when he will reign with a socialist government in office.'

Felipe smiled as he lit a second cigar.

'Intelligent people on the Right – and such people do exist – are taking a very close interest in that proposition,' he told me. 'They know the king and the monarchy will be well and truly established on the day we govern Spain with Don Juan Carlos as head of state. That is when the king will realize his father the Count of Barcelona's old dream and become incontestably "king of all the Spanish people".'

Felipe González's smile became quite venomous as he added, 'And there are some even more intelligent people on the Right who think that the monarchy will be even more firmly established when the socialists lose the next elections, ushering in an alternation of power. That will be the proof that Spain has become truly democratic.'

'Am I right in thinking you never met Don Juan Carlos before Franco's death?'

'No, I never met either him or his father. I know that may seem odd, when so many people were moving heaven and earth to get close to them. The general's fatal illness, slow but irreversible this time, had brought out a good deal of sudden and previously dormant loyalty to the members of the royal family. The *Junta Democrática*, whose spokesman you were in Paris, did its best to give the impression that the Count of Barcelona was about to join its ranks. I think the only person who didn't believe it was Santiago Carrillo;[1] he knew Don Juan was too intelligent and clear-headed to mortgage his independence and liberty of mind at the last minute like that. It was the *Junta* people who were keen for me to go to Estoril and meet Don Juan Carlos and the Count of Barcelona at the count's house, the Villa Giralda. I was told he was the real democrat and his son was only heir to the Francoist dictatorship, so we ought to put our money on the father.'

Felipe González brusquely crushed out his cigar in an ashtray advertising Anís del Mono.

'Those people had absolutely no political vision at all,' he went on. 'They wanted to "legitimize" the father at the son's expense, thereby endangering the only chance of bringing the monarchy back to Spain. I refused to take part in such an idiotic operation. There was really nothing I could do in Estoril. Furthermore, I couldn't believe that the Count of Barcelona – a man whose many sacrifices should be given their just due some day – would come between his son and the Crown. Even if he'd wanted to, it struck me that there was a queen mother in the offing keeping a watchful eye open. But that's just my theory; the royal family has never confided in me on that subject. I've only ever spoken to the Count of Barcelona once, and by then his son was King of Spain, but I still think the game being played in Estoril – the classic game played by courtiers with limited minds – was not just politically stupid but dangerous all round, given the circumstances of Spain at the time. To sum it up, the game was to set father against son and alienate the son more and more from his father. There was a touch of mediaeval drama about it all which was quite out of place in the history of a modern country.

---

[1] Secretary-general of the Spanish Communist Party.

4

'I had no contact with Don Juan Carlos either, before he became king,' Felipe went on. 'The first contact between the Spanish monarchy and the PSOE didn't take place until after the 1977 elections. And on that occasion it was not I but another representative of Spanish socialism who met the king. In fact, that was the first time a King of Spain had ever met a member of my party face to face, as you might say.'

Carmen refilled our coffee cups and Felipe lit another cigar.

'It seems extraordinary to me,' I told him, 'that without ever being in touch with either the Count of Barcelona or Don Juan Carlos, or their entourage, you could see what was brewing in Estoril so clearly. Even the leading actors in that particular psycho-drama sometimes seemed to be floundering in the quicksands. And I know what I'm talking about: I visited the Count of Barcelona myself just before Franco's death.'

'In Paris?'

'Yes, at the Marquis of Marianao's. The marquis, a Catalan, used to lend the Count of Barcelona his flat in the Boulevard Malesherbes when the count was in Paris.'

'Why did you go to see him?'

'It's an odd story. When Franco was dying some members of the *Junta Democrática*, in particular its "coordinator", the notary Antonio García Trevijano, were very anxious to enrol the count in their ranks. They were playing the father-against-son card, calling it a matter of breaking with all that had been contaminated by Francoism, which of course included Don Juan Carlos. The Count of Barcelona, however, had not replied to telephone calls or the messages sent to him by Trevijano, Professor Calvo Serer – a monarchist belonging to Opus Dei – and José Vidal Beneyto, an economist who owned orange groves in Valencia. Santiago Carrillo, far and away the most intelligent of them all, who was keeping well out of this futile manoeuvring, suddenly said, "It's obvious the Count of Barcelona isn't going to respond to any of your advances, but he'll be obliged to respond to Vilallonga." "Why me?" I asked, surprised. "Why, because you're a grandee of Spain and have the privilege of being received by the king at your request." '

'Does such a privilege actually exist?' Felipe asked me, amused.

'I really don't know. But we did know that the secretary-general of the Spanish Communist Party seldom spoke lightly.'

'So did the Count of Barcelona receive you?' asked Felipe.

'Within twenty-four hours.'

'What message were you asked to give him?'

'I was supposed to say that we thought he should join the *Junta Democrática* publicly, that being his only means of access to the throne.'

'Your people were suffering from raging paranoia!'

'Yes; I was so well aware of it that I gave him a very different message. I told him, "Señor, Franco could be dead within a few hours, and monarchists like us will then be in a very awkward situation. We shall find ourselves with two kings: Your Majesty in Estoril, Don Juan Carlos in Madrid. What ought we to do?" The Count of Barcelona looked at me for a long time in silence. He had turned very pale. With great self-control, he replied in grave tones, "You must help the prince in every way you can." I thought that if the count was asking us to help his son Don Juan Carlos, then he meant to do the same himself. And I was right. The Count of Barcelona did help his son in every way he could, first by leaving the way clear for him, and later by renouncing his dynastic rights. All things considered, and in spite of the intriguing that went on in Estoril, it was the Count of Barcelona himself who allowed his son to surprise us all so pleasantly. Because we were all mistaken about Don Juan Carlos, I not least.'

'Speaking for myself,' Carmen Romero put in, 'I never really believed in the part the prince was playing while he lived in Franco's shadow. It was too perfect, and at the same time highly improbable. He was obviously hiding all kinds of contradictory feelings under the sullen, indifferent exterior to which he accustomed us.'

'Perhaps those of us who supported his father Don Juan were too busy wishing he hadn't agreed to succeed Franco "as king",[1] I replied. 'I remember that scarcely two or three days after the Caudillo's death I was asked to do a broadcast in Paris with Santiago Carrillo and a sister of Carlos Hugo de Borbón-Parma, the French prince who had made his way into the bunch of pretenders to the throne of Spain. The first thing the radio presenter asked was what we thought of Don Juan Carlos. Santiago Carrillo said he didn't think anything of him; Don Juan Carlos was only a puppet manipulated by the Francoists, and his reign would be brief. I improved on that by saying I too thought he would go down in history under the name of Juan Carlos *el Breve*, Juan Carlos the Brief. But

---

[1] In designating the prince his 'successor, as king', Franco was *establishing* the monarchy and not *restoring* it, as would have been the case if he had chosen the Count of Barcelona.

then, as you know, something no one had anticipated happened: once he was king, Don Juan Carlos turned out to be extraordinarily clear-headed. He managed the transition from dictatorship to democracy with great expertise, and without the spilling of a single drop of blood. He announced a general amnesty, legalized political parties and trade unions and so on, all with exemplary calm and remarkable political good sense.

'Then another equally striking miracle occurred before the very eyes of the astonished Spaniards. The silent and frequently melancholy young prince was swiftly transformed into a warm, cordial, extrovert character. The metamorphosis came almost as a shock to those of us who had thought him a nonentity, perhaps even not very intelligent. Personally I could have kicked myself for my failure to understand that the prince's gloomy silences and his indifference to the snubs he suffered over the years from Francoist leaders were only a facade hiding a fierce determination to get what he wanted: the restoration of the monarchy in Spain, with or without his father.'

'Indeed, he succeeded in remaining a mysterious enigma until the last minute,' said Felipe González. 'Not long ago I was dining in a Madrid restaurant with some bankers; one of them asked why the socialist deputies had remained seated when the king first spoke in the Cortes after the legalization of the political parties. "I don't think we were alone in remaining seated," I told the banker. "Thirty-eight million Spaniards were sitting in front of their television sets, anxious to know what the young king's message to the nation would be. As soon as he had finished speaking we socialists were the first to rise and applaud him, and so did thirty-eight million Spaniards, leaving aside those few who looked nostalgically back and believed the monarchy would put itself at the service of the privileged classes again."'

There was a short pause, and then Felipe asked me, 'I suppose after what you and Carrillo had said on the radio you can't have been very popular with Don Juan Carlos.'

'I feared that myself; it was a very awkward situation for me, but it came to an end very soon and almost by chance. One evening I was dining at Lucio's[1] with Emilio Romero[2] and a woman friend of his. We

---

[1] Restaurant frequented by politicians and journalists.
[2] Famous journalist of the Francoist period.

7

had a table at the bottom of the stairs up to the second floor. We'd reached the coffee stage when I suddenly saw the king coming downstairs, followed by several people I knew slightly. On seeing us, Don Juan Carlos came over to our table, smiling. Emilio and I rose, and so did Emilio's companion. The king greeted Emilio and his friend warmly and then, still smiling, turned and asked me, "How are you? Why haven't you been to see me yet?" Embarrassed, I made profuse if vague excuses. "Call Mondéjar tomorrow and ask him to give you an appointment," the king told me, and he left us in order to speak to a lawyer dining with his wife at a nearby table. Next day I lost no time in telephoning the Marquis de Mondéjar, head of His Majesty's household, and telling him about my conversation with Don Juan Carlos the previous evening. Mondéjar put me down for an audience at 11.00 a.m. the next Tuesday. I need hardly tell you I was still not entirely reassured when I arrived at La Zarzuela.[1] When an aide-de-camp showed me into the king's office he rose, came around his desk and approached me with his hand held out. I greeted him according to protocol with a brief bow of my head, and got in first by saying, "Señor, I have come to ask for *amán*." '

'*Amán?*' asked Carmen Romero, puzzled.

'When a Moroccan commits a serious offence against the Crown,' Felipe told his wife, 'he throws himself at the sultan's feet and asks him for *amán* – pardon for his errors.'

'Exactly. I didn't throw myself at Don Juan Carlos's feet, but it comes to the same thing.

' "Oh yes? So why are you asking for *amán?*" he enquired, an ironic look in his eyes.

'I had hardly begun going through some of the stupid things I had said and written about him when he interrupted me, no longer smiling. "José Luis, you know I have always felt the greatest respect for all who remained loyal to my father until the last minute." And he added, less gravely, "Anyway, I can hardly hold a grudge against anyone who was living abroad, like yourself, since you weren't properly informed about what went on here in Madrid. It had been a long time since the matter at issue was who would or would not be king: the one thing that mattered was to bring the monarchy back to Spain."

[1] The royal family's residence.

'And immediately after saying that, Don Juan Carlos changed the subject and asked for news of my family.'

'Did you see much of Don Juan Carlos during the last years of the Franco regime?' Felipe González asked me.

'No, I saw him only once or twice when he was passing through Paris. But oddly enough I retained a very clear memory of him as a little boy in army officer's uniform, from a photograph on my father's bedside table. During that audience, which dispelled all my fears, I was principally struck, in spite of the king's peals of laughter, by the indefinable sadness which sometimes clouded his eyes. Many years later, at Palma in Mallorca, I introduced my son Fabrice to him. Fabrice was eighteen at the time. Don Juan Carlos asked him some questions about his studies and his future plans; he was cheerful, charming and witty as he talked to my son. When we left the Marivent palace, however, Fabrice commented, "Good heavens, how sad the man seems!" Old Tarradellas once suggested to me, when he was still president of the Catalonian *Generalitat*,[1] "It may be the profound melancholy he can't hide which makes the king's charm so engaging, so that even if you aren't the kind of royalist who supports the monarchy as an institution, you can't help being a royalist who supports this particular monarch!"'

Not long after that first meeting with the king, for the purposes of my book *Les Sabres, la Couronne et la Rose*, I had a long conversation with José Mario Armero, one of the most curious characters in modern Spain. Those well acquainted with his career have nicknamed him the Pink Panther of power because of his ability to enter the ministerial offices of Right and Left with equal ease. He is a lawyer representing various large American companies, the chairman of Europa Press, an extremely talented diplomat, or rather negotiator, and Franco himself is reported to have said of him, 'If Armero had gone to Munich instead of Chamberlain, we wouldn't have had the Second World War.'

It is to José Mario Armero that we owe the return of Picasso's *Guernica* to Spain, despite all the obstacles put in its way by Roland Dumas as the lawyer acting for the painter's family. In his spare time Armero collects everything which has anything to do with the circus. As a devoted admirer of Don Juan Carlos de Borbón, it was Armero who

---

[1] The autonomous government of Catalonia.

organized his first official visit to the United States while he was Prince of Spain and no one – certainly not the bankers – would have bet a brass farthing on his future as king. In default of money from the financiers, Armero made use of his contacts and friendships with influential figures in the American press.

For the first of our many conversations, I saw José Mario Armero in my library, at my home in the Paseo de la Castellana in Madrid. I had written him a note beforehand, simply saying I wanted to talk to him about the king and the monarchy.

'Why me?' he asked straight away, settling himself in the armchair where I usually sit to read.

'Because you're one of the best informed men in this country, and you can tell me a great deal which no one else knows yet. José Mario, are you a royalist?'

Armero thought for quite a while before replying. What I like about the man is his inability to give way to the temptation of telling lies or even half-truths. 'I wasn't programmed to be a royalist,' he said.

'What do you mean?'

'I simply mean if you're a royalist, you must start by understanding what a king is. Or even more simply, you have to be aware of the fundamental differences between a king and a *normal* human being.'

'I don't quite understand you.'

Armero sketched an impatient gesture. 'The king and I are the products of two different social classes,' he said. 'We weren't brought up by the same rules. We don't have the same mentality. We have nothing in common. I didn't serve in the British Navy, like the Count of Barcelona. I didn't marry a Greek princess, like his son. I've never been an exile from my native land. When I travel abroad I go as an ordinary tourist. My wife is Spanish, and I have the tastes of a normal Spaniard.'

'What are you getting at, José Mario?'

'Just this: neither the Count of Barcelona nor his son has ever led a normal life. And they never will. Those two men, who incidentally are very different from each other, have faced situations and had to make decisions which neither you nor I can imagine.'

Armero rose and paced about my library, then stopped suddenly in front of me. 'For instance, I wonder what the Count of Barcelona felt – what his real gut feeling was – on the day his son ascended the throne which was rightfully his.'

'Perhaps he was thinking it had all been arranged in advance?' I suggested.

'Very likely. But we'll never know just when or how. And then again, I wonder what Don Juan Carlos felt, taking the place of his father, who had been waiting years for the moment when he would wear the crown. I think, indeed I am sure, that none of it was done lightly, and both men must have suffered grievous personal tragedy. But what matters to me is the restoration of the monarchy.'

'Of course.'

Armero sat down again and went on talking, in an almost confidential tone now. 'I'm also interested to know whether kings are "dehumanized" to such a degree that they can disregard feelings and rules of conduct which will always be sacrosanct to us *normal* people.'

'I don't think that the monarchy as an institution has any connection with the monarch's own feelings or lack of them,' I said.

'I do. Governing – and like it or not, reigning means governing at the highest level – is getting more and more like running a multinational company. And you can take my word for it, the multinationals always make very thorough enquiries about anyone who is going to head them. Look at it this way: I know my bank manager very well, I know who he is, but I'm not always sure I know just who the king is. Not a man like you and me, in any case. When Louis XIII said he wouldn't be fit to be king if he gave way to his personal feelings, he was cutting himself off from the world of people like me.'

As I made no comment, Armero added, 'So I wonder what kind of man you have to be to smile all day at people you dislike, and shake hands impassively with people you despise. I couldn't do it myself.'

'You'd make a very bad king.'

'You're absolutely right there. But I told you just now I wasn't programmed to be a royalist, and that held good for almost all the young men of my generation. So I am not a monarchist by upbringing and even less so by tradition, never having lived with monarchists at home or at school, or later on at university. In fact I grew up in an atmosphere of outright hostility to the monarchy, a hostility encouraged and even instigated by the Franco regime. Now, and only now, I am aware of the virulence and savagery brought to bear to oppose and suppress the least impulses of supporters of the monarchy. At the time, everything possible was done to discredit the last kings of Spain and particularly the heir to the throne, Don Juan de Borbón, Count of Barcelona, and it was done with extraordinary and glaring dishonesty. Franco, who was probably a royalist himself in his youth, did nothing at all to halt the vicious campaigns unleashed against Don Alfonso XIII, who had started him on his brilliant career. When I was a young student and intoxicated by the regime's anti-monarchist propaganda, I honestly thought the Bourbons were a set of degenerates who had brought Spain to the brink of ruin. Later, much later, I remember reading the *Cartas a un escéptico en materia de monarquía* (Letters to a Sceptic On the Subject of the Monarchy), by José Maria Pemán,[1] with the intention of "becoming" a monarchist, but I'm afraid the book didn't make much of an impression on me.'

'And of course you didn't become a monarchist. Yet you worked on behalf of Don Juan Carlos when he was only a young prince still with an uncertain future ahead of him, and you –'

Armero interrupted me rather abruptly. 'I liked the man from the first, and I thought everything possible should be done to help him. Yes, I do like the man, very much,' he repeated.

'It's said that Franco regarded him as the son he never had.'

Armero reacted as if stung. 'I never believed that was true.' He sought a more comfortable position in his armchair, and explained. 'To understand the relationship between Franco and Don Juan Carlos properly, you have to go back to the final years of the Francoist regime. Since 1969, that is to say, after he was designated the dictator's successor, "as king", Don Juan Carlos had known his father had no chance of becoming King of Spain. With that certain knowledge, he had only one idea in his head – I would even call it a passion: the monarchy must return, even if it had to be at his father's expense. So far as Franco was concerned, he needed an heir who could safeguard the structures of the regime which had arisen from his victory over the republic in 1936. But although Franco had put all his trust in the young prince he thought he had "brought up" so well, I have the impression that at the end of his life he was tempted to withdraw it more than once.'

'But why? The prince had played his part to perfection! He took us all in!'

'Perhaps not Franco, though. Franco was an extremely suspicious

---

[1] Spanish poet and dramatist.

man. With all those who wanted to bring Don Juan Carlos down pressurizing him – and there were a great many such people – Franco began to have his doubts of the prince. He had learnt, for instance, that Don Juan Carlos had long telephone conversations daily with the Count of Barcelona. To Franco, that meant that father and son were in league with each other. It is quite possible that on several occasions Franco thought of backtracking. The members of his own family, in particular his son-in-law the Marquis de Villaverde,[1] were urging him to get rid of Don Juan Carlos as successor elect and nominate his cousin, the mediocre Don Alfonso de Borbón-Dampierre, Duke of Cadiz, and married to Franco's own granddaughter. The Franco family was thinking very seriously of setting up a new ruling dynasty in Spain, the dynasty of Borbón y Martinez.'

'This is where we leave Shakespearean drama for second-rate operetta.'

'But in any case they were misjudging the dictator, who never went back on his decisions. It was too late by then, anyway. Weakened by illness, Franco was chiefly concerned with his family's future, first and foremost its security. Don Juan Carlos would remain his successor. And quite soon the dictator's terrible death agony began. There was something grandiose and dreadful about that death which reminded me of the *Tirano Banderas* by Valle-Inclan.[2] The chastisement of the gods, so to speak. Franco was literally carved up by a team of surgeons under the orders of the Marquis de Villaverde, who was determined to keep his father-in-law alive if only for a few more hours. A year after the dictator's death, the *Sunday Times* of London published a photographic montage parodying Rembrandt's famous picture *The Anatomy Lesson*. It showed the Marquis de Villaverde giving his father-in-law the *puntilla*.[3] Typical of the black humour of the people of Madrid was a parody of the last bulletins on the Generalissimo's health stating that "His Excellency the Head of State came through his third autopsy very well this morning."'

'What do you think accounts for that obscene determination to keep a man alive when he was already as good as dead?'

'There are several explanations. The most simplistic assumes that the Marquis de Villaverde still thought they might get the general to change

---

[1] Cristóbal Martinez-Bordiu, husband of Franco's daughter.

[2] Spanish dramatist.

[3] Bullfighting term: to finish off the dying bull with a small dagger.

his mind and persuade him to name Borbón-Dampierre his successor, "as king", which would have made Villaverde's daughter Queen of Spain. But Borbón-Dampierre was too much of a nonentity for Franco to think seriously of nominating him. There's another and to my mind more plausible explanation. The general's last illness coincided with the date of an imminent appointment to the position of president of the Cortes.[1] If the chronology of events had worked out differently then Rodriguez de Valcárcel, a staunch adherent of the Franco family, might have been prime minister; that didn't happen because Arias Navarro got in first. Although he was a fanatical Francoist – he wept on television when he read Franco's will – Arias Navarro did not enjoy the entire confidence of Franco himself. Rodriguez de Valcárcel, on the other hand, could have guaranteed the continuity of the regime and with it the security of the dictator's family, or so they thought. The Rodriguez de Valcárcel operation, which Villaverde was so keen on, wasn't a political manoeuvre but simply a bit of survival strategy. And the Franco family had good reason to feel concern. Everything seemed to be crumbling around them. Strikes were proliferating, students demonstrating in the streets in ever greater numbers, the *Junta Democrática* was publicly giving press conferences, and Franco was dying in dreadful torment. All things considered, however, the Franco family extricated themselves from this tangle with impunity, and they are still living quietly in a country which was in a way their private *finca*[2] for almost forty years. The King of Spain's conduct towards them was more civilized than Franco's attitude to the monarchists, whom he hounded in the person of the Count of Barcelona.'

We broke off for a little while to drink lemon tea; then I asked Armero, 'Can we go back to Don Juan Carlos's first visit to the United States for a moment? First, why did he go?'

'The prince was very anxious to tell the Americans about the way he envisaged the monarchy in a modern Spain. He wanted his visit to attract plenty of publicity, and to do that he needed money which he didn't have. So I went to see the great Madrid bankers of the time and ask them to finance the visit. They all said the same: they wouldn't contribute a penny. "What's more," they asked me, "how do we know

---

[1] The chamber of deputies of the Spanish parliament.
[2] Large country estate.

the boy really will be king one day?" These were people with rather limited political vision.'

'May I ask who these bankers were?'

'No, you may not! I'm not Zorro or the Count of Monte Cristo. But the bankers – there were three of them – did not think Don Juan Carlos had a future as king ahead of him. You can't blame them; not many Spaniards did think so. But I believe the main reason for their refusal was fear. They probably felt sure they'd have to pay very dear for any contact with the man in La Zarzuela. Remember that at the time the whole social, political and financial life of Spain was based on a belief that Franco would go on for ever. No one had ever looked ahead to the dictator's death. It was as simple as that.'

'If I remember correctly, the prince's visit was a success.'

'Yes, a great success. I had gone to the States several weeks ahead of him, and for want of financial aid from the bankers I'd made contact with my friends on the *New York Times* and *Washington Post*, and in Associated Press and United Press. The prince appeared on television and gave a speech to Congress in impeccable English, which surprised the Spaniards, used as they were to having prime ministers and a head of state who didn't speak a word of any foreign language. I think Don Juan Carlos has never forgotten that visit; to this day, he often mentions it when we're alone together.'

Armero rose to stretch his legs, and went to look at the shelves in my library.

'Just how many photographs of Don Alfonso XIII do you have in this room?' he asked me. 'You're not like those Russian *émigrés* who fill their houses with icons and souvenirs of the tsar's family, are you? Is it nostalgia?'

'No, it isn't. I've always thought Don Alfonso was a great king. He deserved better than the Spanish people of his time. And he deserved an aristocracy with a more rigorous concept of honour, and military men with more loyalty. However, he was surrounded by mediocre politicians and traitors.'

'You knew him well?'

'I first met him when I was a child, and I saw him for the last time in Rome, a few months before his death. He was a great king.'

'Don Juan Carlos is a very great king too,' murmured José Mario. 'Perhaps a more complete king than his grandfather.'

My smile seemed to annoy him.

'I told you I couldn't have come to monarchism through my up-bringing or family tradition,' he said. 'So when I began acting as a monarchist I had other reasons for it. I became a monarchist by force of circumstances, you might say. Today I firmly support the monarchy because it is what suits my country best. That opinion is shared by many of my friends who have been life-long republicans. The king has acted in a manner which allows many republicans to feel like monarchists, and that in itself tells you how much he has surprised us. Personally I regret not having trusted him entirely from the moment I met him. Even when he was still *el Príncipe* he already had an extraordinary feeling for the state and a profound sense of his historic duties. In a man still so young that was admirable as well as surprising. Once king, he pursued the policies of the heir to a liberal and democratic family. I don't think Don Juan Carlos was ever tempted to set up a post-Francoist regime, still less that he ever felt he was Franco's heir, but that was how a lot of people did see it.'

'To my mind, the great achievement of Don Juan Carlos has been to make reality of his father's old dream.'

'I hope that may be some comfort to the Count of Barcelona, a man who has played one of the saddest parts in contemporary history with great dignity and much courage, continually insulted and humiliated by people who couldn't hold a candle to him, including Franco, the most vicious of his enemies. To my generation, the Count of Barcelona is a perfect example of good ethical conduct.'

Some weeks before this interview of mine with Armero the mortal remains of Don Alfonso XIII, which had been lying in a Roman church ever since his death, were brought back to Spain, following in reverse the route Don Alfonso had taken when he left to go into exile. It was a strange, melancholy ceremony, without much pomp and circumstance.

'What do you think of the return of the old king's ashes to San Lorenzo del Escorial, José Mario?' I asked.

'I have what you may consider a curious theory about that. It was a ceremony in a minor key, so to speak, as if to show that the present monarch wanted to break once and for all with the historical past, or more precisely with a monarchical past which belongs to the nineteenth century. It was right for Don Alfonso to rest among his own in the Escorial. But I repeat, it was a ceremony which the king wanted to keep almost a family occasion. Don Juan Carlos is very anxious to win young people who would normally have been republicans, even Francoist anti-monarchists, over to the Crown, but I don't think he minds too much what Don Alfonso XIII's former courtiers or his father the Count of Barcelona's friends think of him. The ceremony of the return of the ashes strikes me as the consummation of a clean break between the king and the old-style monarchists. Don Juan Carlos is right to look for new supporters among the younger generation. I remember vividly the anti-Bourbon feeling in the universities when I was young, a feeling constantly stirred up by the Franco regime. Fortunately that's all over, and today the monarchy seems to me to be firmly rooted, but in my view it has not yet been sufficiently realized. The people who ought to be promoting the institution lack imagination, and so far we don't have a modern "royal entourage". The king's direct advisers are few in number and don't mind taking a back seat. Suárez's ministers used to go about with more grandeur than surrounds the king. It's time to give Don Juan Carlos's monarchy a brand image which will be uplifting, make people dream. Far be it from me to suggest creating a new court, but I would like to see the person of the monarch given the importance it deserves and to which it has a right.'

Armero paused and then, with a faint smile, added, 'Isn't it odd that we are still fascinated by kings in the twentieth century?'

'Are you really fascinated by them?'

'By ours, yes. He was still very young, you know, when I first met him. At that time I was one of those Spaniards who disagreed with the Count of Barcelona's decision to send his son to study in Spain. I thought too much contact between members of the royal family and the dictator in the Pardo palace was not a good idea. In other words, many of us feared Franco's regime might leave its mark on the man who would be King of Spain some day, whether that man was the Count of Barcelona or his son Juan Carlos. However, subsequent events showed us that Don Juan de Borbón had acted very wisely. He had also shown that he was proof against the influence of his entourage, which was frankly hostile to the prince's going to Spain. But the Bourbons are like that: fiercely independent when there are major decisions to be taken. And believe me, you need a very strong personality to disregard the opinions of those around you, whether they are political advisers or family. In his exile in Estoril, Don Juan was surrounded by people who for the most part belonged to the nobility, and whose ideology was sometimes linked to that of the extreme Right. I had an opportunity to talk to several of them, and I can assure you that they were not noted for either intelligence or common sense. I remember one evening in Estoril when someone treated the Count of Barcelona to an impassioned apologia for Blas Piñar, the ultra-Right leader. Don Juan listened gravely without once interrupting. He merely smiled, his expression inscrutable, but that did not mean he wasn't thinking.'

'Did such things happen in Don Juan Carlos's entourage too?'

'The prince was surrounded by a large number of military men, many of them unwilling to accept the political changes advocated by the Count of Barcelona. Generally speaking, these men supported the idea of a monarchy which would be simply the continuation of Francoism. Don Juan de Borbón, however, held that the only possible monarchy must be a popular and democratic one. The prince – entirely in agreement with his father on that point – broke with Francoism as soon as he came to the throne. It staggered us all; there were people who thought they must be dreaming. If you remember that the entourages of both father and son were one hundred per cent Francoist, that says a lot for the present monarch and his father.

'I remember organizing a dinner in Lausanne in honour of Don Juan de Borbón the day after the funeral of Queen Victoria Eugenia.[1] Thereafter the dinner became an annual occasion, and the Count of Barcelona never missed it. So he would come accompanied by several aides-de-camp – well, they had to be called something. On this particular occasion we were reviewing the political events of the year during the dessert course, everyone freely expressing his opinion. When it came to the aides-de-camp, I could hardly believe my ears. One of them – I think he was a lieutenant-colonel or a colonel – was going on about the Reds who had infiltrated everything, the chaotic situation in Spain, the necessity of muzzling all politicians once and for all, etc., etc. His colleagues all agreed with him. I felt I was back at the beginning of the year 1936. I tell you this to emphasize the Count of Barcelona's independence of mind in relation to the men around him.'

'Why did he surround himself with such people, though?'

[1] Widow of Alfonso XIII.

'They had very clear-cut functions, you know, and no doubt Don Juan de Borbón, a thorough professional himself, merely appreciated what they were good for. He didn't employ them as political advisers. I don't think it would be going too far to say these people were there to open doors for him, play golf with him, go out hunting with him.'

'Superior servants, you mean?' I suggested.

'In a way, yes. In the old days, when formality and etiquette were of considerable importance, the members of the king's entourage were called "gentlemen-in-waiting". They wore golden keys on their uniforms – as a symbol showing that they could enter the monarch's private apartments at any time – and everyone was happy. I don't think it would ever have entered Don Juan de Borbón's head to ask the opinion of one of his aides-de-camp on international politics, though. Myself, I would hate to be surrounded by such nonentities.'

After a long pause, Armero told me, 'You know, the monarchists who were opposed to Francoism didn't talk much about democracy. They were monarchists, anti-Francoists, Juanists, but none of them used the word "democracy". While they were at odds with Franco, they were also ferociously hostile to "liberties"; such liberties, in their view, had led to the assassination of Calvo Sotelo[1] and the burning of the Madrid convents which set off the civil war in 1936. When I hear people today claiming that the men who opposed Francoism were fighting for democracy I say no, that was not the case. I'd go even farther: the only monarchist I heard speak of democracy was the Count of Barcelona himself, and it cost him the throne.'

Another pause, and Armero added, with his usual half-smile, 'Don Juan Carlos had one great piece of luck during the years of the Franco regime.'

'What was that?'

'He was able to keep silent.'

[1] Leader of the Spanish Right.

I

Lisbon, November 1948. A fine, icy drizzle was falling on the pink and white city which had hardly settled down for winter yet. Men in black were drinking the first coffee of the day, elbows leaning on the counters of the Chiado bars. In Ribera Velha in the Alfama, barefoot oyster women were putting up their trestles in the shadow of the baroque facades. The more elegant parts of town were still asleep.

At Rossio railway station, the Lusitania Express was about to leave for Spain. Standing to one side of the crowd thronging the platforms a married couple, still young, were giving last-minute advice to a little boy with fair curls who was visibly struggling not to cry. A few feet away from the couple, several grave-faced gentlemen were watching the scene with emotion. When the little boy waved to them for the last time from the footboard of the train, they all sprang to attention.

The Lusitania Express – driven that day by the Duke of Zaragoza in a boiler suit – finally set off. The Count and Countess of Barcelona waited until the train had disappeared from sight before making their way slowly towards the station exit, followed at a distance of a few feet by their small, discreet and silent court. The count suddenly put his right arm round the countess's shoulders and murmured, his face twisted, 'Maria, remember what I tell you now: today our real troubles are beginning.'

Prophetic words. That morning the little boy with tears in his eyes, His Royal Highness Don Juan Carlos de Borbón y Borbón, son of Don

Juan de Borbón y Battenberg – whom the Spanish monarchists addressed as Your Majesty – and of Doña Maria de las Mercedes de Borbón y Orléans, was leaving his family's home in exile in Portugal and going to Madrid, where his education as crown prince would be supervised by strict mentors. Twenty-seven years later the little boy, now King of Spain and commander-in-chief of the Spanish army, would ascend the throne left vacant by Don Alfonso XIII, not as heir to his father, still alive at the time, but in his capacity as 'successor, as king' to General Franco Bahamonde, and charged with preserving the Francoist order exactly as it was.

For the moment Juanito, as his parents, brother and sisters called him at home, was curled up in a corner of his first-class carriage watching the Portuguese countryside go by. Cork oaks as far as the eye could see, neatly whitewashed cottages, vegetable plots like tiny gardens, and emerald-green meadows with goats grazing under the watchful eye of a herdsman's dog.

Juanito had found it very difficult to hold his sobs back when his parents waved goodbye to him from the station platform. But he was strong enough to swallow his tears, knowing that his father would not like to see him cry. Not that this was the first time he had left Estoril and his family. He had already spent many months away from home at the very exclusive Villa Saint-Jean school in Fribourg. His grandmother Queen Victoria Eugenia, widow of Don Alfonso XIII, used to visit him there when it was not his turn to go and spend the weekend with the old lady, who lived in Lausanne. But this time was different. He had left Portugal and his family for a country still unknown to him, a country of which his father had spoken to him in impassioned tones since his earliest childhood. España! A name he had been taught to revere and love, although in spite of everything it frightened him a little, because he knew it was bound up with the dramas and tragedies the Spanish Bourbons had suffered. He knew, for instance, that on the morning of his grandmother's wedding to Don Alfonso XIII an anarchist called Mateo Morral had thrown a great sheaf of red flowers down on the royal carriage from a balcony. There was a bomb concealed inside it. Doña Victoria Eugenia's wedding dress had been spattered with the blood of the men and horses killed around her. And he knew that in 1931 King Alfonso, surrounded in the Oriente palace by a yelling mob prepared to storm it, had temporarily suspended his royal functions so that 'not a drop of Spanish blood' should be shed for his person. It had often been explained to Juanito that one day his father the Count of Barcelona would be crowned King of Spain, and he himself would inherit that crown, which would lie heavy upon him with the weight of a destiny imposed by history, a destiny of which he was not the master. The little boy was roused from his thoughts by the Duke of Sotomayor, one of his travelling companions, who murmured in his ear, 'The Lusitania has just entered Spain, Highness.'

Juanito immediately glued his forehead to the carriage window, curious to see this country called Spain, a name dinned into his ears ever since he was a tiny child. It certainly did not look at all like Portugal. No more leaves and flowers, no more sparkling white villages, and no more green meadows looking as if they had been mown by an English gardener. The Lusitania had suddenly entered another world. The soil passing by before Juanito's eyes now was desperately dry, cracked and arid. The ancient olive trees which had replaced the cork oaks of Portugal seemed to be rooted deep in the centuries. The train raced through Extremadura as if its driver feared he would have to stop in this countryside where even the dogs looked thinner than elsewhere. The young prince's misgivings grew. If the men and women of Spain were as dry and depressing as this landscape, it didn't look as if the life ahead of him would be easy.

Seventeen years earlier, Juanito's grandfather had left the royal palace in Madrid at the wheel of his car to drive to Cartagena, where he would go on board the cruiser taking him to Marseille, the first stop on his journey into exile. Don Alfonso XIII too had seen the old country now rejecting him for ever pass by, his eyes blurred with emotion. The first light of dawn might be translucent, the sky might look as if it would be very clear, but the dethroned monarch may well have reflected that what really suited Spain was sadness. Only in grief, fire and blood did the country attain its magical proportions. Everything around him looked poor, poor and proud: the colourless houses, their windows still closed, the grey donkeys ridden by old men ignoring the flies, the ageless peasant women, their faces seamed by the dust, lines etched by wind and sun, the silent children, shaven-headed, bare-footed, at the roadside, watching him without moving an inch.

The young prince's first sight of the country which he would rule as king one day probably aroused confused feelings not unlike those constricting the heart of Don Alfonso when he left for ever because, in his own words, he had lost the love of his people.

'Is all Spain like this?' asked Juanito, without taking his eyes off the desolate countryside.

The ghost of a smile showed on his companion's lips. 'Oh no, Highness! Spain is the most varied country on earth! We're passing through Extremadura at the moment; if Your Highness thinks it looks poor and infertile, that's because it hasn't rained for months, so I'm told. Usually this countryside is a real paradise.'

The young prince pretended to be reassured. He had heard his father say, 'Courtiers are always doing a balancing act between truth and half-truth, and they always end up saying whatever they think will be least disagreeable for us to hear.'

The Lusitania Express continued on its way for several more hours. Alone in a corner of his carriage again, the young prince realized, with some dismay, that one chapter of his life had closed for ever and now he must face his destiny, a destiny which would oblige him to leave childhood behind him much sooner than other boys of his age, although subconsciously he had been preparing himself for this eventuality for a long time. He had spent most of his early childhood in Estoril, in the Villa Giralda, where the memory of everything Spanish was elevated to the status of a religion. He had often seen visitors – politicians, aristocrats, soldiers out of uniform, intellectuals – arrive at the villa to closet themselves with the Count of Barcelona for hours on end in the little drawing room he used as an office. Most of them left as they had come, keeping in the shadow of the walls for fear spies in the pay of the Francoist political police might note their names. One day, feeling curious, the prince had asked his father, 'Who are these people? What are they doing here?'

The Count of Barcelona had told him, 'They are my loyal supporters, and they come to talk about Spain.'

Spain, that mysterious and slightly frightening place; the child knew by heart the story of the events which had brought about the fall of the dynasty.

'It is true that your grandfather had to leave Spain,' the Count of Barcelona had told him, 'but he was still the king until the day he died.' And the count had added, in a tone which greatly impressed the young prince, 'A king must never abdicate, you see, Juanito. He has no right to abdicate.'

Words which must have re-echoed in the ears of the child grown to be a man, a man whom many Spaniards – myself included – would call a man sent by Providence. And some among us would add, at times: a man whom we do not always deserve.

The Lusitania Express suddenly stopped at the railway station of Villaverde, a small town only a few kilometres from Madrid. Fearing that monarchists aware of the young prince's presence on Spanish soil might give him too enthusiastic a welcome, the government had preferred him to arrive at this insignificant station where only a few goods trains stopped.

Flanked by the Duke of Sotomayor and the Viscount of Rocamora, the little boy climbed out of his carriage and found himself on the platform, where a dozen or so people he had never seen before in his life were waiting for him. He felt chilly, and turned up the collar of his overcoat to protect himself from the icy wind blowing in gusts from the nearby sierra. His navy blue socks left bare knees still scarred by old scratches. At a loss, the little prince looked at the faces of all these strangers, who in their turn were inspecting him with obvious curiosity. Closed, impenetrable faces. Not a smile, not a spontaneous gesture. Only vague phrases of welcome, all strictly according to protocol. 'Did Your Highness have a pleasant journey?' 'I hope Your Highness is not over-tired?' The Duke of Sotomayor quickly made the introductions. Danvila, Oriol, Rodezno, other names: names which meant nothing to the little boy shaking the hands offered to him one by one.

Most of these reserved and distant men who had come to meet the young prince were monarchists 'of the regime', people who, while they paid regular visits to the Count of Barcelona in Estoril, privately put all their force and all their abilities behind the Francoist regime which guaranteed the order preserving their privileges and their peaceful existence. These men always had a useful phrase ready to cover up all their weaknesses, acts of cowardice and sometimes acts of treachery: '*No es el momento oportuno.*'[1] As they saw things, it was never the right moment to stand up to General Franco and insist on his making way for Don Juan de Borbón, Count of Barcelona, rightful heir to the Crown of

---

[1] This is not the right moment.

Spain. We may guess what anxiety some of them felt at the arrival on Spanish soil of the young Prince of the Asturias (the title borne by the eldest sons of the Kings of Spain), in whom they saw someone who might very likely put a spanner in the works.

The long solitude of Don Juan Carlos de Borbón began then and there on Villaverde station platform, lashed by the keen winds from the steppes of Castile.

'Solitude,' Don Juan Carlos told me, looking back to that day, 'begins with the need to keep silent. I spent years knowing that every word I uttered would be reported in high places, having first been analysed and then interpreted as they pleased by people who did not always wish me well.' And he added, 'But silence can be very dangerous too. It fosters misunderstanding. You know the saying, *Quien calla otorga.*'[1]

A motorcade of big black cars was waiting for the procession at the station entrance. The little prince was put into the first car, which immediately set off at high speed. Danvila, who had taken the front seat beside the chauffeur, ordered curtly, *'Al Cerro de los Angeles.'* Travelling fast, the motorcade skirted Madrid and took the road to Toledo.

The Cerro de los Angeles – the Hill of the Angels – is situated right in the geographical centre of the Iberian peninsula. At the top of the hill a huge devotional statue of the Saviour, curiously like the statue which watches over the sleep of the citizens of Rio de Janeiro, stretches its arms out to the faithful who fall at its feet. In 1919 Don Alfonso XIII, the last King of Spain, solemnly consecrated his country to the Sacred Heart of Jesus. A Carmelite convent was built on the spot in memory of this vow. In 1936, during the early days of the civil war, a revolutionary tribunal from Madrid tried the statue and condemned it to death. It was shot at point-blank range by a firing squad of drunk militiamen. Danvila told all this to the little boy freezing with cold in the back of the car. Once he arrived at the convent, and after hearing a Mass which seemed to go on for ever, Don Juan Carlos learned that to the Spaniards the Cerro de los Angeles had come to symbolize the victory of the Francoist troops over 'Red' barbarianism. It was obvious that these gentlemen who acted as intermediaries between the Pardo palace and Estoril, running with the hare and hunting with the hounds, wanted to show the

[1] He who keeps silent makes an admission.

young prince the picture of a Spain that was always divided: victors on one side, vanquished on the other. A picture diametrically opposed to the image of a Spain reunited some day which was the Count of Barcelona's dream.

On the way out of Mass, Don Juan Carlos was asked to repeat the words spoken by his grandfather when Don Alfonso consecrated Spain to the Sacred Heart. The child did so in a trembling voice, his cheeks blue with cold. Then everyone got back into the motorcade, which now took off for Las Jarillas, an unpretentious residence some twenty kilometres from Madrid but in the immediate vicinity of the Pardo palace, where the young Prince of the Asturias was to pursue his studies.

'Do you remember all this, Señor?'

'I was scarcely eleven at the time,' the king tells me, suddenly turning melancholy. 'But I do remember very well how cold, how terribly cold it was that day!'

II

The king receives me daily in his office on the second floor of the La Zarzuela palace, at exactly five in the afternoon. To be on the safe side, I have fallen into the habit of getting to the palace half an hour before the appointed time. The entrance to La Zarzuela, coming by way of Somontes, only a few kilometres from the dictator's old home in the Pardo palace, is guarded by a detachment of the *Guardia Real*[1] which discreetly screens visitors. For form's sake, since they know who I am and what I am doing here, they check my identity papers and run a detector over the briefcase with my tape recorder and blank cassettes. Then a guard raises the fragile barrier blocking the way into the *finca*, gives me a military salute and finally lets me into the magnificent estate. It covers several hundred hectares planted with cork oaks and olive trees; wild boar, red deer and roe deer roam free beneath their branches. The sky is often so clear a blue that the light seems to tremble as in the paintings of Velásquez.

At La Zarzuela, which resembles a palace in nothing but name, I am met outside a second gate by a secretary acting as something midway between janitor and major-domo. He escorts me to the foot of the staircase, where there is an aide-de-camp already waiting for me at the top – sometimes a naval officer, sometimes a senior army officer. We shake hands, and the aide then indicates that I am to follow him through

[1] Royal Guard.

an antechamber to a huge, polished oak door. He knocks at the door, tapping discreetly. We immediately hear Don Juan Carlos's voice.

'Come in!'

The aide-de-camp opens the door, enters first and announces me: 'Don José Luis de Vilallonga, Marquis of Castellvell, Your Majesty!'

Then he steps aside to let me in. The ceremonial is of a fairly informal nature, nothing like the regal protocol of the Elysée palace in Paris. When I arrived there one evening to dine with Madame Dayan in her official apartment, I had to go through several checkpoints, always accompanied – or rather watched – by guards in white gloves, in boots and caps, their glances stern, their expressions inscrutable. At La Zarzuela, on the other hand, they scarcely glanced at my papers after my third visit, and the aides-de-camp ask with interest, '*Cómo va su trabajo con su majestad el Rey*,[1] Don José Luis?'

As soon as I enter the room Don Juan Carlos rises, walks round his handsome desk with its gilded fittings and comes to meet me with his hand held out, a smile on his lips. The two or three times he has been a few minutes late receiving me he went to the trouble of apologizing, explaining exactly why.

The office – *el despacho* – where the king works and receives his visitors is a large rectangular room with light from the sierra flooding in through a pair of huge French windows reaching from floor to ceiling. The wall opposite the windows is occupied by bookshelves holding neatly arranged books finely bound in leather and stamped with the royal arms. The shelves also display a legacy from the late Duke of Baena, a magnificent collection of solid silver models of caravels, perfect replicas of the ships in which Columbus discovered America, as well as photographs of Doña Sofía, Prince Felipe and the Infantas Elena and Cristina, taken by the king himself.

Behind the armchair where Don Juan Carlos usually sits, the wall is entirely covered by a tapestry from the Real Fábrica[2] depicting the arms of Spain, and in an alcove in the wall close to the window hangs a Dali of his *Virgen esplosiva* period. Not far off, over the fireplace with its polished wooden surround, hangs a very fine sketch of King Alfonso XIII,

---

[1] How is your work with His Majesty the King going?
[2] Famous tapestry factory.

wearing a spiked helmet in the Prussian style and the sky-blue jacket of the cavalry, a work by Laszlo.

The king usually wears grey, with a different Hermès tie every day. These ties are often very striking and set his entourage talking. Don Juan Carlos wears a gold ring with the royal coat of arms on the little finger of his left hand, in the English manner.

During our first conversation, I realize it will be very difficult for me to make Don Juan Carlos keep to chronological order in the story of the events marking the crucial moments of his life. Indeed, he says so himself.

'Don't make me discuss the vicissitudes of my life in their strict order. Let's take it as it comes, talking like a couple of friends, one with plenty to say and the other with plenty to hear.'

So we agree on a method of work which does not seem like work at all. The king will talk about whatever comes into his head, and I will do my best to bring him back to the subjects which interest me. Having said that, it is not easy to give an idea of the full sense of what Don Juan Carlos tells me in words alone. His gestures in particular – not for nothing was he born in Rome – his mimicry, his laughter and his half-smiles all add much to what he says. Some of his silences say more than words too. When he looks me straight in the eye and says nothing, his silence can convey a wealth of meaning.

When I ask him what he learned from Franco, that cunning, wily and inscrutable Galician, during all those years when he lived practically in the dictator's shadow, Don Juan Carlos replies without hesitating, 'I learned to watch, to listen, and to keep my mouth shut.'

The king opens a drawer in his desk and takes out a box of Cohiba cigars. He offers me one, which of course I refuse. Don Juan Carlos never smokes in public, perhaps out of respect for the queen's principles, and that must sometimes be a great sacrifice, since he takes obvious pleasure in the first few puffs at his cigar.

'Franco very rarely talked politics with me,' he tells me, 'and he never gave me advice. Sometimes, when I asked him what I was to do in such or such a situation, he would say: "I really don't know, Highness, but in any case you won't be able to do what I would have done. When you are king, the times will have changed. People then won't be as they are now." If he didn't want to answer a question he pretended not to have heard me and changed the subject.'

Don Juan Carlos was obviously a good pupil, for when he decides not to answer one of my questions he too just looks straight through me, suddenly assumes an abstracted expression, and waits for the next question in silence.

'Franco didn't talk much,' he tells me, 'and he hated giving explanations. If he did give advice his common sense could be disconcerting. When I was still Prince of Spain our top horseman of the time, Ordovás, invited me to be a member of the Spanish show-jumping team. I was very keen, but I told Ordovás I would have to ask Franco's permission before accepting. So I went to see the head of state and told him about Ordovás's proposition. Franco looked at me for quite some time in silence and then said' – here Don Juan Carlos does a perfect imitation of the general's very characteristic voice – ' "No, Highness, impossible." "But why, General?" I asked. "You know I ride very well, and I'd show to advantage in the Spanish team. So why –" He interrupted me with a gesture. "Because if you win they'll say it's because you're the prince, and if you lose it will be very bad for the image of Spain." When I thought it over, I realized he was quite right. So I never did join the Spanish show-jumping team.'

'When did you first meet Franco, Señor?'

'Exactly a fortnight after I arrived in Spain. Danvila and his friends would have liked to take me straight from the Cerro de los Angeles to the Pardo palace to present me to the general. However, they had put it off because Madrid was in turmoil that day. Carlos Méndez was being buried in the Almudena cemetery; he was a monarchist student who had died in prison after a beating from his jailers. The police forces were on the alert, and thousands of people had invaded the cemetery and its surroundings. It definitely was not a good day for me to be introduced to the head of state. However, news of my arrival had spread fast, and quite a number of people went straight from the Almudena cemetery to Las Jarillas to show the son of the Count of Barcelona that they supported the monarchist cause. My father was very anxious about this first meeting with Franco. We often discussed him at home, not always in friendly terms. As a child of eleven, I didn't understand much of what went on around Franco, but I was well aware that he was the man who caused my father such trouble, prevented him from going back to Spain and let the newspapers write unpleasant things about him. I didn't feel much liking for him at first. Before I left for Madrid, my father had given me all sorts of advice. "When you meet Franco," he said, "listen hard to what he tells you but say as little as possible. Be polite and answer his questions briefly. *En boca cerrada no entran moscas.*" [1]

'I was invited to meet Franco on 24 November. It was still very cold, and the sierra was covered with snow. I thought the Pardo palace very impressive with the Moorish Guard at all its gates. The palace was swarming with men in uniform, aides-de-camp, I suppose, talking to each other in low voices as if they were in church. I was taken through a whole series of drawing-rooms veiled in semi-darkness, and suddenly found myself facing Franco. He was smaller than he looked in the photographs I'd seen of him, he had a paunch, and he was smiling at me in what struck me as an unnatural way. However, he was very kind to me and asked after His Highness the Count of Barcelona. I was surprised to hear him say "Highness", because to all the Spaniards who came to see us in Estoril my father was His Majesty the King. Franco seemed interested in my studies, and wanted to know which subjects I found most difficult. At the end of the visit, when I'd already said goodbye, he invited me to go pheasant-shooting with him in Aranjuez so that I could send some game back to Estoril. To be honest, I wasn't paying very much attention to what Franco said to me, because right at the start of the visit I'd spotted a tiny mouse running around the legs of the armchair where the general was sitting as if it did so all the time. To a child of my age at the time, such a brave mouse was much more interesting than this over-kindly gentleman going on about Visigoth kings whose names I knew off by heart.'

'And what about Las Jarillas, Señor? What are your memories of that?'

The king's face lights up with a smile. 'Oh, I have delightful memories of Las Jarillas, a rather beautiful house lent by its owner Alfonso Urquijo, a friend of my father's, so that I could pursue my studies there. It was quite close to the Pardo and also quite close to La Zarzuela, which was to be my official residence later and where you and I are talking at this moment. There were quite extensive grounds around the house, and we were allowed to hunt in them. Eight little boys of my own age

[1] No flies get into a closed mouth.

31

had been assembled at Las Jarillas, all of noble families well known to my father except one, José Luis Leal, who later became Adolfo Suárez's finance minister. I was delighted to find my first cousin Carlos de Borbón-Sicilia among them, because I was very fond of him. He's now married to Anne of France, one of the daughters of the Count of Paris. Luckily I was allowed to share a bedroom with him, or I'd have felt very lonely those first few days. You mustn't think we were indulged, far from it! In fact they made us work much harder at our studies than boys in an ordinary school because "considering who we were, we had to set an example".

'The man who carried the whole responsibility of Las Jarillas on his shoulders was Don José Garrido Casanova, formerly tutor to the Sotomayor children. He was a remarkable character, an Andalusian who had founded a charity called La Paloma to care for poor and homeless children. Don José Garrido was a just and good man. I was very fond of him, and there are sometimes moments when I still ask myself what Garrido would have advised me to do. Then there was Don Heliodoro Ruiz Arias who taught us physical education. I got on very well with him. He was bent on making me a good athlete. His son, another Heliodoro, looked after our health. The elder Don Heliodoro had been gymnastics instructor to José Antonio Primo de Rivera, founder of the Falange party; I had heard a lot about Primo de Rivera at home.

'While both the Ruiz Ariases, father and son, were liberal, tolerant men who could adjust to the times, Father Zulueta had to be handled with kid gloves. He came three times a week to talk religion and morality to us. The people who advised my father about my education had warmly recommended Don Ignacio de Zulueta because he represented the most conservative trends in the Francoist regime. He was a former architect who had become a priest late in life. Tall, aloof and distant, he was a great stickler for protocol. He didn't much like having José Luis Leal among us because he was not of a noble family. On the day of my arrival at Las Jarillas, Zulueta insisted on my future classmates greeting me with a very correct "Welcome, Highness!" which embarrassed me horribly. Luckily I was very soon Juanito to everyone. I can be a stickler for protocol myself when necessary, but in my private life I do my best to make sure I'm not isolated from real contact with other people.'

The king suddenly laughs.

'As a matter of fact protocol has done me a bad turn now and then. When I was a cadet at the Military Academy of Zaragoza, all my friends and the people in my year used the familiar pronoun *tú* to me – some of them still do when we're in private – and called me by my first name. Or else they just called me SAR, pronounced phonetically, the initials of *Su Alteza Real*, His Royal Highness. General the Duke of La Torre, who had taken an active part in my pre-military training before I started at the Academy, came to see me every Saturday. After asking my instructors how my studies were going, he would invite me to lunch at the Grand Hotel, a favourite haunt of high society in Zaragoza at the time. Knowing that I lunched there on Saturdays, people would go there to see me and stay for lunch themselves. My solitary lunches with the duke were rather heavy going, since he was not exactly an amusing companion – he was a military man of the old style with perfect but very starchy manners. He always spoke to me with a respect which left me paralysed. His Royal Highness this, His Royal Highness that. Well, you can imagine! One day he asked me to invite two or three of my fellow cadets to lunch next Saturday. I thanked him effusively, thinking that if I had friends there the atmosphere was bound to be more relaxed. So I asked three of my closest friends, and at two o'clock on the dot we turned up at the Grand Hotel, where the Duke of La Torre was already waiting for us. We hadn't been seated for more than a few minutes when one of my friends turned to me and asked, using the familiar pronoun, "Juan, did you know that –" But he never finished his sentence, because suddenly the duke slammed his fist down on the table so hard he rattled the china. He was white with rage. He pushed back his chair, rose to his feet and shouted, "*Caballero cadete!*[1] Get up and stand to attention!" A deathly hush fell over the dining room. My friend, standing to attention, was pale as death, and the duke went on shouting. "*Caballero cadete*, how dare you use such familiarity in speaking to someone whom I myself, a lieutenant-general, address as Your Royal Highness?"

'If I personally was horrified, so were my three friends. The duke finally simmered down and we finished our lunch in a silence you could have cut with a knife. As soon as the duke left us I did my best to console the man who'd had a strip torn off him. "Some invitation!" he muttered, near tears. "Never again, never!" And indeed I never could persuade any of my friends to accept my invitations to lunch with the duke after that.'

[1] Sir Cadet!

Don Juan Carlos crushes out the remains of his cigar in a cut glass ashtray placed in front of him.

'Señor, may we go back to Las Jarillas? Was that the first time you'd lived away from your family?'

'Oh no. When I was eight I went to boarding school at the Villa Saint-Jean in Fribourg. The school was run by Marianists. I was miserable there at first; I felt my own family had abandoned me and my father and mother had forgotten me. This was in 1946, the year when my parents decided to move closer to Spain and left Switzerland to go and live in Portugal. I waited day after day for a phone call from my mother. It never came. Later I realized my father wouldn't let her phone. "Maria, you must help him to toughen up," he told her. It wasn't cruelty on his part, still less insensitivity; as I realized later on myself, my father knew that princes need a tough upbringing if they are to be men able to bear the whole weight of the state some day. My father had a deep feeling for royalty. He saw me not just as his son but as the heir to a dynasty, and so he owed it to himself to prepare me for my responsibilities. He would not give way to tender impulses for fear of making me a weakling. He was very strict and asked a lot of me, but at the same time he did show me great affection. My father can be forbidding and tender at the same time, as sailors so often are.

'Later, in my adolescence, I found him a very reliable friend and confidant who would give me his full attention. But at Fribourg, far from my father and mother, I discovered that solitude is a heavy burden to bear. Luckily my grandmother Queen Victoria Eugenia was there to keep an eye on me, although I suspect she'd been told not to spoil me too much. I spent weekends with her at the Hotel Royal in Lausanne, where she lived. And she brought me to Portugal in 1946 after a long school term at Fribourg. My parents were living in Estoril by then, in the Villa Bellver, rented from a Portuguese friend. They didn't want me wasting my time, so I was handed over to Eugenio Vegas Latapie, who had already taught me at the Villa Saint-Jean. Eugenio, who ran my father's secretariat, was a splendid man...'

Don Juan Carlos pauses, suddenly lost in thought.

'You know,' he goes on after a moment, 'I have had great luck, all my life, in that I've always had exceptional men near me – first among my tutors, later among my trusted advisers.'

He gives no names, but I know he is thinking of Garrido, Eugenio

34

Vegas, Torcuato Fernández Miranda,[1] the Marquis of Mondéjar – whom Don Juan Carlos described as 'my second father' – and General Don Sabino Fernandez Campo, head of the royal household, recently made Count of Latores and a grandee of Spain. I may well have left out some names, but these are the men the king mentions most frequently.

'When I say that Eugenio Vegas was a splendid man I don't feel I'm exaggerating. His enemies – and all honest men have enemies – said that he lived in the past. That may have been true, since moral rigour isn't a modern virtue. He agreed that the heir to a dynasty should be brought up without any concession to the weaknesses which seem normal to ordinary people. So he educated me to realize that I was someone apart, with far more responsibilities and duties than other people. Someone said jokingly one day, in front of the Count of Barcelona, "Eugenio Vegas is making us another Philip II." Knowing my father, I'd guess he took that as a great compliment.'

'When you speak of exceptional men, Señor, you mention your former teachers, your fellow students, your advisers, but you seldom use the word "friend". Don't you have friends?'

Don Juan Carlos seems momentarily taken aback. 'My father always says, "God gives you a family, but it's up to everyone to find his own friends." '

And some moments later he adds, 'It's difficult for a king to have friends.'

'Difficult or dangerous, Señor?'

'Difficult and dangerous. Dangerous because if a man can say "my friend the king", then he can instantly add, "the king said this, the king told me that", and you never know just where it may lead.'

'Would you agree with Chamfort, then, Señor? He bracketed friendship at court with "the faith of foxes and the society of wolves".'

'I didn't know that saying, but as a matter of fact...' Don Juan Carlos sketches a disillusioned smile. 'We use the word friend too lightly in Spain,' he says. 'It ends up meaning nothing much any more. My own feeling is that friendship should arise from a long relationship of confidence and loyalty. It's a difficult thing to achieve, and it takes time. Personally, I feel the danger lies in the use that may be made of my friendship when I give it to someone. If you're a king it isn't always easy

[1] Don Juan Carlos's mentor during the years before he came to power.

to tell the difference between a friend and a courtier. Having said that, José Luis, I am very seldom mistaken.'

'Señor, princes have infinite power over those who approach them, and those who approach them have infinite weakness in doing so, or so Fénelon says in his *Examen de conscience sur les devoirs de la royauté*. To avoid falling victim to that weakness I always say, if asked whether I am a friend of the king, "No, I am not his friend; I am his loyal subject. If the king honours me with his friendship then I'm the happiest of men." But it doesn't go beyond that. My father often used to tell me what happened on the night of 14 April 1931 in the Oriente palace in Madrid, when Don Alfonso XIII was about to go into exile. An aide-de-camp told the king that about fifty people were waiting for him in the salon known as the Duke of Genoa's Drawing Room to say goodbye. The king's face lit up. Voice husky with sudden emotion, he exclaimed in surprise, "To think of them coming across the Plaza de Oriente at a time like this to say goodbye to me! Those are truly brave people!" My father accompanied the king into the drawing room, where men with strained faces, women in tears and even several children clinging to their mothers' skirts stood motionless under the great Bohemian crystal chandeliers, waiting to say goodbye to Don Alfonso. But none of them had had to brave the anger of the crowd besieging the palace, because they all lived there. They were servants of the royal household: footmen, chambermaids, chauffeurs, errand boys, cooks and some of the *alabarderos*[1] in their uniforms. Taken aback, your grandfather looked at them all for some time in silence, Señor. His lower lip began to tremble. Turning to my father, Don Alfonso said, in a barely audible voice, "Salvador, I see none of my grandees here – none of the men who used to play polo with me, none of those who asked me for appointments and honours." The grandees, Señor, the men who boasted of playing polo and going hunting with the king, or who had obtained favours and sinecures from him, were not his friends. They were only courtiers. And in my opinion, Señor, courtiers are rather poor specimens of the human race.'

Don Juan Carlos has been listening to me, lost in thought. 'Well, your story is a cautionary tale, anyway,' he murmurs. And he remains silent for several moments again, before adding, 'When I was still Prince of Spain, my grandmother Queen Victoria Eugenia told Doña Sofía,

[1] Royal guards.

"You'll need one or more accredited ladies-in-waiting to accompany you wherever you go." But I told Doña Sofía, "No, you won't. If you need someone with you, choose a woman friend of your own, or a secretary, or one of my aides-de-camp, but I don't want the title of lady-in-waiting to be the kind of honour for which aristocratic ladies would fight as they did in my grandfather's time." I know there are people who feel we don't lead a grand enough life, but I'd rather our way of life was on the simple side than see the rebirth around us of an embryonic court out of tune with modern times.'

'You remind me of the advice Don Miguel Maura, the monarchist who was minister of the interior in the first republican government of 1931, offered anyone who might ever become King of Spain, i.e. you, Señor.'

'Yes, in his book *Aso cayó Alfonso XIII*.[1] If I remember correctly, there were three pieces of advice. The first was, "Don't live in the Oriente palace. It is fatal to the monarchy; it is the Spanish Versailles. It should become a museum, like its French equivalent." The second piece of advice was something along the lines of "Close your doors to what is called high society. Surround yourself with intelligent, unassuming men of the middle class which is the real backbone of the country. Those are the people who will bring the fresh air of the street in to you every day."'

Don Juan Carlos pauses and, affecting innocence, asks me, 'Do you remember Miguel Maura's third piece of advice?'

'Yes, Señor, I remember it very well. He advised Your Majesty not to unpack your baggage in case you had no time to repack it if the situation turned out badly. "For perhaps," Don Miguel warned, "things may not end as well another time as they did in 1931."'

Don Juan Carlos looks at me in silence, waiting for my comments.

'Well, that third piece of advice strikes a pessimistic note which isn't relevant today, Señor. Miguel Maura could not foresee that many life-long republicans would be very happy with the present monarchy.'

I am not sure how far Don Juan Carlos likes or does not like boldness of this nature, but I have the distinct impression that on this occasion his almost imperceptible smile grows just a trifle wider.

[1] Thus fell Alfonso XIII.

III

Why do some of us describe Don Juan Carlos as a man sent by Providence? Bossuet stated, a little imprudently, that chance plays no part in the government of human affairs and Fortune is a meaningless word. For his part, Chamfort called Providence the baptismal name of Chance, Chance in its own turn being nothing but the nickname of Providence. All of which boils down to saying that man is not really the master of his fate, and very often Fortune, Chance and Providence unite to choose the road he must follow.

Nothing predestined Don Juan Carlos de Borbón y Borbón to rule Spain one day. His father Don Juan de Borbón y Battenberg, the third son of Alfonso XIII, was well down the list in the line of succession to the Spanish throne at the time of his own birth. But Fortune, Chance and Providence decided, long before Don Juan Carlos was born, that he and not his uncles or his father would one day become the providential figure to guide his country from Francoist dictatorship to democracy, with the wisdom and courage of an astute leader up to all the ruses necessary to gain his ends.

The last king to reign over Spain had been Don Alfonso XIII, Don Juan Carlos's grandfather. He left Madrid on the night of 14 April 1931 and drove to the port of Cartagena, going into an exile which would end only with his death in a suite in the Grand Hotel, Rome, on 28 February 1941. An hour before he left the Oriente palace, besieged by a crowd, General

Cavalcanti came to Don Alfonso offering to bring in a cavalry squadron to charge the yelling mob calling for the king's departure and sometimes even his death. The king refused Cavalcanti's offer in a phrase which later became famous: 'Not a single drop of Spanish blood shall ever be shed for my person.' Cavalcanti took his leave of Don Alfonso to avoid telling him that a king has no right to say such things. In a country where the love of blood – its smell, its taste, its colour – lies deep within the people themselves – and what is the blood of a people if not the price of its history? – the monarch's refusal to see blood shed was a denial of his own high rank. 'I would not be king,' said Louis XIII, cogently, 'if I allowed myself to have personal feelings.' More than one of the king's supporters asked, later, 'Didn't he know you have to spill rivers of blood in Spain to be popular?' Those rivers of blood flowed lavishly during the civil war which began in 1936.

Don Alfonso XIII had written his final proclamation to the people of Spain with his own hand. The typical Spaniard is a man of few words. Concision and clarity are the essence of his race. '*Al pan, pan, y al vino, vino.*'[1] In taking leave of his subjects, Don Alfonso de Borbón y Habsburgo-Lorena wanted to dot the i's and cross the t's. After the elections of Sunday 12 April, he realized, '*Yo no tengo el amor di mi pueblo*',[2] but he doubted whether he had lost it for good. He accepted that a king may be mistaken – and very painful that must have been for the Habsburg he had never ceased to be! – but he remembered that Spain has always found it in her heart to forgive mistakes made without malice. It should be said in passing that he had the necessary means to defend his royal prerogatives by armed force, in an '*eficaz forcejeo con quienes las combaten*',[3] but he said he could not envisage civil war between Spaniards. He gave clear notice that he was not renouncing any of his rights, which were an historical trust and not personal to him. And he ended by stating that he was 'deliberately suspending the exercise of royal power' so that the nation might have sovereign power over its own destiny.

The portrait I painted of Don Alfonso XIII in my book *La Chute* might have been directly inspired by the actual picture hanging over the mantelpiece in the office which is the scene of my meetings with Don Juan Carlos.

[1] To the bread, bread, and the wine, wine.
[2] I no longer have the love of my people.
[3] Efficacious struggle against those who are fighting against them.

'Don Alfonso de Borbón y Habsburgo-Lorena,' I wrote, 'who ruled Spain as Alfonso XIII had not so much the face as the countenance of a king. In profile he resembled a beast of prey, with a lower lip like a gargoyle's and an insolently jutting jaw, the effect of an old, hereditary imperative. His forehead was high, his hair retreating at the temples, his features bony. His dark eyes were extremely compelling, particularly when they first settled on the face of a woman still unknown to him.

'Don Alfonso always held himself very erect, his body almost wedded to its uniform – its many uniforms – and each of his often very abrupt gestures gave his figure a look of menacing majesty which fascinated courtiers and amazed any who saw him pass, even from a distance.

'There was an undeniable Habsburg imperiousness about him: a particular way of carrying his head so that his gaze remained always fixed above the horizon. He displayed a curious lassitude in his relations with people who depended directly on him, and a Teutonic arrogance, appearing suddenly and made up of cold rages and terrible utterances. He also assiduously cultivated – and this was perhaps his most specifically Habsburg trait – an immoderate, blind, Austrian love of all the more tiresome and useless elements of protocol.

'But the Spaniard in him showed more clearly than anything, the ultimate Spaniard, solitary, melancholy and haughty in a world peopled by others whose blood was not his. Only a Bourbon skin-deep, he was courtly, distant, and did not mind giving offence. His humour was black and often macabre, although he did not neglect to show daily a certain condescension which it would have been wrong to take for kindness. He took a hectic delight in hunting and killing game, again very much the Habsburg. He had a mortal hatred of advisers. And a grandiose and sublime pride possessed his hand when he signed, "*Yo el Rey*"[1] at the bottom of a document.'

His wife, Queen Victoria Eugenia, described him as being 'merry as a Latin, courteous as a Habsburg, as much the sportsman as an Englishman, proud as a Spaniard, and as egotistic as any other man'.

Don Alfonso XIII, the posthumous son of Alfonso XII and Doña Maria Cristina de Habsburgo, Archduchess of Austria, had the misfortune to be born a king. Winston Churchill, who knew him well, pitied

[1] I, the king.

him for being surrounded from infancy by flattering courtiers who kept him from learning anything about real life. Educated by tutors who sang his praises, the only people he mixed with later were aristocrats, ecclesiastical dignitaries and high-ranking military men who never dared express opinions contrary to his own. And yet he was a great king who said of himself, 'I sometimes feel I am a good actor performing with other actors as second-rate as the play itself.' However, the play ran for forty years.

Don Alfonso first met his future wife at a ball in London, given in his honour by the Duke of Portland. She stole the king's heart from her cousin Patricia of Connaught, another granddaughter of Queen Victoria, a pretty young girl who had long been regarded as the future fiancée of the King of Spain. But as soon as Don Alfonso saw Victoria Eugenia – Ena to her friends – he had eyes for no one else. Patricia of Connaught consoled herself by letting it be known that she had thought the Spanish king 'perfectly hideous'.

The future Queen of Spain was the daughter of Henry of Battenberg, second son of Prince Alexander of Hesse, and of Princess Beatrice, second daughter of Queen Victoria. The couple had settled in London because the old queen would not be parted from her favourite daughter. They had three boys and a girl whom they baptised Victoria Eugenia in honour of the Queen of England and the Empress of the French, Eugenia de Montijo, born in Spain, who later encouraged Ena's marriage to the Spanish Bourbon. It was this blonde child, with her milky complexion and blue eyes, who was to poison the blood of the Bourbons of Spain by passing on to her own children that terrible and mysterious disease which another granddaughter of Queen Victoria, Alice of Hesse-Darmstadt, wife of Tsar Nicholas II of Russia, transmitted to her son the Tsarevitch Alexis. Ena of Battenberg and the Empress of Russia both came from the house of Hesse-Darmstadt, where the mortal illness whose name people scarcely dared to utter at the time is suspected to have originated.

King Edward VII did not look very kindly on the marriage of his niece Ena to the young King of Spain. 'Spain is nothing like the country where you were born,' he told her. 'I'm afraid you may never get used to it, so don't come complaining to me when things go wrong.'

They began going wrong on the very day of Ena's wedding to Don

Alfonso. As she emerged from the church of Los Jerónimos on her royal husband's arm, already '*la reina guapa*'[1] to the Spaniards, she had no idea that she was about to escape Mateo Morral's assassination attempt unscathed a few minutes later.

But the family tragedy was only just beginning. In 1907, a year after her marriage, Doña Victoria Eugenia gave birth to a male child, Alfonso, Prince of the Asturias, heir to the throne. Ever since the days of the Catholic Kings, it had been a tradition in the Spanish royal family to circumcize newborn babies. As soon as the doctor's lancet cut into the little prince's flesh the baby suffered a violent haemorrhage which seemed as if it would never stop. It told the distraught parents that the Prince of the Asturias had been born a haemophiliac. Next year Doña Victoria Eugenia bore her second child, the Infante Don Jaime. He was a deaf mute. Then, in 1909 and 1911, she had two daughters, the Infantas Beatriz and Cristina, both of them perfectly healthy. A third boy was born in 1913. This was the Infante Don Juan, the future Count of Barcelona. The doctors could find no trace of the terrible malady in Don Alfonso XIII's third son. However, another boy was born the following year, the Infante Don Gonzalo, and he too was affected, although less severely than his brother the Prince of the Asturias, by the 'German disease' which spared females but had already wrought havoc among the royal couple's male children.

Don Alfonso endured these blows of fate without showing any emotion, but all the same he suffered cruelly, holding Doña Victoria Eugenia responsible for the blighted hopes of their family. He adored his eldest son, whose health demanded constant care. As time passed, the Prince of the Asturias grew to be a handsome, very fair-haired young man with his mother's blue eyes. Contemporary photographs of the prince wearing naval officer's uniform show a certain likeness to the late Duke of Windsor when he was Prince of Wales. While his brother Jaime was very dark and looked typically Spanish, the Prince of the Asturias had inherited the looks and features of the Battenbergs. Unable to make great physical efforts, the young prince was at the mercy of the slightest accident, which might cause his immediate death, as indeed was the case with his brother Gonzalo, who died after suffering a tiny contusion

[1] The beautiful queen.

when his car skidded. The prince never left his rooms in the Oriente palace except to go to La Quinta, a charming country estate where he reared pigs and poultry, like a male Marie Antoinette. There was a rumour among the working classes in Madrid that the Prince of the Asturias had to drink a large glass of fresh blood every morning to keep alive. From that it was only a step, and a step readily taken by some, to claiming that the blood had to be human.

For years Don Alfonso XIII had his eldest son brought up as crown prince and treated him as such, as if he would not let himself admit that the young man's illness was real. Today historians agree – Winston Churchill himself confirmed it on several occasions – that when the young King of Spain visited London King Edward VII warned him of the risks he was running in marrying his niece Ena, who was probably a carrier of the 'German disease'. But Don Alfonso, head over heels in love with the young English beauty he was determined to bring home to Madrid at any price, turned a deaf ear to what he considered old wives' tales.

However, he had to bow to the evidence. The Prince of the Asturias would never be King of Spain. The iron entering into his soul, Don Alfonso XIII was preparing to do what must be done to remove his eldest son from the succession to the throne when the prince himself spared him this painful decision, by contracting a morganatic marriage with Edelmira Sampedro, a pretty Cuban girl he had met in a Lausanne clinic where she was nursing him for lung trouble. The prince wrote his father a letter renouncing all rights to the Crown for himself and his descendants. He took the title of Count of Covadonga and retired from public life. As Don Alfonso XIII had foreseen, his eldest son's passion for the pretty Cuban burnt itself out very quickly. The hectic life of Paris, visits to fashionable night-spots, new and sometimes undesirable friendships, and most of all money troubles brought a considerable chill into the couple's relationship. Edelmira abruptly left her husband and took refuge in her native island. They were divorced in Havana in 1937.

Less than two months later the prince fell madly in love with a model of dubious reputation, Marta Rocafort, another Cuban, and married her out of hand. This second marriage was even more disastrous than the first. The couple separated after four months, and the Count of Covadonga obtained his second divorce without any difficulty. On 6 September 1938 the former Prince of the Asturias crashed his car into a telephone pole outside a Miami nightclub. Don Alfonso died very quickly of a haemorrhage which drained him of blood. The mortal remains of Alfonso XIII's eldest son were sent back to Spain in 1985 and buried in the vault reserved for him in the Escorial. Edelmira Sampedro, who had truly loved him, went to Madrid airport and wept over the coffin of the man who had been her husband and would have been King of Spain, had the 'German disease' not made him a poor creature whose mind very soon showed the effects of the physical weakness which, in his last years of life, made him the plaything of all sorts of intriguers and women greedy for honours to which poor Don Alfonso no longer had any right. The Prince of the Asturias was the first obstacle removed from the path to the throne of Don Juan Carlos, himself as yet unborn.

A second obstacle – though it did not seem one at first – proved more difficult to get around. This was the Infante Don Jaime, the deaf mute. It is said today that Don Jaime was not born deaf and dumb, but that his infirmity was the result of an attack of mastoiditis when he was only four, which the doctors could not cure. Although this time Doña Victoria Eugenia bore no responsibility for her child's condition, she paid the price for this new tragedy in the form of a sudden coolness on her husband's part.

Don Jaime, who was not in the least feeble-minded, quickly learned to lipread what people were saying to him, and he 'spoke' not just Spanish but English, French and Italian too in this way. The wall of silence which so cruelly separated him from the rest of the world soon made him a solitary, melancholy character. On 21 June 1933, ten days after his brother had renounced his rights to the throne, the Infante Don Jaime, aware of the physical handicaps which would have prevented him from reigning, renounced all his own dynastic rights 'for himself and his descendants'. There were precedents for a prince to renounce his rights or be set aside because of severe infirmities. Carlos III de Borbón had debarred his son Don Felipe from the throne; Felipe, who was mentally deficient, made way for his brother Carlos IV, famous from Francisco de Goya's terrifying portrait of him and his family.

A year and a half after his renunciation the Infante Don Jaime married Emmanuelle Dampierre in Rome. Emmanuelle was an ambitious girl, the daughter of a French viscount and an Italian princess. Informed of Don Jaime's condition, Pope Pius XI saw fit to intervene.

He warned the fiancée's family of the countless difficulties she would have to face if she married the infante. The Pope even told Emmanuelle's mother that if the marriage did not turn out well, it would never be annulled in his lifetime. But the marriage of their daughter to a royal infante dazzled the Dampierres, and Emmanuelle's mother encouraged her daughter to marry the deaf mute. Horror stories about the newly wed couple's honeymoon were told at the time. It was said that Don Jaime's sexual appetites had frightened his bride, who shut herself up in her rooms and telephoned for help.

Fifty years later Emmanuelle Dampierre was telling anyone who would listen that her marriage to the infante had been arranged in too much haste, and she was never physically attracted to her future husband. According to her the marriage had been arranged by her mother, and her own feelings had hardly been taken into account at all. For his part, Don Jaime said much the same. However, the infante cannot have been quite as repulsive to Emmanuelle as she claimed years later, since two sons, Alfonso and Gonzalo, were soon born to the couple.

It is obvious that Emmanuelle, like the rest of the Dampierre family, was highly flattered by the idea of becoming a Royal Highness, even if that meant marrying a man not altogether to her liking. However, matters were not so simple, nor was King Alfonso XIII so easily manipulated. After much thought, he decided that Emmanuelle would not have the rank of Royal Highness, and must content herself with becoming Duchess of Segovia. This was a severe blow to the young woman's vanity, but Don Alfonso XIII remained inflexible on the subject, and she had to accept his decision.

After the birth of her son Gonzalo, Emmanuelle lived more or less separated from her husband, although under the same roof. It was at this time that she began an intimate relationship with Tonino Sozzani, son of a Milanese stockbroker, whom she was to marry when she was widowed. Emmanuelle left the marital home for good in 1941.

On 15 January 1941, shortly before his death, Don Alfonso XIII made his will in Rome. It ended with these words: 'I offer my country the renunciation of my rights so that my son Don Juan may be automatically designated my sole legitimate heir, beyond any possibility of dispute.'

Don Jaime had raised no objections to his father's will, or to Don

Juan's acceptance of the position of head of the royal house of Spain. On 23 July 1945, he had even ratified his renunciation of all his rights in a curious letter addressed to 'His Majesty King Don Juan III', in which he said: 'When I decided to marry, some time after renouncing my rights to the Crown on behalf of myself and my descendants, I chose my wife from outside the circle of the royal houses of Europe, so that there could be no question of my children's claiming the rights I myself have renounced.'

The indecisive and confused character of Don Jaime – although in many ways he was a good and generous man – led him to change his mind several times about the validity of his renunciation. Poorly advised by intriguers who sought only their own profit, Don Jaime first recognized his brother Don Juan's dynastic inheritance as legitimate, but then proclaimed himself head of the royal house of Spain and Duke of Anjou in his capacity as eldest son of Don Alfonso XIII.

From 1950 onwards the infante was prey to paranoia. In defiance of reason and logic, and ignoring indisputable historical facts, Don Jaime declared himself pretender not only to the throne of Spain but to the throne of France as well. He made his son Alfonso 'Dauphin' and his son Gonzalo Duke of Aquitaine, greatly to the surprise of the reigning houses of Europe. He handed out titles, offices, honours and decorations with the generosity of an oriental satrap. He even gave the Order of the Golden Fleece – whose grand masters are the Count of Barcelona for the Spanish branch, and Otto von Habsburg for the Austrian branch – to persons whose only merit was to have caused him to make his worst mistakes. These decorations were obviously worthless, since the infante had no right to bestow them. Leaving nothing undone, Don Jaime also proclaimed himself Duke of Madrid and heir to the Carlist kings. He even wrote a letter to Franco – always delighted to sow discord in the monarchist ranks – which the general had the good taste to keep secret. 'I have the honour of addressing myself to Your Excellency,' the infante wrote, 'to inform you that my renunciation of the throne of Spain in favour of my brother the Count of Barcelona has been annulled since 1949. I here solemnly renew that annulment, and I claim my rights to the crown of Spain as the eldest son of the late King Don Alfonso XIII.'

None of this was of any great importance, apart from the fact that the ridicule publicly incurred by Don Jaime did considerable harm to the dynasty as a whole. However, matters became more complicated when ten years later, on 8 March 1972 and in the chapel of the Pardo palace, Don Jaime's elder son Alfonso, 'the Dauphin', married María del Carmen Martínez-Bordiu, daughter of the Marquis and Marchioness of Villaverde and General Franco's favourite granddaughter.

This marriage divided the people of Spain down the middle; in one camp were those who still saw Don Juan Carlos as the future King of Spain, and in the other those who told themselves that María del Carmen Martínez-Bordiu's new husband, the ambitious and bitter Alfonso, would do his best to bar his cousin Juan Carlos's path to the throne. Many loyalties changed sides at the time of this marriage.

The wedding of pretty María del Carmen was celebrated with all the pomp and ceremony of a Napoleonic court. Every *parvenu* in the kingdom made a point of attending, and so did some of the nobility who ate at the Francoist table while making a prudent display of loyalty to the monarchy. Ministers, ambassadors and aristocrats of every shade and hue were present, looking very fine in operetta uniforms plastered with crosses, ribbons and medals. There was no comparison between this wedding and the wedding of the dictator's own daughter, mother of today's bride, to the histrionic Marquis of Villaverde; that occasion had been cold-shouldered by the same aristocrats who now saw Alfonso de Borbón-Dampierre as a new candidate for the throne he might occupy one day, if Franco changed his mind about Don Juan Carlos and made his granddaughter the new Queen of Spain.

At the end of the wedding ceremony the Infante Don Jaime gave the dictator one of the Golden Fleeces he handed out so lavishly. Franco accepted it, but never made any use of it.

Urged on by his son Alfonso, now Duke of Cadiz and a Royal Highness, the Infante Don Jaime put out a curious document in which, in his capacity as 'head of the house of Bourbon and the royal house of Spain' – thereby implying that he was head not only of the Spanish Bourbons but of the French branch too – he approved of the decision taken by the Cortes to designate his nephew Juan Carlos successor to Franco 'as king'. This amounted to saying that he did *not* recognize Don Juan Carlos as the legitimate heir to the dynasty.

Taking such a stance, nothing if not ambiguous, was playing with fire. That document would later allow Alfonso de Borbón-Dampierre to assert his dynastic 'rights' as the elder son of the elder son of Don

Alfonso XIII and so, according to himself, the only legitimate dynastic heir. He even let it be known that Don Juan Carlos could only 'establish' a new monarchy, while he, Alfonso de Borbón-Dampierre, was the one person who could 'restore' it.

The last years of the Infante Don Jaime's life were sad. Chronically short of money, he had to leave the Villa Segovia in Rueil-Malmaison because he could not pay the rent. Matters became even worse when, on a sudden impulse, he married Carlota Tiedemann, an alcoholic Prussian cabaret singer who proclaimed herself Duchess of Segovia as soon as she was married; she had no right at all to that title since Spanish law did not recognize divorce, so the only Duchess of Segovia was Emmanuelle Dampierre, still the infante's lawful wife although by now she had contracted a civil marriage with the handsome Tonino. Carlota Tiedemann added to her spurious title of Duchess the style of Royal Highness, which greatly impressed the shady society in which the infante moved.

Relations between Don Jaime and his sons were not always easy. In 1960 the two brothers – Gonzalo, as always, following his brother Alfonso's lead – did not scruple to drag their father through the French courts, accusing him of squandering a fortune he did not possess and of having become mentally unbalanced since his marriage to Carlota Tiedemann. The French courts, after hearing the infante at length, declared him of sound mind and perfectly responsible for his own actions.

Don Jaime breathed his last on 20 March 1975, in strange circumstances, at St Gall Hospital in Switzerland. During a violent argument with Carlota in Paris a few days earlier, the infante had fallen and hurt his head. The doctor who gave him first aid could find no fracture of the skull or cerebral haemorrhage. However, he recommended complete rest for several days. But Carlota, who had just reserved rooms at the hospital in St Gall, where she was going to dry out, decided the infante was well able to stand up to the car journey. Accordingly they left Paris by taxi and arrived in Switzerland. The infante, who was feeling worse and worse, had needed several stops en route. As soon as they reached St Gall, Don Jaime went to bed suffering from exhaustion. He died of a stroke in the night.

His death distressed everyone who knew him well. Isolated from the real world by his affliction, he would confide ingenuously in anyone who showed him the least sympathy or affection, however slight. He was a decent, childlike, credulous man who allowed flatterers and adventurers of all kinds to approach him. His changes of mind and impulsive statements gave his brother Don Juan many headaches. He imprudently encouraged the stupid pretensions of his elder son to thrones to which he had no claim. His death marked the passing of the second son of Don Alfonso XIII who might have been King of Spain had Fortune and Providence not refused their aid.

Alfonso de Borbón-Dampierre, Don Jaime's son, was a sword of Damocles suspended over the head of Don Juan Carlos rather than an obstacle on the path to the throne. Melancholy, vindictive and bitter, Alfonso de Borbón-Dampierre could never accept that he had been born without any of the rights he claimed.

On 17 September 1936 King Alfonso XIII, foreseeing further vacillations such as those already displayed by the Prince of the Asturias and the Infante Don Jaime, told his secretary, the Marquis of Torres Mendoza, to write a letter to Rolf von Kutzschenbach, editor of the prestigious *Almanach de Gotha*, specifying that: 'The elder son of His Royal Highness the Infante Don Jaime, born in Rome in April, is to be entered in your publication without the title of Infante, simply as Don Alfonso de Borbón-Segovia, in accordance with his father's renunciation of all his dynastic rights.' Alfonso de Borbón-Dampierre was therefore born just '*el excelentísimo señor don Alfonso de Borbón*', etc., etc.

Don Alfonso's tragedy was that he could never accept his own destiny. It is true that it was an unfortunate one. The son of a deaf mute and an ambitious and light-minded mother who abandoned him almost at the moment of his birth, lacking any personal fortune, despised by a wife who left him very soon after their marriage, and having seen his eldest child die before his eyes in a car accident caused by his own imprudence, he seemed to carry the weight of all the tragedies in the world on his shoulders. Although he never represented any real danger to his cousin Don Juan Carlos, Franco made use of him as a possible substitute if relations with the Count of Barcelona made the dictator change his mind about the heir he himself had designated. It was not always easy to guess Franco's real intentions over this affair. His granddaughter's family, however, the Villaverde clan, played the Borbón-Dampierre card for all it was worth, sure that in the end the aging dictator would succumb to the temptation to see María del Carmen become Queen of Spain. The ultra-Francoists and most of the leaders in the regime thus believed for some time in the possibility of Don Alfonso's coming to the throne. This was to misjudge the Caudillo, who seldom went back on his own decisions, and who did eventually get the Cortes to vote for Don Juan Carlos as his future successor 'as king'. But before he did that the wily Galician made clever play with the threat represented by the infante's son.

Following in his father's footsteps, Alfonso de Borbón-Dampierre liked to make increasingly ambiguous declarations. Immediately after his marriage, for instance, he let it be known that: 'I recognize the establishment of the monarchy in the person of my cousin Don Juan Carlos by the vote of 22 July 1969, in so far as he will respect the fundamental principles of the *Movimiento*.[1] Should he cease to respect them, I will no longer recognize him.'

One person who very soon tired of these unreal games – which had made her Duchess of Cadiz and even Marie du Carmel of France! – was the young bride. A very pretty woman who had inherited a cool, realistic character from her grandfather, she refused to follow her husband into futile and Utopian dynastic adventures. She left him, and once she had obtained her divorce she married a French antiques dealer of Italian origin, Jean-Marie Rossi, a man with the gift of making her laugh: a pleasant experience to which Borbón-Dampierre had not accustomed her.

Alfonso de Borbón-Dampierre, pretender to the crown of France – the crown of Spain having been refused him – died at Beaver Creek, Colorado, decapitated in a skiing accident. He left behind him the memory of someone too proud to admit that, as Montesquieu put it, a man is not unhappy because he is ambitious, but because his ambition devours him.

---

[1] *Movimiento Nacional*, name given to the Francoist regime.

IV

'Señor, may we go back in time for a moment? You were born in Rome?'

'Yes, on 5 January 1938. The civil war had already been devastating Spain for two years.'

'Why Rome, Señor?'

Don Juan Carlos smiles before replying. 'My father often says it's the duty of the monarchy to be nomadic. He means we ought to keep travelling around the country, seeing and being seen, making contact with people, getting to understand and love them. Well, mine was a family of nomads for years, by force of circumstances. In 1931, when my grandfather Don Alfonso XIII left Spain, he first settled in France and then moved to Rome, where he lived until his death. My parents, who had chosen to live in Cannes, had to leave because of hostile demonstrations against them under the Popular Front government. I believe that once the civil war began the Spanish republican government brought pressure to bear on the French authorities to make them leave France. They went first to Milan and then to Rome, where they stayed at the Hotel Eden for some time before moving into the top floor of the Palazzo Torlonia in the Via Bocca di Leone. Eventually they moved to the Villa Gloria in the Viale Parioli. I don't remember the Villa Gloria, but I know the Viale Parioli was almost on the outskirts of Rome at the time. It was a part of the city inhabited by middle-class people – doctors, lawyers, businessmen – anyway, not a luxurious residential area; my parents couldn't have afforded that kind of place.'

Don Juan Carlos was baptized by Cardinal Pacelli, later Pope Pius XII, in the chapel of the Order of the Knights of Malta.

'Your first forename is Juan, Señor, like your father's. But why Carlos?'

'It was my godfather's name; he was my grandfather the Infante Don Carlos de Borbón-Dos Sicilias, who had married Doña Luisa of Orléans, daughter of the Count of Paris. At my christening my uncle the Infante Don Jaime stood proxy for my godfather, who couldn't get away, being a general with a command in the Spanish army. My godmother was my grandmother Queen Victoria Eugenia.'

'Why did they decide on the chapel of the Maltese Order for your christening?'

'Simply because it was in the Via Condotti, very close to the Palazzo Torlonia whose owner Alessandro Torlonia, Prince of Civitella Cesi, was married to my aunt the Infanta Beatriz, one of my father's sisters. The reception was held in the Palazzo Torlonia, and a few Spaniards who could move about freely came to it. It was not the ideal time for travelling. Spain was in the middle of the civil war, and Italy itself was preparing to enter another war. I've often heard my parents speak of the tense situation at the time of my birth. To my own family, the civil war was a tragedy whose outcome was still uncertain, and to many Italians who hated fascism, the future looked very black indeed.'

An aide-de-camp enters the office to hand the king a note. When we are alone again I ask him, 'Señor, do you remember the moment when you first felt you were Spanish?'

Don Juan Carlos looks at me for a moment, baffled, as if he does not quite understand my question. Then he says, 'Spain has always been present in my mind, always! I think my parents began telling me about Spain while I was still in the cradle! In fact it was the one subject of conversation which really roused my father. He always saw everything in relation to Spain.'

Don Juan Carlos pauses for a moment, and his voice is different, lower and more intimate in tone, as he tells me, 'I think that my father could endure exile only because he lived in the certainty that some day he would be back in Spain, his paradise lost.'

'You have been an exile too, Señor.'

'Yes, but my exile had nothing in common with my father's, José Luis. I was born in exile. I'd never known my country. I couldn't feel the lack of the things exiles always miss: things that aren't written in capital letters, just little things which are as important as life itself. Familiar colours, odours, voices, things you eat and drink at home and nowhere else. My father, on the other hand, was born in Spain. He'd spent his childhood and part of his youth there; he was very well aware of what he'd lost. His regrets were real. I had no regrets, only hope. And a great deal of curiosity, José Luis, a great deal of curiosity. When the Lusitania Express entered Extremadura, I was obsessed by one idea: was the Spain passing by before my eyes really the Spain my father had told me about?'

'And was it?'

'Yes, but you had to look at it with the heart and not the eyes, and that was a question of time so far as I was concerned.'

The king locks his fingers together on the polished wood of his desk.

'To die in exile,' says Don Juan Carlos, 'must be the worst thing that can happen to a man. I am sure that thought must have tormented my father a great deal during his own long exile, particularly during the civil war. If the republicans won the war, it would mean the end of our hopes of return.'

'The republicans lost the war, but it was still years before the Count of Barcelona could go home.'

Again, Don Juan Carlos does not reply, but then he nods and says quietly, 'Yes. And having to decide that I should be the first to go back must have been very painful for him. I sometimes tremble to think what my father must have suffered.'

The telephone rings, and I hear the king speak the name of his sister Doña Pilar. I rise and discreetly leave the office. The Duke of Baena's caravels are shining with a soft light on the bookshelves, touched by the last rays of the sun. When the king has finished his call I come back and sit down in front of him.

'You know,' he continues in a confidential tone, 'it was when I had been studying in Madrid for years while my father was still kicking his heels in Estoril – so near to Spain and yet so far! – that our relationship sometimes became difficult, because when he talked to me about Spain he meant a Spain which was part of his historical memory, his nostalgia, a Spain which had become a dream, a pure reflection of his mind. I was living in Spain, breathing its air, feeling its pulse every day, and I said to myself: the Spain my father tells me about is a thing of the past, Spain has changed, the men and women living there today are nothing like the people my father knew when he was eighteen and began his long exile. But I couldn't flatly contradict him and say, "You're wrong, Father, things aren't like that any more! Your Spain and my Spain are two different places!"'

This time Don Juan Carlos's silence seems endless.

'My father is such a decent man, you know,' the king says at last, stressing the adjective, 'that he was as good as defenceless against the various dirty tricks he's encountered so often during his life. For instance, he had great difficulty in coming to any understanding with Franco because my father is a man who always goes straight to the point, while the general, usually so silent, could talk for hours on end when it suited him for the express purpose of saying nothing at all. My father was exasperated by long monologues during which Franco spoke at length about the war in Africa, which had nothing to do with the subjects they were supposed to be discussing. Where my father was a man as clear as spring water, the general made things extremely complicated: he had a kind of inability to go up stairs without looking as if he were coming down them. It was a talent of which my father thought nothing at all. I was often a victim of Franco's taste for secrecy and dissimulation myself. I remember setting off on holiday for Estoril in June 1969 to spend St John's Day with my family. A number of Spaniards used to go to Portugal at this time to wish the king[1] a happy name-day. My father liked to have his whole family at home with him on that day. Before leaving Madrid I went to the Pardo to say goodbye to the general.

'"When do you expect to be back, Highness?" he asked me.

'"On the twelfth or thirteenth, General. In any case I'll be here for the military review on 18 July."

'"Very good, Highness. But come and see me when you get back, because I shall have something important to tell you."

'These last words of the general's intrigued me, but I very soon forgot them. As soon as I arrived in Estoril my father told me he had reliable information that Franco very soon intended to nominate me his successor, "as king". I said Laureano López Rodó[2] had told me much the

---

[1] The Count of Barcelona, regarded as King Juan III by his supporters.
[2] A monarchist and one of Franco's ministers.

same in Madrid, but it was only rumour so far. "If the nomination were imminent," I explained to my father, "Franco would have told me so when I went to say goodbye before coming here." "So you don't know anything for certain?" persisted my father. "No, absolutely nothing."

'Back in Madrid after my holiday, I went to the Pardo to see the general. As usual he received me in a very friendly manner.

'"How's your family, Highness?"

'"Very well, thank you, General."

'"Good. I have some news for you," he told me without any change in his tone of voice. "I am going to nominate you my successor, 'as king', on 22 July."

'That was only five or six days away. I was staggered.

'"But General, why didn't you say anything to me when I came to see you before I left for Estoril?"

'"I didn't want you to know before seeing your family," he said perfectly calmly.

'"Well, I must let my father know your intentions now, anyway."

'"I'd prefer him not to know."

'"General, I can't lie to my father, still less keep news of such importance from him."

'He looked at me in silence for several seconds, his face impenetrable, and then asked, "Well, what's your decision, Highness?"

'He didn't tell me to take time thinking about my reply; no, he wanted it then, on the spot. The moment I had feared so much had come at last. Standing there facing the general, who was waiting imperturbably, I performed a very simple piece of reasoning, one I'd often been through before. My father, going against the opinion of many of his advisers, had wanted me to study at university and do my military training in Spain, and he knew better than anyone the risks he ran in sending me into the "enemy camp". It didn't take me long to find those out for myself. The real point at stake now was not who would be King of Spain, my father or me: bringing back the monarchy was what really mattered. General Franco had just asked for my decision. If I didn't reply then and there, he could strike me out of his plans; he did not like to be crossed, and he had plenty of other pawns to go on with his game if I vacated my space on the board. And Franco would certainly not be turning to the Count of Barcelona. That being said, José Luis, there was never a moment – and God knows we had some difficult moments – when I thought the general was going to change his mind about me. The fact that he had taken so long to nominate a future king didn't mean he was not a convinced monarchist. Throughout the whole of the Francoist regime, Spain had never ceased to be officially a kingdom, and that seemed to me significant. Naturally I would have liked things to be different, particularly for my father's sake. But Franco had me up against the wall that day. He was waiting for my reply. So I told him, "Very well, General, I agree." He smiled very slightly and shook hands.

'Back at home I called my father in Estoril and told him what had just happened. His reaction struck me as perfectly logical. "That means," he said, in a different tone of voice "you knew when you came here and you didn't want to tell me." I told him he was wrong: I'd known nothing whatsoever when I went to Estoril. I was aware of certain rumours, just as he was, but you can't take rumours at face value in Madrid. I was telling nothing but the truth, but the shock of the news was so great that my father didn't believe me. He was very cold towards me for several months. Then, as time passed by, we went back to our normal relationship. He embraced me and told me, "After all, it was I who put you in this difficult situation, sending you to Spain." And he added, bitterly, "But I would never have believed things would turn out like this."

'It had all been done in the general's characteristic way, which was to strike hard without warning. He could be extremely affable with one of his ministers at the end of a Council meeting, and send a motor-cycle messenger half an hour later with a letter telling the man he was dismissed. Thinking about it so many years later, I consider that Franco behaved with his own very idiosyncratic kind of logic over this business of the succession. He had decided long ago that my father would never succeed to the throne of Spain while he, Franco, was alive, and he took the time he thought necessary to try me out before nominating me instead.'

'To him, Señor, the very act of nominating you must have meant that he saw his personal power coming to an end soon.'

'Yes, but only with his death. He was perhaps one of the very few Spaniards to realize that he actually would die some day. The death of Franco was no part of the programme to those in power around him.'

'What was your relationship with him like, Señor?'

'Considering that he was naturally a cold and secretive man, it was pretty good. He was very friendly to me, often affectionate, and always very respectful of what I represented in his eyes.'

'It's been said that he regarded you as a son, Señor.'

'As the son he never had? Yes, perhaps. However, he was a strange man. When I came back to Spain after my marriage to Doña Sofía in 1962, I didn't know how to fill my time. In spite of my military training I was sure Franco wouldn't allow me to shut myself up in a barracks or serve on board a warship. So I went to see him, and I told him, "General, I have to occupy myself somehow. I'm too young to hang about doing nothing." He looked at me in silence for some time. Franco always took his time about replying to a question that he thought important. Finally he told me, "Let the Spanish people get to know you, Highness." And he added not another word. It was up to me to decide what he meant, and pick the best way of letting my compatriots get to know me. With the assistance of General Vigón, minister of public works, his under-secretary Vicente Mortes, and Laureano López Rodó, I began studying the intricate workings of the civil service by spending two or three months in each of several ministries. Then I followed Franco's advice by going on my travels round Spain, visiting city after city, small town after small town.'

'How were you received by people to whom you were still a completely unknown factor?'

'With great warmth and cordiality. Of course there were exceptions to the rule. I remember one village, near Valladolid, where people threw potatoes as we drove past. The minister of agriculture, who was travelling with me, was horrified. I had to calm him down. "Don't worry, Minister, it's me they're after, not you!" Another day, in Valencia, I was walking down the road with the captain-general of the region. Ever since then I've been in the habit of turning round to see if anyone is following me, and if so who. That day I saw a man running towards us. Instinctively, instead of walking faster, I stepped back, and the captain-general found himself alone in the middle of the road, so he got the volley of tomatoes intended for me. Yet again, I had to explain the tomatoes were meant for me and not the captain-general. *Gajes del oficio*,[1] as my grandfather Don Alfonso XIII would have said.'

'There's a period in Your Majesty's life which has always greatly intrigued me. I meant the time when you used to appear in public behind Franco, always silent, often sullen. You gave the impression of wishing

---

[1] Occupational hazards.

yourself a thousand miles away. Many people considered you a complete enigma, and a great many of us were wrong about you. A number of those who are now committed "Juancarlists" thought that even if you succeeded to the throne, you wouldn't last more than a fortnight. Santiago Carrillo suggested you'd be known as Juan Carlos *el Breve*, and I wasn't so far from agreeing with him myself.'

The king's face lights up with a huge smile. 'Yes, Don Santiago and I often laugh over that prediction. He never misses a chance of reminding me how wrong he was!' The smile vanishes, and his face is grave again. 'Why did I always keep silent? Why didn't I ever say anything? Because at that time no one, not even I, dared to speak. Self-censorship, prudence if you'd rather, was the general rule. Personally I couldn't tell how things were going to turn out. I didn't know if I would succeed Franco in his lifetime, or if I would have to wait for his death to become King of Spain. Nor did I know how the country would react to the suggested change.'

'It has even been said that when Franco was on his deathbed, and you were awaiting the outcome of events here at La Zarzuela with Torcuato Fernández Miranda, you remarked: "We may equally well see people turning up to offer me the crown on a cushion, or the *Guardia Civil*[1] coming with orders to arrest me."'

'Yes, I believe I did say something like that. We were all feeling very nervous.'

'But how could Your Majesty have been so uninformed?'

'I wasn't uninformed. It was only certain information I lacked. I knew Franco had decided to make me King of Spain, but I did not know how the country would react to his decision. Because just how many monarchists were there in Spain at that time, José Luis? Let's be honest: not very many. Realism had to be the order of the day. Even the "back to the monarchy" operation upon which Franco had resolved wasn't without its risks. How would the Left react? What attitude would the Communist Party take? People just did not know. When I thought of that, the general's advice to me in 1962 to let the Spanish people get to know me suddenly assumed its full significance. I had already realized that while rural and small town areas might accept the monarchy without much trouble, the farther up the social scale you went the more openly

[1] Civil Guard.

doubtful people were. I knew the military would accept me, of course, because I had been nominated by Franco, and in the army you didn't argue with Franco's decisions. Moreover I'd been through all the military academies, and made a great many loyal friends there, and I never missed a chance to make contact with my old comrades.'

Suddenly raising his voice, Don Juan Carlos asks, 'If I hadn't had loyal friends in the army, do you think I could have done what I did on the night of 23 February?[1] I'm sure I couldn't.' And resuming his normal tone, Don Juan Carlos tells me, 'You know, I often asked Franco to let me spend time in a barracks with my friends who had trained in the same year, or serve on board a warship. To which Franco replied, "Doing what? Going to the bar to play cards?"'

'General Monasterio, who commanded the cavalry in the civil war and whose aide-de-camp my father was throughout that period, used to claim that Franco felt a certain scorn for the army,' I say.

'Well, he never showed it in front of me,' replies Don Juan Carlos rather drily. 'If he refused to let me be part of the army it was because he knew I had better things to do than play the lieutenant in any one regiment. You were saying that I didn't talk much at the time. That's true, but I was doing a great deal of listening. And I kept travelling around the country, trying to get a real idea of what Spain was. It was only when Franco was dying, however, that I realized what a responsibility was about to be mine. I was chiefly preoccupied with wondering how I was going to set up a democracy when Franco was dead. I remember Torcuato Fernández Miranda telling me, "Don't worry. It will be easier than you think. When people see there is a king in Franco's place they will understand that things can't go on in the same way as before; they won't need to have anything explained to them."

'"Yes," I replied, "but I shall need a minimum amount of time, a kind of parenthesis, to make them understand what I intend to do."

'To that, Torcuato said, "Your first speech will be the keystone of the whole change. You will tell the Spanish people: this is what I intend to do, and how I intend to do it." Torcuato knew that basically my political thinking was the same as my father's: I wanted to be king of all the Spanish people. I contrived to get that phrase into my first speech.'

'What was the reaction, Señor?'

[1] 23 February 1981, the date of the attempted *coup d'état* by Tejero.

'Well,' says Don Juan Carlos, smiling, 'as you can imagine, some people were distinctly worried, but the vast majority of the country breathed a sigh of relief.'

'Señor, do you think Franco really believed in his famous saying "*Lo dejo todo atado y bien atado* (I am leaving everything tied up, and well tied up)"?'

'I never heard those words in his mouth, but it's something that need not be taken literally. I think the general meant to indicate that he was leaving behind him the structures the country needed. He was far too intelligent to believe that things would go on after his death exactly as before.'

'It strikes me as odd that since Franco meant to make you his successor, he didn't ask you to share the responsibilities of state with him, and he gave you no explanations or advice.'

'Franco was well aware that I wouldn't be able to follow most of his advice. Certainly not all of it. But I do remember going to see him when he was already very ill. He took my hand, pressed it very hard, and whispered: "Highness, all I ask of you is to preserve the unity of Spain." It's true that I had often asked him to let me attend a Council of Ministers to see how he "tackled" them' – the verb Don Juan Carlos uses here is *lidiar*, which has connotations of bullfighting – 'and he always replied, "It would be no use to you, since you won't be able to do what I do." As for that phrase *atado y bien atado*: if he ever really did say it, Franco will have intended a double meaning, as he so often did. Franco had a very Spanish type of black humour. I remember that when I was Prince of Spain the press mounted an extraordinarily virulent campaign against my father, describing him as a freemason, a dangerous dema-gogue, even an Englishman, because he had served in the British Navy. I went to complain to the general. "You can't let them treat my father like this," I told him, "not when I am here myself." He looked at me impassively and replied, without the trace of a smile, "Oh, it's just the way of the press, Highness." And that was at a time when not a single newspaper editor would have dared to publish a word which might displease the general!'

'Ironic, then, and cynical with it?'

'The general would have told you, "Politics are politics." When I come to think of it, my relations with Franco were never on the level of the commonplace. I was always perfectly honest with him. When I didn't like something I went and told him so. I sometimes warned him of possible trouble. "I've heard rumours of this or that, general; if I were you I'd check." I think he appreciated my frankness. Anyway he knew I never flattered him.'

'You must have been the only one who didn't, Señor.'

'Probably. I don't know. I had nothing to lose or gain, but I was at peace with myself. The only thing Franco could do to me was say, "Go back to your father in Estoril," and I would have been happy to obey. I've sometimes been asked if the general exercised a great influence over me. Well, he did influence me, by his example, to get into the way of looking at things calmly, at a distance from myself, with a certain detachment. However, I don't think Franco ever tried to influence me on particular subjects. He never went beyond suggestion or veiled advice; he always left me perfectly free to act in my own way. Having said that, he did nothing to smooth difficulties from my path either. When he was already very seriously ill he asked me to preside over the Council of Ministers in his place. I got into the habit of going to see him as soon as the Council meetings were over to tell him what had been discussed. It was a gesture of courtesy on my part towards the man who was still head of state. However, when I reached his bedside I often found that one of the ministers had been ahead of me and had already given him the information. One day, exasperated, I lost my temper. "What's the idea, General? It's for me to come and tell you what happened at the Council meeting, and I have no intention of joining in a motor race with the ministers in order reach you first. If this goes on I'm not presiding over the Council any more." My annoyance seemed to amuse him. I had the impression he was continually putting me to the test so as to get a better idea of my character and discover any weak spots in it. One day when I came to his bedside and was going to tell him about the Council, he stopped me with a gesture. "Don't bother, Highness. The minister of agriculture was ten minutes ahead of you today."'

And the king laughs heartily.

'Señor, when we were talking about your childhood in Rome yesterday you indicated that your family had money troubles at the time?'

'Well, when my grandfather King Alfonso XIII left Spain in 1931, he didn't have what they call a large fortune. Besides, as far as I know kings don't usually make off with the contents of the till. Ever since I was a small child I'd heard our economic problems discussed at home. Money was a constant worry to us. I was five or six years old when I struck the first bad bargain of my life. It was in Lausanne. A Spanish visitor who had come to see my father had given me a gold pen. There was a little shop just outside the Hotel Royal, where we were staying, and we sometimes went there to buy sweets and chocolate. Not having a penny in my pocket, I had the brilliant idea of going to find the hotel porter and showing him my pen. "It's made of gold," I told him. "How much will you give me for it?" The porter offered five francs; I gave him my pen and went straight to the little shop to buy toffees. When my father heard about it he went to see the porter, gave him ten francs and got the pen back. He told me sternly, "You've just lost me five francs."

'Before I became Prince of Spain and had an allowance from the state I was often short of money. I've already told you that Nicolás Mondéjar was like a father to me, and there was a time when he was paying for my suits from Collado.[1] Whatever people may say, neither my father nor any other member of the royal family ever received a penny from the Spanish state during all the years of our exile. In the time of Don Alfonso XIII the king had a civil list, a salary paid by the state if you prefer to put it that way. Don Alfonso had to pay for the maintenance of all the royal palaces out of this salary – the Oriente, El Escorial, La Granja, Los Alcázares, Pedralbes and I forget how many more. All his money went down the drain of those expenses, which must have been astronomical, because they were very grand residences; you couldn't have kept them going with a staff of a mere dozen or so. Hundreds of people were needed, and their wages too came out of the king's privy purse. The figures would stagger you. When I was studying at San Sebastian I lived in the Miramar palace, a private property my father had inherited from Don Alfonso XIII. I lived in a few rooms and the rest of the palace was shut up, because my father didn't have the funds to cover the maintenance of the whole place. When he came back to Spain my father sold Miramar, just as he later sold the Magdalena palace, which was also his personal property.'

'Was it because of Don Miguel Maura's warning that Your Majesty didn't come to live in the Oriente palace in Madrid?' I ask.

'No,' replies the king, laughing, 'although some of his advice does strike me as very sensible. I never thought of taking up residence in the

[1] Famous Madrid tailor.

Oriente palace because ever since 1960 I'd been living here at La Zarzuela, a house which Doña Sofía and I like very much. It's well away from the city, noise, pollution and unwelcome visitors. And I don't know if you've ever visited the private apartments of the Oriente palace, but all I can say is that my grandparents and their children were hardly living in the lap of luxury. If I'd wanted to take up residence in the Oriente in 1975 everything would have needed modernizing – plumbing, wiring, heating, everything. I think General Franco did contemplate restoring one wing of the palace to make it habitable, but nothing got beyond the planning stage, probably because of the expense.'

'They say the King of Spain is the worst-paid king in Europe, Señor.'

'I think it's rather risky to simplify quite so much. If you compare us to the British, well, maybe so. But if the King of Spain isn't too well paid, the state does look after many of his expenses. I have a civil list, but so do the queen, the Prince of the Asturias, and the two infantas. That wasn't the case in the time of Alfonso XIII. The British may be better paid than we are, but we have a *Patrimonio Nacional* ('national patrimony') to take care of many of our expenses, including the upkeep of all the royal palaces. In the past the *Patrimonio Nacional* was the *Patrimonio Real* ('royal patrimony'), comprising all Crown property. After the civil war, the name changed and Crown property became national property. As for those in the service of the Crown today, they aren't recruited in the same way as people used to be recruited in the old days. I wanted such posts filled by civil servants, not people directly linked to the Crown as they were in my grandfather's time.'

The king pauses, looking at his photographs of the queen and their children.

'You were asking just now whether I ever thought of taking up residence in the Oriente. The answer is no, never, and not just for economic reasons. I had a much more important reason: my ambition was to live a life as close as possible to a normal family existence with my wife and children, in a house where we could sometimes forget the burden of the offices of state. For that I needed a house on a human scale, and the Oriente is a palace. An enormous palace. It's an exhausting job being a king, you know, José Luis. You need a chance to forget it from time to time. La Zarzuela is a real home, and the Oriente never could have been that. We can be here together in private, in rooms of normal dimensions. The prince goes to university, comes back for lunch, goes out again. So do the infantas. When we're here together we have the illusion of being a family like any other. The Duke of Edinburgh once complained that he could never get a hot cup of tea at home. There's such a distance between the kitchens and the private apartments in Buckingham Palace that the tea gets cold on the way. They're reduced to boiling water on a hotplate for their own tea, poor things.'

The telephone rings again. The king picks up the receiver, listens in silence for a few moments, and then says, 'I have Vilallonga here.' Placing his hand over the receiver, he tells me, 'It's the queen.' Instinctively, I straighten up. '*Se ha cuadrado*,'[1] the king tells Doña Sofía. Then he rises and gives me his hand across the desk. 'I'll have to leave you now. They're expecting me for dinner.'

[1] He's standing to attention.

V

If there is one thing with which Franco cannot be reproached, it is having neglected the training of the future King of Spain.

'In 1953,' Don Juan Carlos tells me, 'or it may have been 1954 – I'm bad about dates – my father and the general met at Las Cabezas, a *finca* belonging to the Count of Ruiseñada. The subject under discussion that day was when, where and how I was to do my university studies and military training. My father wanted to send me to Bologna University, with its world-famous reputation, or to Louvain University in Belgium. Then he wanted me to return to Spain and study first at the Military Academy of Zaragoza, then at the Naval College of Marín, and finally at San Javier. Franco did not agree with this programme at all. "Highness," he told my father, "if we do as you seem to wish, the prince will be twenty-two or twenty-three by the time he returns to Spain. At that age it will be very difficult for him to fit into military life, surrounded by boys of between seventeen and eighteen. A young man in Spain gets his lieutenant's commission at the age of twenty at the latest. The prince won't feel at all happy with fellow cadets so much younger than himself. My view is that he ought to do his military training first, and then, once he has completed it, go to one of our great Spanish universities. It's out of the question for a prince who is to reign over Spain some day to be brought up abroad." The discussion between the pair of them lasted two hours. Finally my father gave way; he had run out of arguments, but above all he realized that Franco was right. So I entered the Military

Academy of Zaragoza at the age of seventeen. Discipline was very strict, and my father had insisted that I was to be treated like any other cadet. Unfortunately, political circumstances meant I was never able to complete my university studies later, as I would have wished.

'Once my father and the general had agreed, I was sent to Madrid to live with the Duke of Montellano and his family in a *palacete*[1] in the Calle de Eduardo Dato, now the headquarters of a large insurance company. I attended the Colegio de Huéfanos[2] to prepare for my entry into the Military Academy of Zaragoza in 1955. Then, in 1957 and 1958, I went to the Naval College at Marín – I went on a voyage of the training ship *Juan Sebastián Elcano* – and I finished my military studies at the Air Force Academy of San Javier.

'Meanwhile the Duke of La Torre and my father were drawing up the programme for my university studies. The duke had persuaded my father, against the advice of the members of his privy council, to send me to Salamanca University, his main idea being to keep me as far from Madrid as possible, so that I wouldn't be prey to the pernicious influences of the capital and the intrigues of sharks swimming in the waters of power. I think the duke also wanted to spare me too much proximity to General Franco, not a man close to his heart. But once I had my commissions for the land, sea and air forces in my pocket, my father, giving way to pressure from his privy council, decided I was to study at Madrid University and not Salamanca after all. For once Franco agreed with him. While I was attending the various military academies, Franco had quite a heated discussion about me with the Duke of La Torre. The general didn't want me to go to Salamanca University because one of the lecturers there was Don Enrique Tierno Galván, the famous *viejo profesor*,[3] an intellectual of the moderate Left who later became the very popular mayor of Madrid. The Duke of La Torre thought these reasons were ridiculous, and lost his temper. As he saw it, Salamanca was the oldest and most prestigious of the Spanish universities, with a great history and tradition behind it, and therefore suitable for the education of the future King of Spain. My father, fortified by the support of Franco and the members of his privy council,

---

[1] Little palace.
[2] A military college.
[3] Old professor.

put an end to the argument by announcing that I would be staying in Madrid. At this the Duke of La Torre, not a man easily led, bowed out. "You entrusted me with the prince's education," he told my father, "and now Your Majesty, siding with General Franco, has decided to remove that trust from me. I am therefore going home." And the duke went, metaphorically slamming the door behind him. He let me know how sorry he was to have to leave me. The duke's departure distressed me a great deal, but there was nothing I could do for him. Nobody had asked me for my opinion. I was like a football pitch with the ball up in the air, and I had no idea where it was going to fall.

'However, Franco did agree with the Duke of La Torre about Madrid in that he didn't want me to live there. "You need to study in peace and quiet," he told me. "I thought you could live in the Casita de Arriba."[1] This was another *palacete*, fitted out by Franco in case he had to use it as a refuge during the Second World War. It was not at all like a bunker, though; it was a kind of doll's house very close to the Escorial. A drawing room, a dining room, three bedrooms and an office: that was all. But the little house was equipped with a network of ultra-modern communications, though to look at it you wouldn't have thought it could act as a bolthole for a really important person.

'The general offered me the Casita to live in while restoration work on La Zarzuela was still in progress, so I spent several months there. I went to the university at nine every morning, came home for lunch, and had the afternoon free for sporting activities. Since the Casita was fifty kilometres from Madrid I spent several hours a day at the wheel of my car.'

The king looks at me as if expecting a question which I do not ask. Then he says, 'Yes, at the end of the day Franco won all along the line. He had me close to him, and he had removed me from any influence that the men on my father's Privy Council might have exercised over me. He did not like those men because he thought them too liberal.'

'I believe, Señor, it was at this time that a key figure in Spanish politics entered your life.'

'Torcuato Fernández Miranda? Yes. Most of all, he contributed a great deal to my training to be king. He came to the Casita every

[1] Little house up above.

morning to teach me political law. He had a fascinating mind. After a few days I asked him, "Aren't you going to bring me any books?"

' "Your Highness doesn't need them."

' "What do you mean, I don't need them? I need books to study!"

' "No, no, Your Highness must learn by listening, and looking around you."

' "But when I have exams to pass—"

'Torcuato interrupted me. "You don't need books."

' "You're wrong, I do!"

' "No, you do not." And I couldn't get him to budge from that position. When he talked to me about my future job as king, about what I would have to do or not do, I felt anxious. "How am I going to find out about all these things? Who's going to help me?"

' "No one. You'll have to be like a trapeze artiste working without a safety net."

' "No net?"

' "No net."

'These were totally surrealist conversations. Torcuato,' Don Juan Carlos goes on, 'had a cool sense of humour which was sometimes very elusive to grasp, because he seldom smiled. But he taught me patience and serenity, and above all he taught me to see things as they are, without illusions and without trusting appearances too much. He often repeated, "When I tell Your Highness to look around you, it is so that you will understand that apparently identical situations can sometimes be basically very different. History repeats itself, but it is never quite the same. The stake is different every time." '

'That's more or less what Franco told you.'

'Yes, indeed. From the 1960s onwards, Torcuato was almost always at my side. I trusted him completely, and he showed me total, perfect loyalty to the day he died. When I became king on 22 November 1975, the prime minister was Arias Navarro, and Rodriguez de Valcárcel was president of the Cortes: as you know, they had always been loyal supporters of Franco. For political reasons, and to keep the country quiet, I had to retain both in their posts for some time. However, when Arias felt obliged to offer his resignation on 1 July 1976, I asked Torcuato, "Which would you rather be, prime minister or president of the Cortes?" After my own, the position of prime minister, head of government, was the most important in the kingdom. I could offer

68

nothing better to the man to whom I owed so much. Torcuato replied, without a moment's hesitation, "As a political man, which I am, I would like to head your new government, but I can be a great deal more use to you as president of the Cortes." It was a handsome gesture on Torcuato's part. We were going through a difficult, not to say dangerous time just then. The Francoist apparatus was still in place, and it could still wield enormous power. We also had to consider the fact that the Cortes dated back to the preceding regime, and the Council of the Realm numbered the ultra-purist hardliners of Francoism among its members. Of course it also included people like Miguel Primo de Rivera who supported me, and whom I could count on to introduce the change gently. But unfortunately they were in a minority. The only man who could influence the Council of the Realm one way or the other was the president of the Cortes. Torcuato knew it, and that was why he preferred that post to the office of prime minister. For weeks he patiently spun his web, conducting private conversations with those *procuradores*[1] who were most opposed to the slightest change. He did the same with the members of the Council of the Realm, making it customary for them to meet every fortnight. Each time, the press and those in high places thought: the Council of the Realm is meeting, so something must be going to happen. But nothing did. Then, one day, Torcuato came to see me and asked me: "Your Majesty, tell me the name of the man who ought to replace Arias Navarro, and I'll do what I can to get him voted in." He'd been working quietly for weeks, arguing with some people, winning others over. Everyone listened to him and respected him, for he was a man of great moral authority, and he could assess his opponents shrewdly.'

'I know Your Majesty didn't like having to swear to maintain the principles of the *Movimiento* before the Cortes.'

'No, because I knew that even if I did swear to maintain them, the principles of Francoism could not remain in force: that would have been the same as saying that the old regime was still in office. But Torcuato, unperturbed, told me, "Your Majesty has no cause for concern. Swear to maintain the principles of the *Movimiento*, and at a later date we will change them legally, one by one." His favourite saying was, "We must go from the law to the law." And so we did. Finally everyone, even the

[1] The members of the Cortes directly nominated by the regime.

most fervent defenders of the Francoist regime, realized that with Franco himself dead things could not go on exactly as before.'

'Could it be called collective suicide by the Francoist *procuradores*, then?'

'If you like, but it is a phrase I would not want you to put into my mouth.'

'All the same, Señor, it seems almost miraculous that the transition from dictatorship to a constitutional, democratic monarchy went so smoothly and serenely.'

'The miracle was being able to count on the Spanish people, the great majority of whom trusted us while they waited for what, thank God, we have been able to give them.' Don Juan Carlos hesitates for a moment before adding, 'I don't think there is a king in any other country in the world who has been given the opportunity of doing what I have done.'

'I'd like to return to that saying about your being sent by Providence, Señor, because no one else could have done what you did in your place.'

'No, certainly not, but to talk about being sent by Providence sounds a little pompous. Let's say I was the right man in the right place at the right time. And then – why should I deny it? – luck often comes my way, and I have a certain gift for catching it on the wing, even summoning it up. I do fervently believe you must defend your good fortune as doggedly as you defend your rights, but fortune has many different faces. My own good fortune has been to have the men I needed at my side in delicate situations, and there's no doubt about it, Torcuato was one of those men.'

'Why was Adolfo Suárez elected?'

'Because he was young and modern. Because his roots lay in Francoism, and he couldn't be suspected of wishing to introduce excessively radical changes which would have been unacceptable to certain sectors of our society. Adolfo had been within the Francoist fold throughout his career, like all the Spaniards in public office at that time. He had been secretary-general of the *Movimiento*, and later, at my request, director-general of the national television company, where he did a good deal for my image as Prince of Spain. But I repeat, he was young and modern, and ambitious enough to want to be the man who dealt with the period we were going through. As a Francoist, he managed to persuade the anti-Francoists to trust him to introduce change. He was successful beyond our dreams. But don't forget that behind him, behind us, stood the entire Spanish people, wanting peace more than anything else. I believe they forgot their ideologies and thought: let's wait, at least for a while, and see if the thing can be done.'

'What were your first meetings with Felipe González like, Señor?'

'Very easy. He was leader of the opposition, but an opposition which wanted to collaborate in making the change succeed.' And as if paying a great compliment, Don Juan Carlos adds, 'He was a man of my own age.'

'Is it true that during one of your first meetings you asked him, "Why are you socialists republicans?" and Felipe González told you the story of the King of Sweden and his prime minister?'

'Olof Palme?'

'No, long before him.'

This incident occurred at the time of the electoral campaign of 1937 or 1938, when the social democrats, whose leaders had been preaching republicanism, came to power. The Swedish monarch of the time summoned the prime minister *in pectore* and told him, 'Prime Minister, we have two possibilities before us: the first is that you respect your electoral promises and consequently, since you have an absolute majority, there will be not only a political change but a change of regime and you will proclaim a republic. The second possibility is that you continue to respect the institutional system of the monarchy. In either case I am ready to take scrupulous account of the will of the people. But I suggest a compromise: let us go on as we are for a year, so as not to traumatize Swedish society any further. If all goes well we'll discuss the matter again next year. But before you leave, Prime Minister, I will just add this: the monarchy will always cost the Swedish people less than a republic. With me as head of the state, you will save the cost of presidential elections, which as I am sure you know entail the squandering of a great deal of money. Good day, Prime Minister.' A year passed, and the social democrat prime minister never mentioned the subject of a republic again. And things have gone on as before to this very day.

Telling me how he told the king this story, Felipe González added, 'Don Juan Carlos listened to me attentively, still smiling. I think my anecdote was a good reply to his question. The king, who seemed amused, understood that it was not just a good story, and I had chosen this anecdote to show him what was behind my thinking.'

*

'Yes,' says Don Juan Carlos, 'I remember the story very well. As a good Andalusian, Felipe is an excellent raconteur.'

I tell the king, 'When Felipe had finished his story, I said, "The king asked why you socialists were republicans, and you told him this Swedish fable, but you didn't actually answer his question."

'"Yes, I did," Felipe objected. "He was well aware that if we had always been republicans it was because his grandfather's monarchy never made any direct contact with us. When he travelled abroad Don Alfonso XIII sometimes talked at length to the French socialists and the British Labour Party, but he never had a serious conversation with a Spanish socialist."'

'That does seem to be correct,' admits Don Juan Carlos.

'Which amounts to saying, Señor, that the monarchy of the old days was the monarchy of a single class, the Right, and regarded the Left as its enemy.'

'Yes, and that is why, for forty long years, my father went on saying *ad infinitum* – and it cost him the Crown – that he wanted to be king of all the Spanish people. As for me, José Luis, I am very proud to have made my father's old dream an indisputable reality. At present the King of Spain is ruling with a left-wing party in power, the socialists. But I listen to everyone: the Left, the Right, the unions, the employers, the communists. Speaking of communists, I must tell you a story which strikes me as both funny and very significant. When Valéry Giscard d'Estaing was visiting Spain as President of the French Republic, we gave a state banquet in his honour at the Pardo palace. The occasion left much to be desired. Everything went wrong. The cold consommé was warm, the fish which ought to have been hot was cold, the meat was tough, and so on and so forth. To be honest, it was a disastrous dinner, and one of the hundred or so guests present was Santiago Carrillo, then secretary-general of the Spanish Communist Party. Two or three days later, Giscard d'Estaing invited us to the Aranjuez palace. The French laid on a magnificent dinner. Everything was absolutely exquisite. Chefs from Maxim's had been sent from France by special plane, along with the best French wines. The china was marvellous, the service perfect. Don Santiago, who was at that dinner too, took Nicolas Mondéjar's arm as he left the table and told him, "This won't do, Marquis! You dine better with the French than at the King of Spain's table! It mustn't happen again. Official dinners given by Their Majesties should be as good as the dinners given by our foreign guests, if not better! The prestige of our monarchy is at stake!" Don Santiago was really annoyed to think the French had outdone us; the secretary-general of the Spanish Communist Party felt his pride wounded because "his" monarchy hadn't come up to scratch! Don Santiago is a remarkable man!' And the king laughed heartily.

'He's a man to whom the Spanish people owe a very great deal,' I say. 'Because if he had wanted to throw a spanner in the works at the beginning of the transition –'

'Oh, I knew he wouldn't do that,' Don Juan Carlos interrupts me.

'How was that, Señor?'

'Well, it's a long story.' Don Juan Carlos casts a glance at the Breitling on his wrist and murmured, 'I don't know if I'll have time...'

I can sense that he really wants to tell me his 'long story', so I keep prudently quiet.

'Well, I'll try to keep it short. First of all,' the king tells me, 'I must go back to the time when I was still Prince of Spain, a time when few people dared make contact with me openly, for fear it would be noted in high places. I think you asked if I had met Felipe González before becoming King of Spain. I told you no, but I did meet other members of the Socialist Party, for instance Luis Solana, who came to see me at La Zarzuela on his motorbike and entered this room without taking off his helmet, to avoid being recognized. Through Solana and various other people, Felipe González was kept informed of what I planned to do and how it was to be done. With other covert democrats – I'm thinking of Iñigo Cavero, Oreja and Ruiz Jiménez – matters were less complicated. But then there was the Communist Party, and no one knew very much about it. In Spain, no one apart from the communists themselves had any information about the party. How many militants did it contain? What was its real strength? What would the communist leaders do on the death of Franco? What attitude to the monarchy would they adopt? What we did all know was that the Communist Party had been alone in causing General Franco's regime occasional anxiety, by virtue of its efficiency and the means it seemed to have at its command. I was still Prince of Spain when I realized that, once I was king, the government would have to legalize political parties to speed up the move towards democracy. And I was convinced it would be unthinkable to exclude the Communist Party. I therefore had to find out, very fast, all I could about the communists and their intentions in a future which, given the general's state of health, seemed to be coming rapidly closer. I had heard that my father had met Carrillo in Paris, and thought him remarkably intelligent. But I couldn't ask my father to meet him again and sound him out in my name. This was a dangerous game and one I wanted to play alone, without compromising the image of the Count of Barcelona – because there could have been a leak.

'What was clear to me was that some day the Communist Party would have to be legalized, against any opposition, but that did present me with enormous difficulties. Years later, when Adolfo Suárez was in power – and he too was convinced of the necessity of legalizing the Communist Party – the French ambassador Jean-François Deniau told me, "The thing to do with communists is count them. In Portugal, Alvaro Cunhal's party was a constant menace to the government until the day they held elections and the Communist Party won 14.6% of the votes – those were the votes of the people who believed it represented the future, a wonderful tomorrow, a radiant society, etc. But thanks to the elections, it became obvious that 84.4% of the population didn't believe any such nonsense. So the Communist Party lost any right to say it was the people, it represented the people, it was the future. That is what should be done in Spain, Your Majesty," Ambassador Deniau told me, and he added, "Personally I don't think the Spanish Communist Party would be very successful at the polls, but I have a very good idea of all the drawbacks its exclusion would entail. All observers and the entire international press would be saying: your elections aren't real elections, your democracy is not a real democracy!"

'I too thought the Communist Party shouldn't be allowed the monopoly of civic virtue, or privileged access to the mystery of the future. But I didn't know how I was going to convince the Spanish people of it, José Luis. I told myself that first I must find out what Carrillo and his party intended to do the day I came to the throne.'

Don Juan Carlos falls silent for a moment. Then he goes on.

'I really don't know if I ought to be telling you all this. Even today it's a very delicate subject! There are people who, when they find out that even while I was Prince of Spain I was already thinking of legalizing the Communist Party some day, will say to themselves ... oh, I don't know ... they'll think I was already preparing to deceive them or betray them.'

'Señor, with the exception of a minority, I believe people will think, as I do, that first and foremost you had a very accurate political vision of the state of affairs: today no one would venture to claim you were wrong to legalize the Communist Party and thus unveil the secret of its strength, or rather its weakness.'

'Well, you may be right. But I repeat, it's a very delicate subject. Still, let's take the risk. I'll tell you how it happened. My problem, you see, was this: how to make contact with Carrillo through some third person. But what third person? Then, one day, I remembered that in 1975 I'd been invited by the Shah of Iran to the commemorative celebrations at Persepolis, and there, in a kind of residential area reserved for heads of state and persons of note, I'd been introduced to Ceauşescu – a megalomaniac, a raving lunatic if you ask me – and I had a short conversation with him. I also remembered that Ceauşescu had told me he was well acquainted with Carrillo, who used to go to Romania on holiday. Remembering this conversation, I said to myself: I'll find out what Carrillo has in mind through Ceauşescu. So I sent for a very close friend, someone you know well, whose name I won't mention because I don't think he would like it publicly known he was involved in this story. Our friend came to see me, and I told him, "I want you to go to Romania, old fellow." From the expression on his face, I could see he didn't like the idea at all. I explained that he was the only person I could trust. The message I wanted to get to Ceauşescu had to be delivered verbally, for I feared that any blunder would set off a scandal which would spare no one, least of all me. So our friend flew to Paris or maybe Zürich, I don't remember which, and from there on to Bucharest, where in spite of my letter of introduction they locked him up for two days in a kind of basement where he couldn't see the light of day except through a fanlight with stout bars over it. This fanlight was at pavement level, so our friend saw the feet of passers-by going along, and those feet were shod in heavy army boots more often than he liked, so he was inclined to think he'd been shut up in a barracks. He was distinctly worried, poor fellow, because in Romania at that time ... well! The whole time he was kicking his heels there in his basement they showed him videos extolling the wonders of Ceauşescu's regime. Every now and then our friend rebelled: "I came to Romania to deliver a message to your president from the future King of Spain!" They shrugged their shoulders and advised him to suffer in silence. "There were moments," he confessed to me later, "when I thought I'd never see my native land or my family again." Finally Ceauşescu saw him. The message that I had asked him to deliver to Ceauşescu by word of mouth was, roughly speaking, this: I asked him to be kind enough to communicate to his friend Carrillo that Don Juan Carlos de Borbón, the future King of Spain, intended to recognize the Spanish Communist Party along with all other political parties when he came to the throne. Ceauşescu was also asked to advise Carrillo to trust Don Juan Carlos. If he would go along with this, all would be for the best. If he didn't, he ought to know that the prince thought things might get very difficult and complicated in Spain if he had to expect opposition from the Communist Party. I waited a long two weeks for a reply. Finally our friend came back from Romania and told me he had delivered my message to Ceauşescu, who had promised to pass it on very soon.'

'When did all this happen, Señor?'

'In 1975, a month or so before I was made head of state for the second time.[1] Then, one day, our friend heard that a Romanian minister had arrived in Madrid and would like to meet the prince. Of course no one in the government had wind of this visit. When I met the minister, I asked, "How did you manage to get into Spain without the authorities concerned knowing?" The man smiled and murmured, "We have the necessary contacts." Those obviously couldn't have been anything but contacts with Spanish communists. A very efficient set of people. Ceauşescu's reply to my message was: "Carrillo will not move his little finger until you are king. After that you will have to agree on a period of time, not too long a one, within which to make your promise of legalization good." I breathed a sigh of relief, my mind easier than it had been for a long time. Carrillo would not send his people out into the streets, so we could work in peace and quiet. I thanked the Romanian minister, who left without any fuss, just as he had come.

'Then, on 22 November 1975, I became King of Spain. But before we could discuss legalizing the Communist Party any further, we had to wait for the resignation of Carlos Arias Navarro and the appointment of Adolfo Suárez as head of the new government.'

An aide-de-camp knocks on the office door and enters, reminding His Majesty that he has a visitor to receive in quarter of an hour's time.

[1] Cf. p. 170

The king rises, comes around his desk and says goodbye to me with a smile. 'Always the same old story, José Luis. As soon as you start discussing something interesting, you have to stop and put the rest off until tomorrow. *Hasta mañana.*'[1]

---

[1] See you tomorrow.

VI

As French ambassador in Madrid, a man with a ringside seat to the transition, Jean-François Deniau spoke to me, in an interview, about the Communist Party of Spain.

'The whole affair of the legalization of the Communist Party was manna from heaven to everyone with an interest in destroying the Spanish democratic process. If they got what they wanted, they would simultaneously and successfully be reintroducing the atmosphere which preceded the civil war. The Communist Party would be operating under cover again, and the Left, including the Christian democrats, would show solidarity with the communists, obliging the Right to regroup around the pure, hardline nationalists, so that the democratic process would be halted for good. That was their grand strategy, an idea surreptitiously backed by certain political leaders who thought it was for them to guide the transition in a direction which would be a continuation of Francoism, with those cosmetic touches necessary to give an illusion of change. To these men, Adolfo Suárez was merely a young Francoist functionary who should be at their command. They also expected the king (*ese niñato*,[1] as Arias Navarro called him) to content himself with acting as a figurehead presiding symbolically over a post-Francoist state whose evolution, if it evolved at all, would be very slow and very prudent. However, things did not turn out as they expected.

[1] That child.

Neither the king nor Adolfo Suárez would play their game. Don Juan Carlos had very precise ends in view. He had already succeeded in getting the Francoist Cortes to commit collective suicide. Later, there was much praise for the courageous initiative he took during the long night of Tejero's *coup d'état*, an initiative recognized even by Carrillo, who said on the day after the enactment of that tragi-comedy, "Your Majesty, you have saved our lives." In my view, however, it's much more difficult to reign day after day *cuando no pasa nada*[1] than to stand firm for a night, however dangerous. You have to know what you are after every day. You have to avoid falling into traps set for you every day. And the most dangerous of all traps set for the king was the trap of the Communist Party, which he had to legalize at any price. The king understood perfectly well – even while he was still at the mercy of any change of mind on General Franco's part – that he could no more keep Santiago Carrillo's party out of political life than he could ban a party of any other political hue. He had said he was king of all the Spanish people.

'Myself, I told my friends on the Right to wake up. "Your king is not a communist," I told them, "he's logical, that's all. I'm not a communist either, but I would never tolerate the banning of Monsieur Marchais's party in my own country. That's how democracies work!" And I often told the king, "The real trap is to allow a climate favouring another civil war to spread through the country. If you are to prevent that you have to act fast." It was during one of our conversations that I told Don Juan Carlos, "You and Adolfo Suárez, Your Majesty, are the only people who can tackle the problem of the Communist Party unimpeded by preconceived ideas, because neither of you was involved in the civil war, and the people of Spain need to be able to identify with men who did not take part in that stupid fratricidal struggle at last. You are the only person who can turn the page, Your Majesty. The past must be forgotten once and for all."

'But the legalization of the Communist Party was still a difficult pill to swallow. The army wouldn't hear of it, of course. And there were people highly placed within the new power structure who quietly made their way to the general staff of the armed forces and told the staff officers not to worry, there would be no legalization of the Communist Party

[1] When nothing is happening.

while they were around. Then there were those who were working, sometimes successfully, to recreate a climate similar to that which preceded the civil war of 1936, with a view to speeding up the collapse of the democratic process. For that to work, Spain had to be divided into two camps once more: good on one side, bad on the other. Their trump card consisted of reference to the mysterious affair of Paracuellos del Jarama, not known to many people outside Spain.

'During the first year of the civil war, one of Franco's officers, General Mola, held a press conference in Burgos. When a foreign correspondent asked him when he was going to take Madrid, Mola replied, "I have four columns marching on the capital, and a fifth already inside it." Hence the expression "fifth column"; not everyone outside Spain knows its origin. Of course this enigmatic remark alarmed a great many of the republican general staff. That meant, so some of them thought, that there were armed men in Madrid itself ready to seize power right behind the Madrid front line, which took in the Manzanares and the University. And not far from there was the Cárcel Modelo,[1] where five thousand prisoners arrested by the republicans and most notably by the communists were being held. The security chief in charge was Comrade Santiago Carrillo, aged twenty-three. Not one of those five thousand prisoners had been arrested for any criminal offence. They'd been picked up in the streets or taken from their homes at night because they were guilty of wearing hats and ties, the insignia of a bourgeois the world over. Putting it simply, they were enemies of the working class: lawyers, engineers, doctors, diplomats, and of course noblemen and aristocrats.

'When Mola let slip his venomous little phrase, the republican staff officers immediately said to themselves: it's those thousands of prisoners in the Cárcel Modelo who are going to rise. The nationalists will try to pierce the front with commando troops, reach the Modelo, not eight hundred metres from their front lines, and liberate five thousand prisoners all at once; those five thousand will immediately join the enemy camp. So a decision was taken to evacuate these five thousand dangerous prisoners to a more secure jail: to be specific, Valencia prison. The transfer began in great haste, but none of the five thousand prisoners ever reached Valencia. The municipal buses with the first

[1] Model prison.

groups of detainees on board stopped on waste land on the outskirts of Madrid, near a village called Paracuellos del Jarama. The prisoners were made to get out, forced to dig a trench, and shot in the back of the neck. The trench was filled in and the buses set off again empty, to return a little later with a new batch of victims. Another trench was dug and filled with corpses. The macabre round trip went on until four thousand five hundred people had been massacred.

'So those working to overturn the democratic process said to themselves, with some justification: the crime of Paracuellos was a crime against humanity, and a prosecution can still be brought. Carrillo must be tried and the Spanish people reminded that the hands of the communists are stained with the blood of thousands of victims. That will be the best way to stop the legalization of the Communist Party.

'Believe me, it was a very difficult time. Even within the government opinions differed widely. There were supporters of legalization, of course, but the great majority thought it too risky a step to take. In ten years, maybe, not now. And they would strike up the eternal refrain: this is not the right moment. Eventually the government found a judge whose opinion they sought on the possibility of taking legal action against the Communist Party in the person of Santiago Carrillo, to be accused of crimes against humanity. This judge was a man whose father and brother had been massacred at Paracuellos del Jarama, so he could be expected to come down hard on the communists. Well, the judge gave his opinion: neither the Communist Party nor Santiago Carrillo could be tried for crimes against humanity, since the concept of "crimes against humanity" did not even exist when the crimes in question were committed, and moreover, the judge pointed out, the law cannot be retroactive. He therefore thought there were no grounds for prosecution. He couldn't apply a law first devised by the Allies at the Nuremberg trials, years after the Paracuellos crimes had been committed. The judge concerned, and let me point out again that his own father and brother had been killed at Paracuellos, was on morally unassailable ground, and the supporters of legal action against Carrillo had to shut their big mouths.

'Meanwhile Don Santiago, as the king always calls him, was coming and going in and out of Spain exactly as he liked. All he did was wear a wig which fooled no one. In the end he was arrested in the street by members of a para-police force – there were plenty of people around interested in making things more complicated – and taken, though with proper respect, to Carabanchel prison. He was carrying a forged French passport in the name, believe it or not, of Giscard. I told him later, "Santiago, you were out of your mind! That forged passport is a provocation bound to stir up the fires of an anti-French campaign which accuses France of being behind the legalization of the Communist Party in Spain!" To which Don Santiago, with his usual cheerful demeanour, said, "No such thing! I'd gone to ground in Clermont-Ferrand, that's all, and when I got this passport done I thought I might as well take a local name, it would look better."

'Don Santiago has always had a great sense of humour. I heard the story of his last conversation with Stalin from Carrillo himself. They were arguing ferociously, and at one point Stalin told him, "You Spaniards are hopeless! You know nothing about proletarian internationalism, nothing about historical materialism, nothing about scientific Marxism! Well, that's not so surprising; you're not interested in anything but stupid nonsense like God and the Virgin Mary." Very much on his dignity, Carrillo interrupted the dictator. "Comrade Secretary-General, say what you like about God, but lay off the Virgin Mary in my presence!"

'Well then,' Jean-François Deniau went on, 'Carrillo was in Carabanchel jail. It was still thought that he'd be brought to trial and the democratic process halted. And now comes an incident which is curious, to say the least of it. A very high-ranking emissary of the Spanish Communist Party came to see me at the French embassy and said, "Ambassador, I've come to ask you to convey a message to the highest authorities in the French Communist Party."

' "You know I have no special access to the authorities to which you refer," I told him, "but tell me what it's about, and then we'll see."

'So the messenger explained. "As you know, our secretary-general, Comrade Carrillo, is in prison at Carabanchel, and we've heard that the French Communist Party has decided to organize a demonstration showing solidarity with him in front of the Spanish embassy in the Avenue George V in Paris. Which is all very well and good, but could you please ask them not to overdo it? You see, Ambassador, the moment the French start getting involved in Spanish affairs we'll have a million Spaniards out in the Plaza de Oriente shouting, 'Viva Franco,

Viva España, Una, Grande y Libre!' So Ambassador, would you tell Monsieur Marchais that a small demonstration of solidarity is fine, but please keep it as discreet as possible."

'Rather surprised by the messenger's request, I asked him, "Why don't you give this message to your French comrades yourselves?"

'The messenger replied, sadly, "Because they won't believe us. They'll believe you, because they respect you. But they don't respect us."

'I felt almost sorry for the poor fellow, he looked so downcast. So I promised to make sure that his message reached the Place du Colonel-Fabien in good time, and it all passed off very well. Two hundred hand-picked militants gathered outside the Spanish embassy in the Avenue George V. There was a little obligatory shouting, nothing over the top, no broken windows. Everything had been perfectly organized, the communists being good at discipline. My friend the Spanish communist came back to see me at the embassy and thank me for my good offices. At the end of our conversation, he said, "Anyway, Ambassador, it wasn't worth their putting themselves out in Paris. Our secretary-general is leaving prison any moment now."

'I was staggered, because I was sure very few people – and no communists – knew that Santiago Carrillo was about to be set free. In fact before they let him out the judge had to state formally that in law no case could be brought against either Santiago Carrillo or the Communist Party, since the crimes of which they might have been accused didn't fall at the right time. Freeing the communist leader just like that would have been seen as unjustifiable provocation by a large part of the army. When I spoke to my Spanish friends about the necessity of legalizing the Communist Party they said, "You're a good chap, Jean-François, but you're out of your mind! You're not Spanish, you didn't go through the civil war as we did, or you wouldn't speak like that." Even my friends on the Left wouldn't have understood. Many of them still thought that legalizing the Communist Party was a great mistake. "Can you imagine," they asked me, "a Communist Party headquarters in the middle of Madrid, and the Red Flag with the hammer and sickle on the balcony? That could set off serious incidents with hundreds of deaths!" I did my best to reassure them. "If Santiago Carrillo is an intelligent man – and I know he is – he'll hang a large Spanish flag on the balcony of his headquarters beside the party flag. Carrillo is clever enough to play the game, and you ought to play it too, by defusing this business of its drama before it becomes a canker in the democracy."

'Before leaving me, the emissary of the Spanish Communist Party repeated again, "I can assure you, Ambassador, it wasn't worth their while going to so much trouble in Paris."

'I did my best to look like a man who knew nothing about anything. "But how do you know Carrillo is going to leave prison?"

' "We have evidence. And there are unmistakable signs, you know."

'If there had been any leaks, it could have been a very serious matter, for those opposed to legalizing the Communist Party would be quick to find some other excuse to check the democratic process. "What evidence?" I asked. "What signs?"

' "Oh, it's perfectly simple," the man told me. "The Carabanchel prison wardens have stopped addressing our secretary-general as *tú*. They're already calling him Don Santiago."

'Now if the warders in Carabanchel prison were addressing Carrillo as "Don", it meant they knew he was shortly going to become a person of some importance. Really important people don't languish long in Spanish prisons.

'Directly after the communist emissary's visit to me something rather dramatic happened: the judge investigating the Carrillo affair died suddenly of a heart attack. Another judge had to be found in a hurry, one as sure as the first that applying laws retrospectively could leave the door open for all kinds of appalling excesses. Such a judge was found, and no action was taken against the Communist Party and Carrillo.

'Then time passed very quickly, and the first really free elections took place. The UCD (*Unión de Centro Democrático*), Adolfo Suárez's party, won convincingly. The Spanish people as a whole had not voted for either the extreme Right or the extreme Left; they voted for the centre. Finally free of its old demons, the country seemed to be settling down. And the Communist Party had gained only 9% of the votes. The monster was demystified once and for all.'

During my long conversation with Ambassador Deniau, I asked him 'How many people realized that the king had known for quite some time that Santiago Carrillo would play the democratic game?'

'Not many, I'd say.'

'How did the king manage to persuade the military that legalizing the Communist Party was a necessary step?'

'I don't think he did really convince them of that. My few friends in the army accused me – me, the French ambassador! – of bringing negative influence to bear on the king by advising him to legalize it. I told them I had not brought any influence to bear on the king at all, either negative or positive. The king is the king. He listens to those whose views he thinks he ought to hear, and then he takes his decisions by himself. Myself, I'd explained to him that in the long term it was more dangerous not to legalize the Communist Party than to legalize it. That's politics. You assess the risks and then you opt for whatever represents the least danger for the country!

'As the military saw it – and they were very disconcerted – openly admitting the political existence of the communists was as good as giving in to the enemy they had soundly defeated in the civil war in 1936. But Carrillo, a man who could tell which way the wind was blowing, acted very discreetly. There were no mass demonstrations – and anyway, what masses could he have summoned up to demonstrate? – no incendiary speeches, no red flags waved like a *capote*[1] in front of his opponents' noses. The only person who still believed in the Stalinist era was La Pasionaria.[2] When she seized a microphone at meetings to call out slogans in her beautiful, impassioned voice about "our Soviet comrades who represent the future ... we must fight with all our might against Western corruption ...", there was always someone present to call her to order. "Not here, Dolores, not now." By this time Santiago Carrillo was openly anti-Soviet and the unfortunate Pasionaria represented nothing but the past.

'What did seem surprising, however, was the admirable restraint of the Spanish people as a whole. Individually, no one could give you an explanation of such unusual moderation in a nation with a reputation for always acting on impulse and giving the passions free rein. You really felt that, while they didn't fully understand what was going on around them, the people of Spain were well aware of living through a great moment in their history. Do you remember Ortega's saying? "What is Spain? An eddy of dust on the road of history after a great people has passed at the gallop." In the end the Communist Party was legalized.

[1] Red cloth waved by the bullfighter in front of the bull.
[1] Dolores Ibarruri, the Egeria of the Spanish Communist Party.

85

There was a new constitution, and all the political parties took their due places in the political life of Spain.'

'How do you explain the fact that the army didn't react at all at the moment when the Communist Party was legalized?'

'First, because the whole thing seemed to them such an enormity that, at heart, they had never believed the Communist Party actually *would* be legalized. Second, much to their surprise, the Spanish people did not come swarming out into the streets to kill each other. And finally, when the Communist Party turned out to have gained only 9% of the vote in the elections, i.e. not much at all, everyone calmed down.

'However, those still plotting to halt the democratic process saw another chance to get the clash of swords heard. The unity of Spain was at risk. Catalonia and the Basque country were talking rather too loudly about independence. The opinion polls taken before the elections suggested the possibility of a Popular Front majority in Catalonia. To the eternal conspirators, this was the chance they dreamed of to rebel again. The unity of Spain was sacred. There could be no question of independence for either the Catalans or the Basques. However, the military, taken aback, had to bow to the evidence once again. No one would follow their lead. The great majority of Spaniards did not want intervention by the army, either to ban Santiago Carrillo's Communist Party or to resolve the problems of Basque and Catalan separatism. The idea of intervention by the army, in fact, was not popular with anyone now; it was definitively outmoded.

'All the same, dismembering Spain was a much more serious matter than accepting Carrillo's place in the national community. The military, who had not reacted quickly enough over the Communist Party affair, vowed to act efficiently in the face of the Catalan problem.

'The king had extremely reliable sources of information within the army itself. I myself was kept in touch with events by my own networks, which were as reliable as the king's. The army, they told me, would pour out of its barracks if there was a large Popular Front majority in Catalonia in the elections. But I was also warned that there was much discussion going on in the barracks themselves. If the Popular Front won 15% of the votes, we would see tanks in the streets, but not if the figure was 12%. The possibility of electoral success for the Catalan Popular Front, then, was the last chance the army would have of avenging itself on the communists who had got the better of it. The military men thought they could kill two birds with one stone. They could say the communists and the Popular Front had seized power in Barcelona and were about to proclaim independence. Then the army, the guarantor of Spanish unity, would come out of barracks to defend it. My sources told me there was a lot of excitement among the elite army units, the paratroopers and the general staff of the División Acorazada Brunete. They were getting everything ready to recapture Barcelona, when they could fire on the communists at last. We were really only a step or so away from the beginning of a civil war.

'It was then that the king backed the brilliant idea of recalling Don Josep Tarradellas from his exile in Saint-Martin-le-Beau. Tarradellas was a figure of extraordinary moral authority, a man of great dignity who had lived in poverty throughout the entire Francoist period, obstinately refusing to form a Catalan government in exile, which he was in a position to do as the last president of the *Generalitat* of Catalonia.'

I told Ambassador Deniau that I had known Tarradellas well. 'I admired him very much. Often, when he came to Paris, I went to see him at the Mont-Thabor, the very modest hotel where he used to stay. When we parted he would say, "Forgive me for not inviting you to dinner, but I can't afford it." At Saint-Martin-le-Beau there were two buckets on the floor of the drawing room where he saw his visitors to catch the water dripping from the ceiling. Then Tarradellas moved from the Mont-Thabor to the Hôtel Crillon in the Place de la Concorde one day. And when I learned that the Spanish state was paying the bills for the president of the *Generalitat* I realized that something of importance was about to happen in Catalonia.'

'Yes, the procedure for returning him to his country had just begun. Tarradellas was no longer a poverty-stricken politician in exile, but president of the *Generalitat* of Catalonia, on the point of resuming his position. In fact the king was the first to speak to me about the old man's return. Tarradellas was a living legend to the Catalans. "We intend to go and find him in France and ask him to come back; what do you think of the idea, Jean-François?" I told Don Juan Carlos it was a brilliant bit of poker play. By bringing Tarradellas home the king would be soothing Catalan impatience on the one hand, and putting an abrupt stop any violent action on the part of the army on the other, since with Tarradellas back there was no danger of the pro-separatist Left gaining electoral success.

'So a plane was sent to fetch the exile from Paris. The king received him at La Zarzuela at ten in the morning. The two men got on extremely well. To the day of his death Tarradellas, a life-long republican, was lavish in his praise for Don Juan Carlos de Borbón. When he left the king, Tarradellas came to see me at the embassy. He wanted to thank France in the person of its ambassador for giving him hospitality during his long years of exile. This was both a courteous and a natural gesture on his part, and was studiously ignored by the press, for reasons which can only have been petty.

'Tarradellas, a tall, imposing, handsome man in spite of his age, had a fine sense of humour. As he was about to get into the plane taking him to Barcelona, he said, "My predecessor as president of the *Generalitat* of Catalonia was shot in the trenches of Montjuic. Tell me, who's guaranteeing that the same thing won't happen to me when I arrive?" Going pale, one of the officials with him replied, "You have the personal guarantee of Don Adolfo Suárez, Señor President." It was obvious that the indisputable guarantee of Tarradellas's safety was the king himself, but they carefully avoided mentioning his name. That's how it's done in the curious business of high politics. At this Tarradellas disappeared inside the plane muttering, "After all, there's only one guarantee I want: spare me ridicule."

'The arrival of Tarradellas in Barcelona set off a wave of enthusiasm among the crowd waiting at the airport. Catalonia was finally going to have its government, headed by the honourable figure of Don Josep Tarradellas. Gone was the fear of new popularity for the Popular Front of the Left. Tarradellas was not the man to let anyone encroach upon his terrain. Once again, the people plotting in the shadows to disrupt the democratic process had let slip the occasion to make their point by force of arms. But this time I can tell you there really had been imminent danger of another civil war. The great majority of Spaniards – but not Catalans – lived through these serious events hardly realizing what was going on. In his usual way, the king had acted resourcefully and without giving the enemy time to turn round. All danger was suddenly averted as if at the wave of a magic wand. Like the good sailor he is, the king never forgets that you can't navigate well if you don't know where you're going. Your king, however, always knows where he is going and why. His historic mission – of which he is very much aware – is to make sure that the Spanish people do not come to blows with each other again, as

88

so often in the past. That is his daily work, and it's a hard and difficult job. As for the Tejero business, yes, that was fine, indeed magnificent. A splendid picture: Don Juan Carlos in his uniform as commander-in-chief of the armed forces, with the little Prince of the Asturias, very sleepy, at his side, and millions of Spaniards hanging on the lips of a king whom many people had an interest in presenting as one of those involved in the *coup d'état* which would take Spain back to the Dark Ages. Yes, I agree, most impressive, but I can tell you, because I saw it, that the night we passed before the arrival of Tarradellas in Barcelona was not far behind. We were all asking the same question: would everything collapse or would things settle down in the end? I repeat, it was a brilliant bit of poker play on the king's part, because suppose the mayonnaise failed to "take" ... but it did. And everything stopped as if by magic. The army made no move, because there had been no drama, and without any drama there was no reason to come out of barracks. When you send tanks into the streets, you have to explain why afterwards.'

VII

Don Juan Carlos injured his leg at the end of the winter and is undergoing treatment to rehabilitate it; today he walks with some difficulty, which obviously annoys him. He takes his time over sitting down at his desk and putting his crutches on the floor.

'Where did we get to yesterday, José Luis?'

'The reply to the message the Romanians had conveyed to Carrillo. It was positive. He wouldn't take any action.'

'Yes. I've been thinking a good deal of what I told you yesterday, about the legalization of the Communist Party, and the army. There's something I would like you to explain clearly. My entire philosophy, my entire strategy before, during and after the legalization of the Communist Party centred around a single idea: I did not want to make the victors of the civil war into the vanquished of the democracy. The guiding principle of all my political thinking was to ensure that the Spanish people would never again be divided into conquerors and conquered.' And after a few seconds, Don Juan Carlos adds, 'The victors seldom take the despair of the vanquished into account. And you can't do much with desperate people. There were many wounds to be healed in Spain before both sides could be convinced that dialogue is the best way to settle any kind of problem.'

With a grimace of pain, Don Juan Carlos takes his leg in both hands to change its position.

'One morning,' he continues a moment or so later, 'Adolfo Suárez came and told me, "Now is the time to legalize the political parties. All of them." I told him, "I have something to say in this business too, Adolfo. The army won't give us any problems so far as the Socialist Party is concerned, but it might well give us problems, and major ones, when it learns that we intend to legalize the Communist Party. So I am asking you not to do anything without consulting me first, Adolfo." At this point, José Luis, we must be very careful how we put things.'

I realize that Don Juan Carlos may fear the reaction of certain military men.

'I believe that many young officers would say the Prince of Spain saw farther and more clearly than most politicians of the time,' I tell him. 'And they will also think that if Your Majesty had not succeeded in keeping Carrillo quiet, the Communist Party could have halted the transition process before it had even really begun.'

Don Juan Carlos remains thoughtful for a moment. 'I don't know. You may be right.' Then, suddenly, with that slightly melancholy smile to which I can't accustom myself, he adds, 'Very well, you see to the phrasing. After all, you're the writer!'

Turning grave again, the king continues his explanation to me. 'Long before the legalization of the Communist Party, I had told Manolo Gutiérrez Mellado[1] how I made contact with Carrillo using the Romanians as intermediaries. "Manolo," I told him, "Santiago Carrillo is not going to make any move. I have his word. If we legalize his party, he'll accept both the monarchy and the Spanish flag." Gutiérrez Mellado heaved a sigh of relief. Adolfo knew about my pact with the secretary-general too, but I had a feeling that at this moment Adolfo didn't entirely trust Carrillo, so I emphasized my point again. "Adolfo, I have his promise, and I am sure he will keep his word. Having said that, we must now deal with the feelings of the military. We mustn't give them the impression that we're acting behind their backs. I know the military; I'm a military man myself. They hate surprises, subterfuge and secrecy, and they will never tolerate a lie. I would like to talk to them about this business myself, but it's for you as head of government to let them know what we intend to do. So it would be a good idea if you were to get the captain-generals to come here to Madrid and tell them, "Gentlemen, the time has now come to legalize the political parties, including the

[1] A general, and vice-president of the Suárez government.

91

Communist Party." They will probably protest, but you will explain that we shall have nothing more to fear from the communists once they are operating out in the open; it is very much in our interests to let the Spanish people see that the Communist Party is a minority party, and if we keep it operating under cover we are only boosting its prestige." Adolfo did not seem to feel any great enthusiasm for the meeting with the captain-generals I was suggesting. Manolo Gutiérrez Mellado offered to talk to them instead, but Adolfo wouldn't hear of it: it was for him, as head of government, to take the bull by the horns.'

'But Suárez never did manage to get the military men together.'

'Oh yes, he did. He had a preliminary meeting with them which, contrary to all expectations, was a considerable personal success, if you take into account the fact that most of these men had come intending to do some plain speaking. According to what General Fernández Campo, who was present, told me later, there was even one colonel who was so overcome by the charisma of the young Suárez that he cried out, "*Viva la madre que te parió!*",[1] the ultimate compliment in the mouth of a Spaniard. Suárez had explained to the military men that the time to legalize the political parties had come. When he became head of government, the penal code was reformed and the crime of illicit association ceased to exist. Armed with this piece of legislation, Suárez met the captain-generals and explained what the political reform approved by the government would be. He told me that one of the captain-generals asked him if he intended to legalize the Communist Party. Suárez simply replied that legalization of the Communist Party was not possible while the party statutes remained as they were.'

'At this period Suárez had the reputation of not being particularly popular with the military. Was he afraid of them?'

Don Juan Carlos looks at me in surprise. 'Afraid? I don't think that's the right word. On the night of the *coup d'état* Adolfo showed that he was a man of great physical courage. He and Carrillo were the only ones to remain seated facing the sub-machine guns aimed at the deputies in the Cortes. No, I don't think Adolfo was afraid of the military. Let's say the military were part of a world which was foreign to him.'

*

[1] Long live the mother who bore you!

Enrico Berlinguer, secretary-general of the Italian Communist Party, and Georges Marchais, his French counterpart, had arrived in Madrid on 2 March to take part in the Eurocommunist summit, but most of all to offer support to the Spanish Communist Party, not yet a legal body, while emphasizing the tense and distant nature of their relations with Moscow in order to soothe Spanish fears in general.

Carrillo, who had already left Carabanchel prison, could move about Madrid freely. Rumours reached Suárez that the Spanish secretary-general was beginning to get impatient. It was necessary to keep the promise to legalize the communists. Accordingly, on the Monday of Holy Week, Suárez held a meeting with Gutiérrez Mellado and Alfonso Osorio, both of them vice-presidents of his government, along with Landelino Lavilla, minister of justice, and the minister of the interior Rodolfo Martín Villa. He told them that juridical support had to be found as soon as possible to justify the legalization of the Communist Party in the eyes of the country, and above all of the military. Someone remarked that the public prosecutor could grant a *nihil obstat*, since the supreme court had declared itself unqualified to judge the illegality or otherwise of the Spanish Communist Party. On 9 April, the public prosecutor of the kingdom stated that there was nothing to justify the illegal status of Carrillo's party.

The following Saturday, the Saturday before Easter, the Spanish people were informed through the media that the Communist Party had just been legalized.

'What was the reaction of the military, Señor?'

'Not very good. No one resigned, but many military men felt they had been tricked. In the old days they had fought and beaten the communists, and now the communists were back and this time, in a way, were victorious. I had to talk to a great many of them to explain that nothing was going to happen, Carrillo would keep quiet, there would be no communist demonstrations or red flags in the streets. These interviews were very difficult for me. But finally things calmed down, and Santiago Carrillo kept his word.'

'I sometimes get the impression, Señor, that to some extent you are – well, let's say fascinated by Carrillo?'

Don Juan Carlos looks at me in what may well have been the way Franco used to look at him when he asked a question which the general did not want to answer. However, Don Juan Carlos always ends up reacting positively to my questions.

'Fascinated, you said? That's not quite the word for it, I think. Let's say I feel an ever-increasing regard for people who keep their word. In all that concerns the legalization of the Communist Party I cannot but acknowledge that Carrillo behaved very correctly. He never breathed a word of all I have just told you. Since then he and I have often had occasion to talk together. Sometimes he insists on informing me that he is not a monarchist. I smile and tell him, "Maybe not, Don Santiago, but you should rename your party *El Real Partido Comunista de España*.[1] No one would be surprised."'

It is an old tradition of the Bourbons of Spain to call their subjects by the familiar pronoun, *tú*. However, Don Juan Carlos often departs from this rule when he is speaking to people who have earned his respect. In the case of Santiago Carrillo, the king's use of the more formal *usted* to him is for a very particular reason. Carrillo himself has told me that when he was about to meet Don Juan Carlos for the first time, it was explained to him that the king would probably use the familiar pronoun to him. Santiago Carrillo, not yet the convinced 'Juancarlist' he has become today, replied in some annoyance, 'So far as I know, we aren't old acquaintances. If he calls me *tú* I shall call him *tú* back.' This remark of the communist secretary-general was apparently relayed to Don Juan Carlos, and when Carrillo went to the palace for the first time, the king shook hands and used the formal pronoun as he said, 'I am delighted to meet you, Don Santiago!' Later I asked Carrillo if he would really have returned the king *tú* for *tú*. 'No, I don't think so,' he said, 'because although Don Juan Carlos is much younger than me he is a man for whom I feel great respect.'

In the more retrograde sectors of Spanish society, the king's esteem for the secretary-general of the Communist Party is far from being properly understood.

'Do you know, Señor, that a Spanish duchess not exactly famous for her brilliant intelligence actually asked Jean-François Deniau if he didn't think the king was a communist?'

[1] The Royal Communist Party of Spain.

94

Don Juan Carlos does not even smile. He simply murmurs, 'Well, in any case we Spaniards owe Don Santiago a great deal.' And he adds, amused, 'I believe you've been criticized for your friendship with Carrillo yourself?'

'That's true, by the same people who don't understand that the King of Spain can be grateful to a communist for allowing him to put the transition through successfully.'

'Did you know him very well?'

I told Don Juan Carlos that I did indeed know Santiago Carrillo well when I was spokesman for the *Junta Democrática* in Paris during the year preceding the death of General Franco. At the time, whenever the French press mentioned the *Junta*, it always added the phrase 'of communist allegiance', which was totally inaccurate. I had the job of visiting the editors of the various newspapers in turn and explaining to them that the *Junta* was far from obeying the orders of the Communist Party alone, and Santiago Carrillo had no more authority within our organization than any other of its members, who included members of Opus Dei such as Professor Calvo Serer and dyed-in-the-wool liberals like José Vidal Beneyto, the owner of orange groves in Valencia and a well-known essayist. The only member of the *Junta* on whom I can't pin any ideological label was Antonio García Trevijano – 'coordinator' of all the political tendencies within the *Junta* – a former provincial lawyer and a firm supporter of a total break with the old regime, wishing to sever all contact with those who had been in any kind of contact, close or distant, with the Francoist administration. This was a Utopian stance, to say the least of it. Thin, moustached and swarthy, Antonio García Trevijano was a kind of implacable Saint-Just. Carrillo, unlike García Trevijano, was in favour of entente with those who, even if they had held positions of responsibility under the Francoist regime, could collaborate in a positive way with the monarchy.

From my first contact with Carrillo I was attracted by his solid common sense – he liked to say, 'My years of exile in France reinforced my natural Cartesianism' – and by a sense of humour unusual among communists. Two or three days after we met, Carrillo suggested dinner together. I hesitated to accept, since the murky affair of Paracuellos del Jarama, in which several members of my mother's family had been brutally murdered, stood between us. But my curiosity got the better of my scruples and I went to dine with him in a bistro in Saint-Germain-des-Prés.

As soon as we were seated opposite each other I came clean with Carrillo. I told him how I had come home on leave from the front at Valencia, and my father, meeting me at San Sebastian, told me, "Be very gentle with your mother; she's just heard that several of her cousins in Madrid were shot at Paracuellos del Jarama.'

'So at the moment,' I told Santiago, 'there is a barrier between us, and I don't know how to cross it. I don't even know if I can.'

Carrillo looked at me for a long time, his wineglass in his hand. Then he asked me, 'Do you know how old I was at the time of Paracuellos?'

I didn't. He told me he had been three or four years older than me, only just nineteen. 'Do you think, José Luis, that at such an age I'd have been given responsibility for arranging the assassination of hundreds of prisoners who might, if the occasion arose, have been of exceptional importance to us?'

What could I say? Carrillo added, 'If you like, I can give you the real story of Paracuellos del Jarama in writing on a couple of sheets of paper; the anarchists played a much greater part than I did in the affair.'

He kept his word. Forty-eight hours later he laid several typewritten sheets on my desk. What I read convinced me it was possible that Carrillo was innocent of the Paracuellos massacre.

'But tell me,' I asked him, 'if things were really as you say, why the devil don't you explain it publicly, through the press or in a book?'

He answered me with that indefinable smile which gave a touch of bitterness to his words. 'Because in this country of ours when you're landed with a story of that kind, you're encumbered with it for life. It's not worth the trouble of protesting my innocence. We Spaniards have always preferred the guilty to the innocent. You yourself will be known as the Red Marquis to the day you die, and I shall be the assassin of Paracuellos del Jarama for all eternity.'

Don Juan Carlos makes no comment at all on this story, but his silence is more eloquent than words. I then tell him that towards the end of the Francoist era, certain persons close to the general's entourage thought fit to get in touch with the 'assassin of Paracuellos' to find out what the attitude of the Communist Party would be in the event of any change of regime.

'Good heavens. Don Santiago never mentioned that to me,' says Don Juan Carlos, surprised.

'You weren't the only one, Señor, to wonder what attitude the Communist Party would take faced with an inevitable change of regime. The Francoists were concerned too, although for different reasons.

'One morning Carrillo told me a member of the general's entourage had suggested lunching privately with him at the Vert Galant, near the Palais de Justice. The person concerned didn't want to give his name. "The idea of this lunch is intriguing," Carrillo told me. "It's always useful to know what's worrying the enemy. But I want to know who it is I'm lunching with. So I'd like you to come to the Vert Galant too and sit at a table not too far away from mine. A few minutes after this mysterious person arrives I'll go to the cloakroom, where you can join me and tell me if you recognize my companion." So that was what we did. I sat with a woman friend at a table from which I could see Carrillo and his companion. After a while I saw a man enter the restaurant. He was quite tall, with a sad face and a gangling manner. I knew him immediately; he was the son of Nicolás Franco, the general's brother.'

'Nicolás Franco Pascual del Pobil?' asks the king.

'That's right, Señor. When I joined Carrillo in the cloakroom I told him, "Santiago, you're lunching with General Franco's nephew." "The son of the ambassador to Portugal?" Carrillo went back to his table looking delighted. His lunch with the general's nephew came to an end very quickly. As soon as Nicolás Franco Pascual del Pobil had left, I went to finish my coffee at Carrillo's table. "What did he want to know?" I asked. "Oh, the same as everyone else. Am I going to play the big bad ogre, or will I behave myself when his uncle dies?" "So what did you tell him?" "Not a lot. I simply took the chance to throw him off the scent, and the 'messenger' left feeling rather more worried than when he had come." And that was all Santiago Carrillo told me about this startling meeting.'

Despite the esteem which the king publicly showed him, it took Spanish society a long time to accept – the word 'tolerate' would be nearer the mark – the secretary-general of the Communist Party. 'The first time I went to a reception at the palace,' he told me one day, 'I was received on my arrival by a colonel in full dress uniform, who didn't even deign to speak to me, and when I moved towards the king and queen to greet them I heard voices as I passed audibly apostrophizing me as *"Asesino, asesino!"* [1]

Today, perhaps because of his political disappointments, the former secretary-general turned journalist is regarded as a kind of historical legend. He goes about Madrid on his own and receives many marks of esteem and friendship – particularly from the middle classes, who have finally realized what they owe him.

'As I see it,' says Don Juan Carlos, 'the important point in this whole business of the legalization of the Communist Party is that we managed to get the transition through without bloodshed. No one will deny that such a thing is unusual in Spain. I wanted a transition which would take place without any spirit of revenge, personal animosity or the settling of accounts. I wanted it all to go quietly and smoothly, in a civilized manner. And I think the Spanish people realized we were not simply passing from one regime to another. It was much more than that: we were passing from an era already concluded to a new era, with all its imponderables, its dangers and its hopes. If that transition was to succeed new people were needed, young people, with a vision of the world their elders dared not entertain. Under Francoism, absolute power was wielded by an old man. And I, the newcomer, was a young man with an almost physical need to surround myself with others of my own age.'

'Men like Suárez, and later on Felipe González?'

'Exactly. At those difficult times, I was lucky that most Spaniards could understand the necessity for what was happening. Of course there were exceptions. Men who feared change and remained faithful to their old ideas.'

'That isn't fidelity, Señor, it's arteriosclerosis.'

'Yes, but you're the one who said it.'

'Señor, do you think Torcuato Fernández Miranda, who was no longer a young man, would have legalized the Communist Party lightly?'

'He might have found the idea in itself unwelcome, but if he had been prime minister I'm sure he would have legalized it, in spite of his age and his conservative leanings. Intelligent men are always young in spirit, and Torcuato was an exceptionally intelligent man.'

[1] Assassin, assassin!

'You've surrounded yourself with young men since you were free to do so, but you did pass a great part of your life among men of middle age, people who could boast of experience.'

'Experience is only the end product of a certain number of errors. Personally I wouldn't boast of that.'

'Señor, could you have got on with someone like José Maria de Areilza[1] if he had become prime minister instead of Suárez?'

'I've always got on very well with Areilza. He has a very good mind, in spite of his age.'

'And a very good pen.'

'Yes, he writes extremely well.'

'But you preferred Suárez to Areilza.'

I have to content myself with Don Juan Carlos's famous way of looking you straight in the eye by way of reply. I explain myself further. 'Right up to the evening of the day when Suárez was appointed to head your new government, Areilza still thought he had a very good chance of being chosen.'

'Really?' says Don Juan Carlos.

Ingenuousness is not the king's line, but he can make a good shot at acting the part.

'Areilza was disappointed, I might even say upset, by the choice of Suárez.'

'Yes, a pity, because the Count of Motrico is a man of great merit.'

What Don Juan Carlos will never admit is that he would not have cared to have his new government headed by a former staunch supporter of the Count of Barcelona, a man who had been on the privy council of 'His Majesty Don Juan III'. In a Shakespearean drama, Areilza would have represented the 'guilty conscience' of the young king who had occupied the old king's throne.

'Tell me, Señor, did Ceauşescu ever present you with the bill for his good offices?'

'You often ask me questions I ought not to answer. However, after all this time ... I believe I've already told you that I am a lucky person. I didn't like knowing that some day I would have to receive Ceauşescu here to thank him, but I was in luck again. Ceauşescu twice gave notice

---

[1] J. M. de Areilza, Count of Motrico, minister and ambassador to France and the USA.

that he was coming, and twice serious events – earthquakes in Romania, I think – prevented him from doing so. He finally came in 1979 or 1980, I don't remember which, but a good deal of time had passed, and no one could connect the Romanian leader's visit with the legalization of the Communist Party. Except for Carrillo himself, of course. Most people supposed that Ceauşescu had come to Madrid on a courtesy visit, like so many others.'

The telephone on the king's desk rings. I rise and move away to let him talk privately. Once again I go to take a closer look at the Dalí, which is like an explosion in that sober but sumptuous room. Dalí does not appeal to me as either a man or a painter. The man was an infant prodigy who refused to grow up all his life, and as for the painter, I agreed with Marie-Laure de Noailles when she said, 'Dalí's tragedy is that he wanted to build Saint Sophia, but what he produced was the Sacré-Coeur of Montmartre.' However, I am careful not to say so to the king, who showed his admiration of Dalí by making him Marquis of Púbol, from the name of the place where the painter lived for several years in old age and where he died.

When I come back to sit down in front of Don Juan Carlos again, I tell him, 'There's a very interesting book, *Anatomia de un cambio de regimen* ('Anatomy of a Change of Regime'), by José Oneto, the editor of *Tiempo*, with an afterword written by Suárez in which he says he had to legalize the Communist Party on his own initiative.'

'That's true.'

'All the same, it was Your Majesty who embarked on a strategy which would allow the party to be legalized some day, while you were still Prince of Spain.'

'Yes, you are right, but it was Adolfo Suárez who took the affair in hand when the moment came.'

'But do you think that, without the Romanian contacts Your Majesty had made, Adolfo could have –'

Don Juan Carlos interrupts me. 'What are you trying to say?'

'Only this, Señor: Adolfo legalized the Communist Party – not, in my opinion, exactly as it should have been done – but none the less it was the Crown which smoothed the way so that some day he would indeed be able to act "on his own initiative".'

Don Juan Carlos nods, smiling.

'Apparently your mother and my father were discussing the return of the monarchy one day in Paris,' he tells me. 'Your mother felt that matters were not moving fast enough. After a while, and running out of arguments, my father told her, "Carmen, do remember that I'm a royalist too!"'

'Why do you tell me that story, Señor?'

'Because you too sometimes strike me as being more royalist than the king.'

When Don Juan Carlos laughs, his youthful appearance becomes almost too much.

'You know, Señor, before I knew Adolfo personally I attacked him a good deal in my journalism, sometimes unjustly. Then we were introduced one day in Dr Redondo's surgery – he was the dentist we both went to – and like so many before me, I fell for the legendary charm of Suárez. However, I think that under the mask of what is sometimes excessive cordiality, Adolfo was hiding an inferiority complex which he tried to conceal by theatrical attitudes which give a false, prefabricated image of him. It is clear that he's not at ease with people more powerful than himself, and he isn't at his best with highly cultivated people either – men like President Tarradellas, to whom he was very aggressive on their first meeting in Madrid. However, the old man dealt with him beautifully. When the journalists asked him how the interview had gone, Tarradellas replied, "Very well. President Suárez and I got on splendidly." Months later, when we were lunching together at the Palais San Jordi in Barcelona, Tarradellas, now president of the *Generalitat* of Catalonia again, recalling that stormy meeting in Madrid, told me, "Suárez thought he was doing me a favour by receiving me at La Moncloa. He was wrong. I was doing *him* the favour by pulling out the rug from under the feet of the military who were prepared for anything if Catalonia moved. And with me there they knew it was not going to move, or at least not in the direction they feared. But after all, you know, the only opinion that mattered to me was His Majesty's. So you'll understand that the state of mind of Adolfo Suárez..."'

'Tarradellas was absolutely loyal to me until the day he died,' says Don Juan Carlos. 'He told me, several times, "I am a staunch defender of Your Majesty's monarchy." I'd rather he had simply said "the monarchy", for there is quite a difference.'

'The difference is what allows many life-long republicans to identify with the monarchy today.'

'I know, but all the same ... Did you see much of Tarradellas in Barcelona?'

'I sometimes went to see him with Antonio de Senillosa.[1] Antonio and I agreed in thinking Tarradellas felt confined in his beloved Catalonia. "Rather as de Gaulle might have felt if he'd been sent to govern Corsica," said Senillosa, who was extremely fond of the old man, and it is true that there was something very much like de Gaulle about Tarradellas. He shared the general's bearing and his ambitions.'

'Something I liked in him very much,' says the king, 'was the way he could stand back from problems when the solution wasn't obvious. Very few politicians today are able to distance themselves from events which can't be properly assessed without a certain perspective. In that, Tarradellas resembled Franco.'

A clock strikes the hour somewhere in the office.

'What shall we talk about tomorrow?' asks Don Juan Carlos, rising to shake hands.

'Your military studies, if that's all right, Señor.'

This is a subject on which the king always has something new to say.

[1] Writer and politician.

VIII

It is raining hard over the sierra, with the wind blowing in violent gusts, making the deer and wild boar take refuge under the branches of the cork oaks. The aide-de-camp awaiting me at the top of the stairs, one of the sons of the Duke del Infantado, tells me His Majesty will be five minutes late today. I am taken to a small drawing room where I hardly have time to look around me – there is a model ship on a console table which I would like to examine more closely – when the aide-de-camp comes back for me. 'I said five minutes, José Luis; I was wrong, I should have said four.'

The first thing the king does as I enter his office is apologize for that four minutes' delay. 'I had someone I couldn't get rid of here with me, though heaven knows I know how to do it!' he explains, smiling.

I sit down opposite the king, as usual. Today he is wearing light grey, with a tie striking enough to divert my attention for some moments. I decide to look in at Hermès next day to see if I can get one like it, although the king's ties are probably one-off models.

'I think you wanted us to talk about my military studies today, but I have the impression we've already discussed them.'

'Yes, Señor, but there's one aspect of your time in the various military academies which I'd like to return to.'

'What's that?'

'You are the son of the Count of Barcelona, Señor, and at the time we monarchists saw your father as the only legitimate heir to the Crown of Spain. Did you often discuss the subject with your friends?'

'Very seldom. Sometimes with very close friends, perhaps. But as you know, I was very keen to be just another cadet. You can avoid a great many problems by losing yourself in the crowd. Everyone knew who I was, but they pretended to have forgotten, not always successfully. To my really close friends I was Juan or Juanito, to others I knew quite well I was Borbón, and to everyone else I was SAR, but without any emphasis on it.'

'What about your instructors, Señor?'

'They addressed me as Highness.'

'When Your Majesty was attending the academies, what would now be described as a major smear campaign against your father was being conducted daily in Spain. The Borbóns as a whole were discredited in the person of the Count of Barcelona, who was accused of being a freemason, a womanizer, and having served in the British Navy – the ultimate insult. The campaign even smirched the memory of Don Alfonso XIII, who had done so much for Franco's military career when, thanks to your grandfather's goodwill, he so swiftly became the young-est general in Europe. The idea of slandering your father and your grandfather was to get at the entire Borbón dynasty, accusing it of having led Spain to the brink of the abyss. You can't have been unaware of all this, Señor.'

'I certainly was not! On the contrary. I had several fights with comrades who had said things I didn't like about my father in front of me. We used to arrange to meet in the riding school of the academy at night to settle our differences with our fists. I came out of these encounters with a black eye several times. It didn't happen very often, I'm glad to say. My fellow cadets knew I was in a very difficult situation, and they avoided such subjects in front of me. As for Franco himself, I have already told you how, when I complained to him of the treatment of my father in the newspapers, he shrugged his shoulders and told me he couldn't intervene, the press was free to express its opinions. This was such a bare-faced enormity I could only laugh at it.'

'Why exactly did Franco hate the Count of Barcelona so much?'

Don Juan Carlos looks at the coat of arms engraved on his gold ring for some time. 'I think,' he says at last, 'that Franco saw my father as the one person who could contest the legitimacy of his own power. I also told myself that perhaps Franco had ended up believing the stories his propaganda services spread about my father. He must genuinely have seen him as a dangerous liberal who might turn everything he, Franco, had done upside down. A dangerous liberal leaning towards the Reds. When my father said, "I want to be king of all the Spanish people", Franco probably translated that as, "I want to be king of the victors and the vanquished alike."'

'Wasn't that true, though?'

'Yes, of course, but it would have been an intolerable idea to Franco. Yet the general knew that this "dangerous liberal" had turned up at the Spanish border in 1936 with the intention of fighting the Reds as a volunteer in any unit to which Franco would assign him. On that occasion the general wrote my father a very nice letter, thanking him for his gesture, and telling him his life was too precious for the future of Spain, he could not let him risk it on the battlefield. Why was my father's life so precious if not because he was heir to the throne? But there you are, José Luis, Franco was like that. A pragmatic character, acting according to the dictates of the present moment. Sometimes that was very difficult to bear. But you know, I told myself once and for all that I would have to bear quite a lot to get where I wanted. The game was worth the candle.'

'And for you the game meant the monarchy.'

'Of course. What else?'

'Do you really think Franco was a monarchist, Señor?'

'I have no doubt whatsoever about it. When he organized the 1947 referendum which he won so conclusively with 98% of the votes, Franco was in a position to do absolutely anything.'

'Such as what, Señor?'

'How can we know? I don't like speculation. In any case, he could have done various things which he did not do. On the contrary, he reiterated that Spain was a monarchy and one day it would have a king. The general's philosophy was very simple, you see, José Luis. He had great confidence in the benefits of the passage of time. And it's true, no one can deny it, that time does settle many problems which seem to have no immediate solution. Franco believed in the merit of old sayings and proverbs deriving from folk wisdom. Of Gibraltar, a problem which did not seem to trouble him unduly, I heard him say, "*Eso como una fruta, cuande madure caera.*"[1]

---

[1] It is like a fruit, it will fall when it's ripe.

'If we go to the heart of the matter, Señor, who do you think had more influence on you, General Franco or your father?'

Don Juan Carlos seems quite shocked by the question. 'Why, my father, of course! I never doubted my father's sincerity when he advised me on this or that. It was very different with Franco. I always wanted to follow my father's advice, but often I wasn't very keen to take the path Franco showed me, and I could have wished I was unable to.'

'I often hear people say, "The king has done what his father would have liked to do." Myself, I feel you have sometimes gone farther than your father's objectives.'

'No one can tell what the Count of Barcelona would have done if he had come to the throne,' replies Don Juan Carlos in a rather dry tone.

We are both silent for quite a while. Then Don Juan Carlos continues, doubt in his voice, 'I don't know whether one should believe too much in the influence people around us or family members can exert. Obviously, if my father had never spoken to me so passionately about Spain when I was a child, I would not now be as much in love with the idea of my country as I am. If I sometimes think, act and speak as my father would have done, that's not just the result of influence, but more simply because when I was still very young I was set an example by someone I love and admire, my father. From Franco, I learned chiefly what must not be done any more. Notice that I don't say "must not be done", but "must not be done any more". Anyway, he himself told me not to ask him for advice I wouldn't be able to follow. At the end of the day, what does influencing a person mean?'

'Oscar Wilde said it meant giving him his soul.'

'In that case I was influenced by my father and no one else.' And after a very short hesitation, Don Juan Carlos adds, 'Up to the point when I began to influence my father.'

'How was that, Señor?'

'You know that when exile lasts too long – we were speaking of this the other day – it ends up distorting your idea of the paradise from which you've been expelled. My father was living surrounded by men most of whom had been exiles since the end of the civil war. They talked to him of a Spain which no longer existed except in books. When they thought of the monarchy they were remembering the reign of Don Alfonso XIII. They were building the future of Spain on old dreams.

Ramón Padilla, one of those who followed my father into exile, told me one day, "When I speak of Spain to His Majesty, I wonder afterwards if that Spain still exists." When I went to Estoril on leave – I'm talking about the time when I was at the academy in Zaragoza – and we were discussing this or that problem, my father would often get annoyed. "Good God, you're looking at it from Franco's point of view!" What else could I do? I was living in Franco's Spain. And when Franco himself spoke to me of Spain he was speaking of a Spain I knew, and whose existence my father found it difficult to acknowledge. My father dreamed of Spain. I was living in it. So gradually my father began to listen to me and trust me, and I do think that in certain circumstances I helped him to see more clearly. But I don't know if he liked that.'

'People of a certain age find it hard to admit that young people may be right.'

'That may be because, never having suffered from nostalgia, young people live in reality as fish live in water, whereas reality is very difficult for those who think the past was always better.'

'You know, Señor, when I came back from exile after the general amnesty of 1975 – and don't forget that for over thirty years I had been considered as dangerous a Red as your father, if not more so – I arrived in Spain full of illusions, like those old African elephants who travel thousands of kilometres to find their families again before they die. But the Spain to which I came home was nothing like the Spain I'd left, the country I had dreamed of for so many long years. Even the physical appearance of the Spaniards had changed. In my time they were short, hairy and rather ugly. The modern Spaniards often look quite Nordic.'

'That's because they've learnt to eat a proper diet.'

I stop to give Don Juan Carlos time to light one of the cigars he has given up offering me, because I always refuse.

'Señor, at what point in your life did you really feel the burden of solitude?'

The king gives me that famous look – slightly abstracted, slightly melancholy – which I know signifies that he does not like what I am saying.

'One is always alone to some extent when things are going badly. And unfortunately things almost never go entirely well for whoever's at the top of the pyramid.'

'"Authority is not without prestige, nor prestige without remoteness," de Gaulle wrote in *Au fil de l'épée*. Would you agree with that, Señor?'

'Yes, I would. Authority, even when you're living in its shadow – as I was while Franco was alive – means that people treat you in a rather unnatural, sometimes very artificial way. If I am to be frank with you, José Luis, I have always been solitary to some extent. But I felt the burden of that solitude most when I was designated Prince of Spain and Franco was thinking of choosing me to succeed him "as king". That was a period when it was thought that I would be king, but no one could be absolutely sure of it. Franco might change his mind and nominate someone else instead. So it was a good idea to be "nice" to me, but not too nice. I was alone, but at the same time surrounded by a great many people. Now my father knew genuine solitude for years. Apart from a few loyal friends who were always at his side, people hesitated before going to see him in Estoril. For a long time it was more than awkward to be seen around the Count of Barcelona, it was a political misdemeanour. It might cost you your position, or the import permit for a car you wanted. My father couldn't trust those who did approach him too much either, because many of them rushed straight to the Pardo to report the moment they were back in Madrid: the count said this, the count said that, and so on. Most of the time he was credited with saying things that had never even crossed his mind, but when he did say something of real importance it was suppressed, for fear people might think the person reporting it approved of it. My father's solitude seemed to go on so long he never reached the end of it. I learned a great deal from his sufferings. In a way I armoured myself for fear of being crushed by what might happen to me some day. And I realized very early on that silence was a safe investment. As Prince of Spain, I saw people who were openly on Franco's side and against me as a Borbón, but who came to see me just in case. Others boasted of being anti-Franco and thought that gave them the right to be in my confidence. I couldn't trust either sort. So when I didn't talk much, many people thought I was keeping my mouth shut because I had nothing to say. On the contrary; I had plenty to say, but I preferred to keep quiet because the least little remark, the slightest word could be interpreted in a way that would harm me. Sometimes I even had to watch my body language. He smiled, so he's in favour; he didn't smile, so he's against.'

'It must be very tiring to impose such control on oneself all day long.'

'Very tiring, José Luis, and very hard on the nerves.'

'You must often have felt like walking out and slamming the door.'

'That would have been taking the easy way out, and a way my adversaries would have liked to see me take. Anyone can walk out when things get difficult. My father always told me that a king must not abdicate. He has no right to do so. I wasn't king yet, but it came to the same thing.'

'If I may, Señor, I'll read you an extract from an article which appeared in *L'Express* of 12 December 1991, under Jacques Renard's by-line.'

'Go ahead.'

I take the article in question out of my briefcase and read from it: '... Juan Carlos explained to Santiago Carrillo himself that he had to "play the idiot for twenty years, which is not easy", and that he "succeeded, because everyone believed it".'

'I don't remember saying exactly that, but if Carrillo tells the story it's probably true,' says the king in a neutral tone.

'The same article says, a little farther on, that "François Mitterrand fell for the same mistake, writing in *L'Abeille et l'architecte* of 12 October 1975: 'I have never believed in that third-hand king Juan Carlos, but I could almost feel sorry for him when I think of the tide which will overwhelm him. Being Franco's heir is unlikely to be much use when you are making straight for the abyss!'"'

The king listens, smiling.

'Shall I go on, Señor?'

The king nods assent, and I continue reading. '"It is also said that some years later the French president, on an official visit to Spain and in La Zarzuela, stopped in front of some photographs showing Franco with the future king behind him. Juan Carlos commented with a smile: 'Waiting makes one look very stupid ... as I'm sure you know, President.'" Is that story true, Señor?'

Don Juan Carlos shrugs his shoulders. 'Well, you know, even invented anecdotes sometimes become true by dint of repetition.'

I suspect Don Juan Carlos of forgetting on purpose, so far as the president of the French Republic is concerned.

'Carrillo's story,' he murmured, 'yes, perhaps, at a pinch ... although in Spanish the word *idiota* has connotations of irreversible idiocy; I don't know if that's the word I'd have used.'

'The anecdote was told in French, Señor, and *faire l'idiot* in French is sometimes proof of intelligence.'

'Oh, well, José Luis, then that's my case exactly!' says Don Juan Carlos, with a brief burst of laughter.

IX

The aide-de-camp showing me into the king's office this afternoon, a naval officer with very blue eyes, tells me in a low voice, 'His Majesty has taken several steps without his crutches this morning. He's in a very good mood.' I am glad to hear it, because Don Juan Carlos's moods are having a considerable effect on the way my work goes. When the king is relaxed, he talks a great deal and insists on getting details straight. When he is preoccupied, you can tell it from the way he speaks.

As soon as I enter the office, Don Juan Carlos gives me a broad smile. His pale blue tie has a pattern of tiny seagulls flying over it. His crutches are not on the floor by his chair today, but leaning against another chair a little way off. It looks as if the king has been exercising, walking around the room where he spends most of the day.

'Well, what would you like to talk about today?'

His tone is open and confident. The sailor with the bright blue eyes wasn't wrong; the king is in a very good mood.

'When we were talking about Your Majesty's training in the military academies the other day, Señor, you said something which struck me forcibly.'

'What was that?'

'You asked if I thought you could have done what you did on the night of the *coup d'état* engineered by Tejero and Milans if you hadn't had loyal friends in the army.'

'Yes, I remember. Does it surprise you?'

'No, Señor. It answers another question I had been going to ask you, but I needn't ask it now.'

'What question?'

'I'd been going to ask if such a rigorous military training as yours was really necessary for a future king.'

'I think the events of 23 February 1981 are the best reply to that. The military obeyed me not just because I was one of them, but also, indeed primarily, because I was commander-in-chief of the armed forces. What kind of authority could I have had exercised if I couldn't bring it to bear on these men, many of whom genuinely believed that Spain was going downhill and were ready to plunge into the spiral of violence represented by the trap the ETA terrorists were offering? Who would have taken me seriously if I hadn't been able to wear the uniform of a captain-general to address them before the television cameras?'

On the night of 23 February 1981, Don Juan Carlos ceased, for millions of Spaniards, to be the man who had been General Franco's successor, 'as king', and became King of Spain in his own right. The Spanish people discovered during that dramatic night that Don Juan Carlos possessed the three specific virtues of the Bourbons of Spain: common sense, a long memory, and courage – a calm courage in which boldness and patience were united. He also had the certainty that he was doing right.

'It gets me very annoyed,' Don Juan Carlos tells me, 'when I hear the *coup d'état* of Milans and Tejero described as an "operetta conspiracy". It only looked like an operetta conspiracy because it failed. But what would have happened if the *coup* had succeeded, José Luis? Neither of us would be here discussing it today.'

'Not long after the failure of the *coup d'état*, Señor, a magazine, – I think it was *Tiempo* – published a list of several hundred names – politicians, journalists, actors, writers, even some army men – whom the conspirators led by Milans and Tejero had decided to eliminate during the forty-eight hours after their victory. My own name was on it.'

'Where were you on the night of the *coup d'état*?' Don Juan Carlos asks me.

'Here in Madrid, at home in the Paseo de la Castellana. I heard what had happened in the Cortes on the radio. A little later my wife came back from her hairdresser and told me she had seen a great many lorries full of civil guards in the street.'

'You didn't think of leaving, going somewhere else?'

'No, Señor. Don't ask me why, but though I was apprehensive I didn't for a moment believe the insurrection would succeed. Like millions of other Spaniards, I was waiting for Your Majesty to speak on radio or television. And speaking of radio, Señor, the thing I really found blood-chilling was hearing military music dating back to 1936 for several hours on end. The Hymn of the Legion, and so on. I could already see Spain taking a mighty leap forty years back. I remember phoning my friend Enrique Meneses, a journalist with much experience of all kinds of civil and tribal warfare.'

The word 'tribal' makes Don Juan Carlos smile. He is listening to me attentively.

'I asked Enrique what he thought of the situation, and he said coolly, "Nothing will happen. They've neglected to take the Campsa,[1] and you can't win wars without petrol."'

The king smiles very slightly, and changes his tone. 'The *coup d'état* led by Milans and Tejero took a great many people by surprise.'

He is right there. It even surprised those who ought to have expected it. It is always a mistake not to have an ear open for the *ruido de sables*[2] in Spain. It was a mistake not to take Operation Galaxia seriously, regarding it as a ridiculous conspiracy between old companions in arms well known as habitual malcontents. Operation Galaxia was in fact a kind of dress rehearsal for the *coup d'état* of 23 February. It was so called because the conspirators met at the Galaxia cafeteria, and it was constructed out of nothing by Lieutenant-Colonel Antonio Tejero of the *Guardia Civil* and Captain Sáenz de Ynestrillas, later assassinated in his car by an ETA commando. The aim was to take the palace of La Moncloa[3] by storm with two hundred men and seize Adolfo Suárez and the members of his government while the Council of Ministers was meeting. Tejero's ruling idea, his obsession, was to capture and hold prisoner the entire government. Operation Galaxia was to take place while the king was away on a state visit to Mexico. Tejero and his accomplices believed Don Juan

[1] The oil refinery.
[2] Noise of swords.
[3] The prime minister's palace.

Carlos would rubber-stamp the operation when he got back to Spain. However, the idea was not just to take Suárez and his ministers prisoner; they were also to be humiliated. Later, when Tejero invaded the Cortes with his guards, he humiliated all Spain by making all the government ministers and deputies get down on the floor under their seats.

'What do you think, Señor, were the reasons why the military...'
    'Some of the military,' the king corrects me.
    '...some of the military put on rather too swashbuckling a show?'
    'The reasons?' murmurs Don Juan Carlos thoughtfully. 'Hm...'

There were many reasons. To these men who lived in a world of their own, a kind of closed capsule, there seemed to be plenty of causes for disquiet: the almost daily assassinations carried out by ETA, the Basque separatist movement, the more muted, almost marginal, separatist movement of Catalonia. The army felt there could be no discussion about the unity of Spain.

'You will remember,' Don Juan Carlos tells me, 'that on his deathbed Franco took my hands between his and said "All I ask of you, Highness, is to preserve the unity of Spain."'
    'How far do you identify with the military, Señor?'
    Momentarily taken aback, Don Juan Carlos recovers very quickly. 'As far as a man can identify with them who knows and loves them as I do. I know how they think and how they may react when they are up against the wall. Over the years, almost all my fellow cadets have become high-ranking officers, generals. Many of them have reached the very top of the tree, and like me, they are men of middle age. So I often turn to the friends of my son, the Prince of the Asturias, to keep in touch with what young officers are thinking today.'
    'Is the mentality of these young officers very different from that of their elders?'
    'Yes, very. They're more open, more interested in the changes taking place in the world. They no longer question democracy, still less the monarchy. I do what I can as king and commander-in-chief of the armed forces to get people to understand the military and realize that they belong to the Spanish people too. With the aid of the general staff, I'm trying to abolish military ghettos. I mean I want to give soldiers a

On the morning of Tuesday, 9 November 1948, Don Juan Carlos de Borbón set off from Lisbon for Spain on the Lusitania Express. Escorted by the Duke of Sotomayor and the Viscount of Rocamora, the boy left the train at Villaverde station near Madrid, stepping down on to the platform where half a dozen people he had never seen before were waiting for him. Among them (left to right) were José Aguinaga, Julio Danvila, Juan Antonio Macaya, Father Ventura Gutiérrez, and Juan Caro.

The young prince at a hunting party.

Don Juan Carlos during his training in the armed forces. 'Everyone knew who I was, but they pretended to have forgotten, not always successfully. To my really close friends I was Juan or Juanito, to others I knew quite well I was Borbón, and to everyone else I was SAR [His Royal Highness], but without any emphasis on it.'

Skiing, one of Don Juan Carlos's favourite sports.

The king delivering his televised message to the nation on the night of the attempted coup
d'état *of 23 February 1981. On hearing his final words, all Spain breathed a huge sigh of
relief. The* coup d'état *had failed. That night has been felicitously described by Philippe
Nourry as his 'night of consecration' as king.*

Don Juan Carlos coming out of a Council of Ministers presided over by General Franco in 1974. Carlos Arias Navarro (on the right) was prime minister at the time.

'... *in my first speech from the throne, I made it very clear that I wanted to be "king of all the Spanish people".*'

'The queen and I are very fortunate parents. Our son and our two daughters are very special people in their own different ways.'

chance to live like normal people, not in great blocks of buildings entirely occupied by the military. Mao said that soldiers ought to live within the people like fish in water. He was right. Spaniards must stop regarding the military as people from another planet. Oddly enough, and although it may seem paradoxical, terrorism has been a help to some extent there, forcing us to disperse military personnel so that they won't present the bombers with too easy a target. Yes, the military have changed a great deal over the last few years, José Luis. They take far more interest than their elders used to in history, geopolitics, foreign languages...'

'So you have a great deal of contact with young army officers, Señor?'

'Not as much as I'd like. But whenever I visit a brigade in Cordóba or Badajoz, for instance, I dine with the officers and invite them to talk to me about their problems and ambitions. It isn't always easy; just because they are young, they find it difficult to speak to me freely. So I rely on the Prince, another young officer who knows all about his young friends' problems.'

'Speaking of Don Felipe, Señor, you encouraged him to study law?'

'Yes, and economics too. It never hurt anyone to have two professional strings to his bow.' Don Juan Carlos pushes his chair back to change the position of his legs. 'Things are changing very fast in the military world, you know. I'm a king who had a sound military training, and I can try to resolve the forces' problems with inside knowledge of what they're about. Chiefly, of course, lack of money. I would like my armed forces to be even better adapted to trends in the modern world. For instance, ever since the occupation of Spain by Napoleon's troops, it has been customary to appoint a captain-general to every region, in effect commanding his own army.'

'Warlords, in fact?'

'Let's not exaggerate. We just want the army to depend a little less on the captain-generals and a little more on the local general staff. We need smaller, faster-moving units. Those we already have – the parachute brigade and the airborne brigade – have proved very satisfactory. Large divisions work well in theory, you see, but taking geography and above all our mentality into account, small units work best in practice. To sum it up briefly, let's say I'd back the efficiency of David against the power of Goliath.'

'Have you had to face much resistance over these changes?'

'Well, yes – some of them.'

'Coming from the older officers, of course?'

'There's no denying it.'

'We older folk can sometimes be rather a nuisance, Señor.'

'I'd prefer to say,' says Don Juan Carlos, 'that there are some men, still young, who distrust anything new, and that makes them old before their time.'

The king dismisses the memory of old confrontations with a wave of his hand and goes on explaining.

'Our present objective is to get the army out of the big cities. But moving all those soldiers costs an enormous amount of money. Merely installing the brigade which was a part of the Acorazada Brunete[1] division in Badajoz cost forty thousand million pesetas.'

'Yes, but it can't be denied that having the Acorazada Brunete only a few kilometres from Madrid represents a constant danger for the establishment if the army should ever challenge its power.'

The king agrees with an impatient nod. 'I've spent a good deal of time trying to eliminate suspicion of the army from the minds of politicians. They always feel suspicious, and there's no real foundation for it. I know the military well and I know you can trust them, so long as you're straight with them, of course. But politicians in general just don't trust the military. The military have a different way of thinking, that's all, so you have to make an effort to understand them.'

I can always sense when Don Juan Carlos is torn between a wish to talk and the need to say nothing, but his silences are often as significant as his words.

Several times already, when my questions about the night of 23 February have become too precise, he has told me, 'It's not for me to do anything but express a personal opinion of matters which have already been judged by a military tribunal.' But I know, for instance – there are leaks even in royal palaces – that when he telephoned the captain-generals one by one to ask them to make it clear where they stood on the *coup d'état*, they all said the same thing. 'I am at your Majesty's command *para lo que sea*.' This last phrase will translate as 'for whatever is necessary', but it loses some of its force out of context. *Para lo que sea* implied a

---

[1] Armoured division stationed very close to Madrid.

frank response to the king: 'If you support the action being taken by Milans and Tejero, I am with you. If you are against it, I will help you to bring them down.' That key opened wide the door to the question that many Spaniards asked themselves that night during the hours before the king appeared on their television screens. Was he for or against the military rising?

Let us go back in time. On 23 February 1981, at 6.20 p.m. precisely, Lieutenant-Colonel Antonio Tejero, pistol in hand and followed by civil guards armed with sub-machine guns, stepped into the semi-circle of the Cortes at the moment when Landelino Lavilla, president of the assembly, was proceeding to the nominal voting for the installation of the new prime minister.

Tejero – physically a character who might have come straight out of Edwardian light opera – mounted the few steps which brought him level with President Lavilla and shouted, 'Get down! Everyone on the floor!'

General Gutiérrez Mellado – a frail man with the finely drawn face of an intellectual – jumped up and faced the guards, who turned their guns on him.

'Lay down your arms at once!' he cried.

'We take orders only from the general,' replied Tejero.

Gutiérrez Mellado was indignant. 'What general? I am the only general here!'

Tejero, his boorish behaviour fitting his grotesque appearance, jostled Gutiérrez Mellado and shouted again, 'I want everyone on the floor!'

Ministers and deputies obeyed him almost to a man, crouching under their seats. The full weight of Gregorio Peces Barba came down on the young Felipe González, who was unable to dodge in time. Only Adolfo Suárez and Santiago Carrillo remained seated, determined to die with dignity if need be. Meanwhile General Gutiérrez Mellado was still on his feet, hands on his hips, a few feet away from Adolfo Suárez, lip curled in an expression of unutterable scorn.

Tejero announced through the loudspeakers that he was acting 'on the orders of the king and General Milans del Bosch, captain-general of Valencia, which city he has just occupied with his tanks'. And so began what Antonio de Senillosa, one of the deputies, a man of wide culture and an inveterate night bird, described next day as 'the longest night of my life'.

'Tell me, Señor, out of all the captain-generals you telephoned, did none of them hover half-way between loyalty and rebellion?'

Don Juan Carlos replies without a moment's hesitation, 'There *is* no half-way between loyalty and rebellion. The only one who responded with a statement I could not accept was Milans del Bosch himself when he said, in a husky voice, "Majesty, I have done this to save the monarchy!" '

'Save it from what, Señor?'

'I didn't stop to ask. We'd have wasted too much time in pointless explanations.'

There was also the captain-general of the Canaries, Gonzalez del Yerro, who simply replied, when he realized what the king's attitude was, 'I will obey Your Majesty's orders ... *pero es una pena!*'[1]

'Can Milans del Bosch's monarchist feeling be doubted?'

'Certainly not.'

'So he was acting in good faith?'

'I think he was the victim of subtle poisoning of the mind more than anything else. But he didn't deny hating all the changes that had come about in Spain, *en bloc.'*

The king is a strange man. At no time during our conversations has he allowed himself to say anything at all about people who did him harm which might wound them, even today.

However, he was right in suggesting that Milans was rather a baffling character. One evening, dining with the Count of Barcelona in his chalet of La Moraleja, he stated to the astonishment of his fellow guests, 'I will bring my tanks out into the streets before I retire.' It was no empty threat; he ended up doing exactly that in Valencia. However, after dispersing throughout the city, his tanks stopped very correctly at all the red lights.

Does a man's nature triumph over his appearance, or is it the other way around? The problem does not even arise in the case of Milans del Bosch. He looks what he is: an old soldier rather than a 'military man'. Tall, broad-shouldered, he has the arrogant bearing of a man never

---

[1] ... but it's a pity!

troubled by doubt, and his upper lip sports one of those fine horizontal moustaches which have become the trademark of every self-respecting old fascist in Spain. His mental processes, authoritative rather than persuasive, move as heavily as his tanks. It is quite possible that Milans really thought he would be saving the monarchy by rendering armed aid to Tejero, without realizing that by such an action – pointless anyway, since there was nothing that needed saving – he was putting the democracy, and with it the monarchy, in grave danger. He equivocated a good deal before obeying the king's order to take his tanks back to barracks. At four in the morning, when Don Juan Carlos spoke to him on the telephone for the second time, he still had not done it. Instead, he had made contact with the colonel commanding the Manises air base to order him and his fighter planes to join him. The colonel in question, one of the king's former fellow cadets, called Don Juan Carlos at La Zarzuela immediately to tell him what was going on. 'I told General Milans del Bosch,' said the colonel, 'that I took no orders except from the chief of air force general staff, and in case he dared approach Manises with his tanks, I had positioned my aircraft where they could defend the entrance to the base with missiles.'

'I know the colonel would have done it, too,' says Don Juan Carlos. 'That would have been the first time aircraft ever engaged in anti-tank combat while still grounded! You see how useful I found it that night to have friends and comrades in all the three branches of the armed forces, José Luis.'

However, the army as a whole was far from being as loyal to the king as he believed, or at least as he said he believed. Milans del Bosch – the son and grandson of soldiers who had gone in for conspiracy themselves in their spare time – was not the only hatcher of plots. *Pronunciamientos* are very much a part of the history of Spain. From the beginning of the nineteenth century until 1936 *pronunciamientos*, mutinies and rebellions were of frequent occurrence. A general on horseback, sword in hand, would enter an official building and seize power for a time, until another general took his place. Sometimes these military ventures were pitiful failures, but the rebels seldom ended up facing a firing squad. Neither Milans nor Tejero was risking his skin in the venture of 23 February; the death penalty had been abolished in 1978.

Don Juan Carlos was right when he said it was a mistake to make light of such 'operetta conspiracies' as Operation Galaxia, for that plot could have succeeded, and so could the *coup* of 23 February. It must not be thought that the military were alone in their plotting. Civilians on the most conservative wing of the Right – bankers, great industrialists, and even the occasional ecclesiastical dignitary – surreptitiously encouraged them by means of money and political influence.

'Was the identity of the civilians supporting the military *coup* known for sure, Señor?'

The king waves a hand in the air, his favourite gesture when he wants to evade a question which would take too much explanation.

'N … no. Well, we know and we don't know.'

Like Operation Galaxia, the meeting which took place at Játiva on 13 to 16 November 1977 between General Milans del Bosch, his colleague Coloma Gallegos, captain-general of Catalonia, and Admiral Pita da Veiga, who came with Generals de Santiago and Alvarez Arenas, was not taken seriously. The meeting confirmed what many observers feared: the army was restless and discontented. The Játiva conspirators claimed that they were going to form a government of 'national salvation' which would have stopped Spain's movement towards progress in its tracks, forcibly hauling the country back into the Dark Ages. These were men determined to put an end to the democracy which, in their view, had handed power to the losers of 1936. Without Don Juan Carlos as head of the state, they might have overthrown the government in office long ago. However, the king was a difficult obstacle for them to circumnavigate. Some of them thought that, if a *coup d'état* against democracy were to succeed, the first thing to do was remove him. It was only a short step from that to thinking that he should actually be assassinated.

'Did you sometimes feel you were in danger, Señor – physical danger?'

Don Juan Carlos reflects before replying, 'I never think about death. You can't live your life in the fear of death. Especially when you're a king, which is not the safest of jobs.'

'How can you decide not to think of death, though?'

'I don't remember the name of the bullfighter who was asked if he was afraid at the moment of entering the arena, but he replied, "The fear of being afraid prevents me from being afraid."'

'I remember going to interview Indira Gandhi in New Delhi; she used to receive several thousand people every morning during the *darshan* ceremony, in the gardens of her residence in Safdarjang Road. Sometimes they came from the most remote corners of India. She used to walk among this crowd of strangers, umbrella in hand, talking to this one or that one. One morning I asked her, "Madame, aren't you afraid of being assassinated some day by one of the fanatics who have sworn to kill you?" Indira Gandhi told me, "I never think of it. But if they kill me ... well, that is destiny."'

'And they did kill her in those very gardens, didn't they?'

'Yes, the murderer was one of her own bodyguards.'

'"That is destiny..."' murmurs Don Juan Carlos. 'She was right. Destiny comes to us all.'

'Has there been any assassination attempt on Your Majesty's life?'

'Hmmm – no.'

'I thought I heard of a bomb that was going to be placed under the platform where you stood to review a march past of the armed forces.'

'Oh, yes. In La Coruña. It seems they'd dug a tunnel under the platform, but –' his hand waves these unpleasant memories away, exorcising them – 'but I never heard any more about it.' His tone is one of the utmost indifference.

'Señor, do you feel well protected by your security services?'

'Yes, they do an excellent job. But I think the important part of security is to deter anyone from approaching you with aggressive intent. All the same, no one can do anything about a madman or a fanatic, and terrorists are all fanatics. Better to believe in the good fortune watching over you than think about death. And you need to know you can react in the right way at a moment when others might be panic-stricken. Don Alfonso XIII saved his own life by riding down a man who was pointing a revolver at him. However, poor Mountbatten couldn't do anything to stop the IRA terrorist who pressed a button several hundred metres away from the boat he was going to blow up. Kennedy was assassinated before the eyes of several dozen FBI agents too, and Reagan was nearly murdered by an unbalanced man obsessed with a film star and trying to impress her. The people who organize my security are more preoccupied by my presence at official engagements planned months in advance than my occasional visits with the queen to restaurants where we aren't expected. I believe the best way to avoid assassination attempts is to act on impulse, which isn't always easy in my job. Most of the military men assassinated by ETA have been killed on their usual way to work every morning. If Admiral Carrero Blanco hadn't gone to Mass in the same church at the same time for years, he'd probably still be alive today.'

'Yes, that certainly makes things even easier for terrorists. But Señor, haven't you often thought it amusing to shake off your own escorts?'

Don Juan Carlos leans back in his chair and lets out a shout of laughter. 'Oh, those times are past now! All the same, José Luis, it was enjoyable riding through Madrid on my motorbike with a helmet preserving my anonymity. I sometime used to take it off at the red lights, and the people around me would be transfixed at the wheels of their cars. Those were the days!'

I leave the king immersed in his memories for a few moments, and when the smile finally fades from his face, I say, 'Señor. we've strayed quite a way from our subject, the *coup d'état* of 23 February.'

'No, we haven't! The *coup d'état* itself was an assassination attempt against Spain as a whole. And that's how the people of Spain took it, reacting as they would have reacted to the threat of another civil war. Before I appeared on TV, the *Comisiones Obreras* [1] people telephoned me several times to tell me, "We're going to burn our files and take to the maquis!" I told them, "For heaven's sake, don't do that! I have it all in hand."'

'And did you really, Señor?'

'Yes, because I'd already talked to most of the captain-generals.'

'And you didn't for a moment doubt the loyalty of the men who put themselves at your disposal *para lo que sea*?'

'No, I had no reason to doubt it.'

His tone of voice is not entirely convincing; he sounds like a man reluctant to revive doubts of the loyalty of people he more or less trusted. The lesson Don Juan Carlos learned on the night of 23 February was harsh enough to shake the certainties of this generous and trusting king.

Milans del Bosch and Armada were companions in arms, but not made to like or understand each other. They had nothing in common but the uniform they wore, one to go on manoeuvres in the open country, the

[1] Communist-affiliated trades union.

other to go to his office. Milans was very popular in the army, where they admire the loud-mouthed and pugnacious type. Under the legendary General Moscardí, he had been one of the defenders of the besieged Alcázar de Toledo during the civil war. A great admirer of Franco, he felt a Francoist nostalgia which in no way impaired his loyalty to the monarchy. Don Juan Carlos often showed a liking for him.

The king knew that Milans bore the Suárez government a grudge for not making him army chief-of-staff. He saw this as an injustice, and it was eating him alive. Everyone knew, however, that Milans was not the right man for the post, still less for the position of defence minister, which he also coveted. Milans personified the conventional idea of a man of war. He could be a rather disturbing man. Long before the *coup d'état*, while he was commanding the Acorazada Brunete division, he had boasted that he could take Madrid with his tanks any time he liked. He had all the diplomas and medals a high-ranking military man could desire, but he was far from being intelligent. If he had been, he would never have let himself become embroiled in a *coup d'état* with a man like Tejero, who detested the king as much as he detested the monarchy.

The fact that Milans the fighting man exploded into action did not particularly surprise Don Juan Carlos.

'He'd said so often that he'd bring his tanks out into the streets some day, no one ought to have been surprised when he did it in Valencia. All the same, I was staggered myself when I heard that Milans had decided to "save" me.'

'Were you as surprised by Armada's treachery?'

'Oh, Armada ... I think I've already told you I don't care to go back over matters already dealt with by military tribunals.'

The King slowly shakes his head, his eyes on his hands, which he has laid on his office desk.

The only person to spot the double game Armada was playing was Suárez. When General Gabeiras appointed Armada his second-in-command on the army general staff, Suárez tried to oppose the appointment in any way he could. Everyone would have done better to listen to him.

The plan devised by Armada began to take shape when it became publicly obvious that the Suárez government was in trouble. Suárez's party was drifting like a ship without a rudder. He was felt to be powerless in the face of the ETA terrorist escalation which was infuriating the army, its main target. Attacked on all sides, Suárez did not know where to turn. The military could not forgive him for legalizing the Communist Party. The right wing of his own party blamed him for being the first head of government to receive the terrorist Arafat and embrace him in public. The employers were waging an apparently endless war of attrition against him. The bankers had decided they could no longer stand the audacity of a man who prided himself on scorning money. The Church uttered loud cries of horror on hearing of a bill on divorce to be put forward by Fernández Ordóñez. The unions had ceased to believe in promises which were never put into practice. Now extremely unpopular, Suárez finally gave way. It was then that a number of high-ranking military men, surreptitiously encouraged by Alfonso Armada, 'the king's friend', launched the idea of an abrupt change of tack in the de Gaulle style. Several highly placed socialists seemed to like it. In their turn, right-wing politicians admitted that they could see nothing wrong in a radical change, within the legal framework of existing institutions. They failed to realize that all this could easily degenerate into violence. 'Win the battle with Suárez and then we'll see,' was the watchword.

The king could not do much about all the animosity Adolfo Suárez had aroused. Moreover, even the most discreet intervention on the monarch's part might call his powers of arbitration into question. Josep Meliá, a state secretary at the time, remarked that 'although the king's trust had weighed heavily in the balance when Suárez became prime minister, it would be self-defeating if used to keep him in office'. Illogically, the discretion the king displayed at this point gave rise to all kinds of increasingly malicious rumours.

'I was accused of letting Adolfo down,' says Don Juan Carlos. 'Such accusations disregarded the part which it is proper for the king to play in a parliamentary regime. I had no powers to impose a political solution of my own liking.'

This attitude on Don Juan Carlos's part, absolutely correct on the constitutional level, encouraged some military commanders to say later that the king's 'significant silence' had impelled them to take those initiatives of which 23 February was the outcome. That, again, was to ignore the fact that it was not the king's prerogative to bring about political change, still less an abrupt change of tack giving power to the military.

'I saw some senior officers – people I always did see at their request – who wanted a private interview in which they could put their point of view to me,' Don Juan Carlos tells me. 'I listened to them carefully, and when their arguments struck me as departing too far from reality I tried to make them see reason. But I also made it clear that in no case could they count on me to cover up for the slightest action against a constitutional government like our own. Any such action, I told them, would be regarded by the king as a direct attack on the Crown.'

In spite of this firm attitude taken by Don Juan Carlos, General Armada concluded that the only way of getting the army to act was to call on the authority of the king. Patiently, Alfonso Armada set about weaving a web in which men of the stamp of Milans del Bosch were to become enmeshed. Armada knew that at all costs he must use the prestige of the Crown to cover up for future participants in the *coup*. As he had long been a close friend of the royal family, no one in the military world ever challenged what Armada said when he stated, in confidential tones, 'The king thinks … the king would like … the king told me …' etc.

On 29 September 1981 Adolfo Suárez, back from a troubled visit to the Basque country, went on television to announce that he was going to resign. He had previously had a long conversation with the king, offering him his head on a platter – 'It's the only way,' he told him, 'of sparing Your Majesty the political risks of resolving the coming crisis.' He then addressed the Spanish people, his tone bitter. 'I am resigning because I do not want the democratic system we have all desired to become no more than a parenthesis in the history of Spain.'

After the fall of Suárez, General Armada stepped up his activities. He too was bitter. And vindictive. He had served the Prince of Spain for almost twenty years as secretary-general of his household. Once Don Juan Carlos was king, he had kept Armada near him. But then, to Armada's great vexation, he had been removed from La Zarzuela and given command of a mountain division in Lérida in Catalonia. He was bored to death in his mountains, and let the fact be known in the relevant quarters. He thought he had taken a great stride forward when

Gabeiras appointed him his second-in-command on the army general staff. Paradoxically, Armada made no use of that position when the participants in the *coup* went into action. On his frequent visits to other high-ranking officers, Armada explained tirelessly that the only solution to Spain's problems was a government of 'national salvation', to be presided over, he further specified, 'by a general of great prestige, loyal to the king and respecting democracy'. Politicians who knew about these confidences thought that this 'general of great prestige' could only be Lieutenant-General Gutiérrez Mellado, vice-president of the Suárez government. But part of the army detested Gutiérrez Mellado for the very fact of his deep respect for the democratic system. Armada therefore knew that Gutiérrez Mellado would never be an obstacle in his path.

In Madrid, people were speaking openly of the 'Armada solution'. Armada himself took care to keep on the fringe of any operation upon which persons other than himself might embark. He was well aware that Lieutenant-Colonel Tejero, for instance, would not scruple to put both the monarchy and the democracy at risk. At that point people would turn to him, General Armada, to save the situation.

While Armada was playing Machiavelli, Tejero got in touch with Major Mas Oliver, Milans del Bosch's aide-de-camp, to place himself at the latter's disposal and explain his intention of giving the failed La Moncloa operation a repeat performance, but this time in the Cortes, where he could hold the entire government while they were electing Suárez's successor.

Of all these plots Armada's was the most dangerous, because his was a far better constructed plan than those of the other conspirators. Milans, intending to get rid of Tejero when the latter's *coup* in Madrid had succeeded, very quickly realized that he needed Armada to guarantee the king's cooperation or at least his complaisance. The military men, when Milans asked them to support the insurrection, would all ask the same question: does the king agree? The best reply to that was to mention Armada's name. Everyone involved in the affair intended to deceive everyone else. Milans was going to drop Tejero at the first chance he got, and Armada was going to use Milans so as to become the last-minute 'saviour' of the monarchy and of that democracy which, in his opinion, needed its wings clipped a little.

*

'We all know Milans was not a very subtle character, Señor,' I say to the king, 'but was he obtuse enough to think Your Majesty would cover up for the *coup d'état?*'

'No, but I believe he thought that faced with a *fait accompli*, I could only go along with it. He didn't know me very well.'

'How did you first discover what was going on in the Cortes, Señor?'

'From someone here at La Zarzuela who had just heard it on the radio. I was getting ready for a game of squash when they came to tell me that armed civil guards had entered the Cortes. That was quite some surprise, believe me. I went straight to the phone and called the chief of the army general staff.

'"What exactly is going on in Madrid?" I asked.

'"That's what we're trying to find out, Señor, but if you'd like to speak to General Armada he's right here beside me."

'I said, "Put him on the line. Alfonso, what's all this about?"

'Armada replied calmly, "Let me just pick up a few documents from my desk and I'll come up to La Zarzuela and speak to you in person, Señor."'

Up to this point all seemed normal. It was perfectly natural for Armada, second-in-command on the general staff, to suggest coming to La Zarzuela to tell the king what was going on in Madrid. Suddenly, however, and extraordinary as it may seem, a rather strange thing happened. The king felt intuitively that there would be some danger linked to the presence of Alfonso Armada at La Zarzuela. Armada's voice, too calm, almost indifferent, was the voice of someone who did not appear at all surprised by the events in the Cortes. That voice rang an alarm bell in the king's mind. He knew he must not receive Armada at La Zarzuela. Just at that moment, Lieutenant-General Sabino Fernández Campo came into his office and signed to him to cover the receiver with his hand. The king guessed what was up. Once again, luck had been on his side. Before he called Gabeiras at general staff headquarters, he had told Sabino, 'Phone the general commanding the Acorazada division while I make this call and ask him if everything there is normal.' Still with a hand over the receiver, he looked enquiringly at Sabino, who replied, in a low voice, 'It's about Armada.' The king uncovered the receiver again and apologized to Armada at the other end. 'Hold on a few minutes, Alfonso, they've brought me some papers to sign.' He covered the receiver again. Sabino, still in a low voice, told him, 'If that's Armada on the line, go very carefully. General Juste[1] has just told me, "Ask the king to do nothing if General Armada gets in touch with him. Ask him to wait for me to call you back before taking any decision." ' Don Juan Carlos nodded, and returned to his conversation with Armada. 'Alfonso, try to find out in detail what's going on in the Cortes before you come here. I can't receive you at the moment, but I'll try to see you later.' And he hung up without giving Armada time to reply. Sabino immediately gave the necessary orders to prevent Armada from reaching the palace. He and the king had realized what was afoot. 'If Armada is involved in this business in any way at all,' the king told Sabino, 'then logically he must come here and offer to make contact with the captain-generals of the various regions in my name, to spare me possible awkward conversations. And what would that look like? It would seem to show that the king knew about the *coup* and was going along with it.'

'Tell me, José Luis, who would have believed the king wasn't *en al ajo*[2] if Alfonso Armada took up his station by the telephones in La Zarzuela?' says Don Juan Carlos, his voice rising in sudden indignation. 'Sabino agreed with me entirely. We decided it was for the king to call all the captain-generals personally, one by one, and you know the outcome.'

Meanwhile in the Cortes, Tejero, still with his pistol in his hand, finally allowed the ministers and deputies to get up off the floor and take their usual seats again. From the dais where the president of the Cortes sits, Tejero announced through loudspeakers that he was acting 'in the name of the king and General Milans del Bosch'. Carried away by his own momentum, Tejero added that other military commands, including the Fourth in Barcelona, the Second in Seville, the Seventh in Valladolid and the Fifth in Zaragoza had joined the rising of General Milans del Bosch.

An officer under Tejero's orders announced, in his own turn, the formation of the next government, to be presided over by 'a general of prestige', and said that shortly a person of importance – 'a military man, of course' – would come to the Cortes to give the relevant explanations. This mysterious person of importance – Armada or perhaps Milans

[1] Commanding officer of the Acorazada Brunete division.
[2] In the secret.

himself? – never did put in an appearance, and became known thereafter as *el Elefante Blanco,* the White Elephant.

Directly after announcing the forthcoming arrival of this mythical character, Tejero ordered Suárez to be brought out of the semi-circle of the Cortes. He then called out in turn General Gutiérrez Mellado, the minister of defence Rodríguez Sahagún, Santiago Carrillo, and finally Felipe González and Alfonso Guerra. Later, when he was prime minister, Felipe González told me he was sure at that moment they were all going to be killed. However, Tejero confined himself to shutting them up in a room known as the Clock Room, close to the bar, where the guards had been drinking hard since they arrived.

The rest of the deputies settled down to await the arrival of the White Elephant. The Catalan deputy Antonio de Senillosa, who spent the night reading a novel by Marguerite Yourcenar, whispered to his neighbour, 'I don't for a moment believe the king has anything whatever to do with any armed *coup* carried out by that sinister idiot Tejero.'

Ever since the start of the incident, and unnoticed by anyone, a close-circuit camera had been filming the course of the most grotesque *pronunciamiento* in Spanish history.

At La Zarzuela, meanwhile, the telephones were working overtime. The Marquis of Mondéjar, head of the royal household, General Valenzuela, head of the king's military cabinet, and General Sabino Fernández Campo were answering calls from all over the world.

General Juste called La Zarzuela again and asked if Armada was there.

'No, and we don't expect him here tonight,' General Fernández Campo told him.

General Juste understood at once, and heaved a sigh of relief. Some minutes later, he assembled his officers and told them that the Acorazada division would not move and that 'the king is not involved in the *coup*'. Only Major Pardo Zancada managed to join his friend Tejero in the Cortes, with fifty men. As aid this was derisory, simply a symbolic gesture.

General Gabeiras, chief of the army general staff, who had himself called Milans del Bosch to order him to get his tanks back to barracks, received the brusque reply, 'I'm speaking to no one but General Armada.' However, Armada was not there, and Milans was mistaken in believing that his accomplice must already be in La Zarzuela.

*

At La Zarzuela, in fact, Sabino Fernández Campo, the Marquis of Mondéjar and Fernando Gutiérrez, head of the royal household's public relations office, were all vainly trying to get in touch with Prado del Rey, the Radio Televisión Española buildings. When Fernández Campo finally had the director-general of Spanish radio and television on the line and asked him to send a team to La Zarzuela as a matter of urgency, to record a message from the king to the nation, the director-general gave him to understand, by hints, that he was a prisoner in his own office, and the rest of the buildings were occupied by various companies of the Villaviciosa 14th Regiment, whose quarters were close by.

The king knew that once the first news of the insurrection was out, millions of Spaniards, waiting at home, would be wondering anxiously: *que hace el Rey?*[1] So long as he made no public statement his adversaries would be able to spread rumours of all kinds, just as they pleased. He therefore needed a camera team at La Zarzuela as soon as possible to record his reply to the conspirators. When Mondéjar managed to get one of the officers who had occupied Prado del Rey on the line, he passed the phone to the king.

'Con quién hablo?'[2] asked Don Juan Carlos.

The man on the other end of the line was a young captain. The king announced, in his turn, *'Soy el Rey.'*[3]

There was a momentary hesitation, and then the reply as laid down in regulations came at once. 'At your orders, Your Majesty.'

'Good. These are my orders, then: you will facilitate the departure from Prado del Rey of the television team we are expecting here at La Zarzuela.'

'At your orders, Majesty,' repeated the captain before hanging up.

A television team headed by Jesús Picatoste[4] arrived half an hour later. It was decided that Picatoste would record two copies of the king's message, and each of the copies would take a different route on leaving La Zarzuela, since no one knew exactly what was going on outside the palace. Was the place surrounded by troops? Were the access roads under surveillance? Picatoste had not seen anything, but it was

[1] What is the king doing?
[2] Who am I speaking to?
[3] This is the king.
[4] Famous television personality.

as well to be cautious all the same. The *Guardia Real* was ready for any eventuality, but only inside the *finca*. Later, it was discovered that the occupation of La Zarzuela had not been part of the conspirators' plans. They had not even cut the telephone wires. In fact it was a very amateurish affair.

'If I had wanted to carry out an operation "in the king's name" but without his consent,' comments Don Juan Carlos, 'the first thing I'd have thought of doing would have been to isolate him from everyone, by preventing him from communicating with the world outside. Well, that night I could have gone in and out of La Zarzuela exactly as I pleased, and as for the telephone, I had more phone calls within a few hours than in a month at any other time! Calls from my father in Estoril – who himself was very surprised to find he could get in touch with me – from my sisters, who were both in Madrid, and from friendly heads of state telephoning to encourage me to stand firm. It was a *coup d'état* mounted in defiance of common sense.' And Don Juan Carlos adds, 'Thank God, too, because if I hadn't been able to get in touch with the captain-generals as I did, I don't even like to imagine what might have happened!'

While they were waiting at La Zarzuela for Jesús Picatoste to arrive, General Aramburu Topete, director-general of the *Guardia Civil*, set up his HQ in the offices of the manager of the Hotel Palace, quite close to the Cortes. Aramburu, a strongly built man of medium height, was furious. He took it as a personal affront that some of his men had shut themselves up with that madman Tejero in the palace they were threatening to turn into another Alcázar de Toledo if the GEOS[1] ventured to attack. A crowd of officers surrounded General Aramburu to keep him in permanent touch with the army general staff, and if necessary with other centres of military power.

Around seven in the evening Aramburu, losing patience, courageously entered the Cortes followed by an aide-de-camp. When he came face to face with Tejero he exploded with anger. In a loud voice and no uncertain terms, he ordered Tejero to surrender. 'Surrender?' said Tejero, laughing. 'I'll put a bullet through my head sooner, and I'll take you out first!' Exasperated, Aramburu made as if to draw his own

[1] Special intervention troops.

gun. He was immediately surrounded by guards pointing their sub-machine guns at him.

A short distance away, in the defence ministry, General Gabeiras, a handsome man with the very British look of an Indian Army officer, was in his office with General Armada, whom he now knew to be involved in the plot. Don Juan Carlos had told him to keep Armada under constant surveillance and above all not let him come to La Zarzuela. Gabeiras had decided that Armada himself must help to defuse the *coup*. For a start he asked him to give the Villaviciosa 14th Regiment orders to withdraw from the radio and television buildings, and tell the men to go back to their quarters. But when Gabeiras was called away to join the other chiefs-of-staff, Armada seized his chance to make telephone contact with Milans del Bosch again. Milans knew already that the other captain-generals had not joined the rising. What Armada now had to tell him was even more depressing. Things were not going as expected in Madrid either. Tejero was alone with his guards inside the Cortes, and everyone who knew him feared he might let himself commit some irreparable action. And as for the Acorazada division, they could no longer count on it. Its commanding officer, General Juste, had kept it firmly immobilized. Without interrupting, Milans listened to Armada's toneless report, which left him no hope. The captain-generals had given in, and the king had not fallen into the trap. Only Tejero still believed in reinforcements which would never arrive. Eventually Milans said, in a weary voice, 'Call La Zarzuela again and suggest the formation of a new government with you as prime minister, a government able to start immediate negotiations with a view to making Tejero see reason.' As for him, Milans, he would order the tanks back to barracks.

As soon as Milans del Bosch had hung up, Armada got back in touch with La Zarzuela and placed himself at the king's disposal to negotiate Tejero's surrender. Once again Don Juan Carlos rejected the offer of his old colleague's good offices. Informed of what Armada had been doing, Gabeiras saw no reason not to use the disloyal general, running out of steam as he was, to defuse the time bomb represented by Lieutenant-Colonel Tejero. He gave Armada the necessary orders. 'Go to the Cortes, see Tejero, and if he will agree to surrender offer him two planes to take him and his men to a country of his choice. You may make no other arrangements except on your own behalf, and you will not involve either His Majesty the King or the army general staff. It's up to you.'

After brief and intensive thought, Armada's hopes revived and he decided to stake everything on his last throw. With a bit of luck he might yet figure as the man who 'saved the situation'.

When Jesús Picatoste and his team finally reached La Zarzuela the king was already in his commander-in-chief's uniform.

'In a few moments I was going to take the responsibility of confronting the country with its destiny,' Don Juan Carlos tells me. 'If there had been a single minister still at liberty, then as a constitutional king I would have been bound to agree to any initiative he saw fit to take. But all the members of the government were prisoners inside the Cortes. The only civil power still in working order was that of the secretaries and under-secretaries meeting at the ministry of the interior under the chairmanship of Francisco Laína, director of security, who was in constant contact with me. I was therefore free to act as I thought proper as commander-in-chief of the army. That night, José Luis, I learned how heavy the burden of solitude can be.'

Don Juan Carlos seems lost in his memories for a moment, but quickly returning to the present, he adds, 'There were people who said later I had exceeded the rights granted me by the Constitution that night.'

'I've never heard anything of the sort said myself.'

'They did say so, all the same, but my conscience is clear. One of my chief concerns during those dramatic hours was to be scrupulously careful in preserving democratic legality.'

When Don Juan Carlos went in front of Jesús Picatoste's cameras he knew he was staking not just his crown but his life. However, he has the legendary Bourbon courage, and a profound sense of his royal duty as king of all the Spanish people. So he stood firm and prevailed. His voice very calm but muted by emotion, he looked his people in the eye and said, carefully enunciating every word of his message:

'In addressing myself to all the people of Spain, and in the extraordinary circumstances of the present moment, I intend to be brief and concise. I am asking everyone to remain very calm and confident.

'I give the following order to all the military authorities: in view of the situation provoked by incidents which have taken place in the Cortes, and to avoid any possible confusion, I confirm that I have ordered the civil authorities and *junta* of the chiefs-of-staff of the armed forces to take all necessary measures to maintain the constitutional order within the legal framework.

'All measures of a military nature which may be taken must be previously approved by the *junta* of the chiefs-of-staff. The Crown, symbol of the permanence and unity of the country, cannot in any way tolerate the attempts of any persons, by their actions or their attitude, to interrupt by force the democratic process determined by the Constitution and approved by the Spanish people by means of a referendum.'

On hearing these last words from the king, all Spain heaved a huge sigh of relief. The king – contrary to what many had believed – was at the helm and free to act. The *coup d'état* had failed. For Don Juan Carlos the night of 23 February 1981 was, in the felicitous expression of Philippe Nourry,[1] his 'night of consecration' as king.

When Picatoste's cameras had finished rolling, the king telephoned the 3rd military region again, and when he had Milans del Bosch on the line he told him, with all the firmness of which he was capable, 'I am ordering you to withdraw your proclamation, which I regard as subversive, to send your tanks back to barracks, and to order Tejero to surrender and leave the Cortes. Up to this point I have made myself believe you were not a rebel. From now on, however, I shall have to regard you as such, and I will not be able to go back on that.'

Milans del Bosch's voice on the telephone trembled. 'Majesty, I acted as I did to save the monarchy!'

Don Juan Carlos answered immediately, 'You would have to shoot me before you gained your ends!' And he hung up abruptly.

Immediately after this extraordinarily violent exchange, La Zarzuela sent Milans del Bosch a telex. The text ran:

'In confirmation of what I have already told you, I wish to make the following points abundantly clear:

1. I state my firm determination to maintain the constitutional order in force. These words should suffice, and I do not intend to waste more.

2. No *coup d'état* of any kind whatever can shelter behind the person of the king. It is against the king.

3. I am more determined than ever to keep my oath to the Spanish

[1] Author of the book *Juan Carlos*.

flag. In all conscience, and thinking only of Spain, I command you to withdraw the units you have ordered into action.

4. I command you to make Tejero surrender.

5. I swear to you that I will neither abdicate nor leave Spain. The responsibility for civil war lies with any inclined to provoke it by insurrection.

6. I do not doubt the love my generals feel for Spain. For Spain first, and then for the Crown, I order you to do as I say.'

The telex was signed *Juan Carlos Rey*.

'And Milans obeyed when he received this telex?'

'Yes, but he took his time about it, all the same. I know he spoke to his subalterns, several times, about his honour as a soldier and his reluctance to abandon those who had cast in their lot with him. At four in the morning he finally ordered his tanks back to barracks. Then he telephoned me – I shall never forget his tone of voice – to say that, in obedience to my orders, he had just written countermanding the manifesto which had begun the insurrection. I did not want to engage in conversation with him, so I handed the receiver to Sabino. Milans read him the message which he said he would make public immediately, but he was still speaking of the possibility of an "Armada solution" which would allow everyone to save face. However, his heart wasn't in it. Once we had heard the text of Milans's message at La Zarzuela, we sent it on to all the other military commands.'

'Do you think it was actually your telex which made Milans decide to lay down his arms, Señor?'

'Well, yes, I believe the telex more than anything else convinced him that whatever happened, he couldn't count on me. Then again, he must have been under great pressure from his closest colleagues to give up, we mustn't forget that. But Milans is a tough character. When General Caruana, military governor of Valencia, who had orders from Gabeiras to arrest Milans, went to his superior's office and told him, "I am here to arrest you on the orders of the chief-of-staff," Milans put his gun on the desk in front of him and told him, "*Atrévete!*"[1] However, by then he knew it was all over.'

Could the *coup d'état* planned by Milans have succeeded? He had some good cards in his hands: the vacuum of civil power, a certain discontent

---

[1] You dare!

in the army, and General Armada, who had undertaken to join in once Tejero had got things under way. But everything collapsed, beginning with Armada, who later maintained before the military tribunal that he had never known about the plan devised by Milans and Tejero. For that plan to succeed it was necessary for Armada to go to La Zarzuela to convince the king of the necessity of forming a royalist government headed by a military man, i.e. himself.

'A very dangerous idea, Señor,' I suggest. 'Particularly for the monarchy.'

Don Juan Carlos nods. 'So far as I know,' he says, 'no monarchy has survived that kind of government. The one *raison d'être* of a modern monarchy is to place itself above political parties.'

Were the conspirators really convinced that Armada would get the king's consent to such a solution? In any case they were sure that Armada had access to La Zarzuela, or even if they were not entirely sure at heart, they so much wanted to believe it! Milans, who boasted of despising politics, gave a free hand to Armada, a master of the art of disinformation. To Milans, Armada was a vital piece in the jigsaw puzzle, since he guaranteed the king's complaisance. As for Tejero, he cared nothing at all for Armada, whom he saw as merely a bureaucrat defending the monarchical principle in which he, Tejero, did not believe. On the other hand Tejero too was convinced that Armada had the favour of the king, since Milans had told him so. The whole thing was a vast operation of delusion which ended by deluding its devisers themselves.

It is true, as Don Juan Carlos said, that the chances of success of an 'operetta conspiracy' should not be underestimated because it has failed. There were several factors that could have helped Milans bring the *coup* off: Tejero's holding of the entire government hostage; his own in-surrection at Valencia, which ought to have set off a domino effect in the other military commands; the understanding believed to exist between Armada and the king. And finally, there was the support of the Acorazada division, with forty thousand men massed at the very gates of Madrid. But nothing came of these assets. Armada did not manage to implicate the king in the venture. Tejero would not even listen to the propositions made to him by Armada. And Armada showed his hand at the beginning of the operation. As for the Acorazada division, it refused to invest Madrid with its tanks.

Don Juan Carlos hesitates before telling me, 'It's difficult for me to say this, José Luis, but the real mistake Milans made in the whole business was his total misreading of my character. He never tried to find out what I was like or what I thought. Where I was concerned, he could see no farther than the end of his own nose. Since I was the king, I was bound to like the royalist government he was going to suggest to me. Since I was a military man, I must necessarily share his ideas on matters which to him were fundamental truths. He thought he could take my complaisance for granted.'

Don Juan Carlos pauses again, and adds, 'You see, José Luis, I think that Milans – and some others too – have never understood or accepted that I could be the devoted servant of the will of the people. In other words, that the king could really be a democrat who respected the Constitution. If they had known me better, Milans, Armada and Tejero would not have staged their *coup* so lightly.'

I refrain from telling the king the comment of a cavalry officer, son of one of the conspirators, who saw no sense in the concept of democracy at all. 'Next time they'd better start by bombarding La Zarzuela.'

X

'Who was at the palace with you, Señor, on the night of 23 February?' I ask.

'My usual colleagues, of course. Nicolás Mondéjar, Sabino Fernández Campo, General Valenzuela, several aides-de-camp, and Fernando Gutiérrez.[1] Oh yes, and Manolo Prado, who had come on a visit to discuss something on behalf of the Institute of Iberian-American Cooperation, of which he was then president.'

Colleagues, the king calls them, but several of them were more than colleagues, even than friends. Don Juan Carlos has told me he has always been lucky in having exceptional men around him at difficult moments. The oldest of these exceptional men, Nicolás Cotoner y Cotoner, a cavalry general, Marquis of Mondéjar, a grandee of Spain, holder of the Golden Fleece and descended from a very ancient family of the island of Mallorca, was head of the royal household for a long time. He had also acted as proxy father to Don Juan Carlos during his youth. At over eighty years old the Marquis of Mondéjar still comes in to his old office in La Zarzuela.

The other exceptional man in Don Juan Carlos's entourage is Sabino Fernández Campo, a general in the juridical corps of the army, recently elevated to the dignity of Count of Latores and grandee of Spain for services to the Crown. A handsome man and attractive to women, he is

---

[1] Head of the palace's public relations.

the king's loyal vassal in all the old romantic sense of the word. He is famous for his ability to say no in the kind of tone generally used to pay compliments. Head of the royal household since the Marquis of Mondéjar's retirement, this very discreet Asturian can speak out clearly and straight to the point when necessary, although he greatly prefers to use hints accompanied by a half-smile which says a great deal.

Manuel Prado y Colón de Carvajal, Don Juan Carlos's childhood friend and an ambassador of Spain, is another man to be relied upon for missions which could be confided to no one else.

'Also in the palace,' Don Juan Carlos goes on, 'were the queen, her sister Princess Irene of Greece, my two daughters the Infantas Doña Elena and Doña Cristina, and my son Don Felipe, Prince of the Asturias. Well, the whole family.'

'Is it true that you told Don Felipe—'

The king interrupts me with a gesture he must have made dozens of times. 'Yes, it is. I made the Prince of the Asturias spend the night in my office, watching me do my job as king.'

'How old was he then, Señor?'

'Thirteen. The ideal age to learn what life will otherwise teach him when it may be too late. At the start of that long night he asked me, "Papa, what's going to happen?" I turned to the image of a football in the air again; you don't know just where it may fall to the ground. "It's the same with the Crown, Felipe," I told him. "At moments like these it is up in the air, and I am doing everything I can to see it falls in the right place!" Several times – he was only thirteen, poor lad! – he fell asleep in his chair, and each time I made him wake up, saying, "Felipe, *no te duermas!*[1] Watch: this is what you have to do when you are a king." That night, José Luis, the Prince of the Asturias learned more in a few hours than he may learn in the rest of his life. Later on my sisters Doña Pilar and Doña Margarita arrived, with their husbands. They all settled down somewhere in the house, and I stayed in my office with my son, Mondéjar, Sabino, and the aides-de-camp answering the phones. When I woke him up for the second or third time, Don Felipe murmured, *"Jo, papá, qué mes!"*[2] Poor boy, he'd had a difficult month, first with his studies at school and now with this business of the Crown up in the air.

[1] Don't go to sleep!
[2] Oh, Papa, what a month!

It was all a bit much for him. Next day my children asked if they had to go to school. I told them that since everything was back to normal there was no reason at all for them to skip their lessons.'

While the king was appearing on the nation's television screens, there were frantic comings and goings between the general staff and the Cortes. Obeying the order General Gabeiras had given him, Armada went to the Hotel Palace where General Aramburu Topete had set up his HQ, with the wild hope of figuring as the man who put an honourable end to the drama of which he himself was co-author with Milans and Tejero. Having betrayed the king and left the captain-general of Valencia to his fate, he now prepared to turn on Tejero. General Alfonso Armada had the looks for the part he played. Pale-faced, hollow-cheeked, with furtive eyes, his narrow-shouldered, round-bellied figure would have looked better in a cassock than his army uniform, which gave him the appearance of an old nightclub doorman.

Armada got Aramburu Topete to accompany him to the gates of the Cortes, where he gave the armed guards the password, 'Duque de Ahumada', in homage to the founder of the *Guardia Civil.*

After a moment or so Tejero came to meet the two generals surrounded by his guards, several of whom were in a state of intoxication. Tejero himself was abnormally excited. Moustache bristling, forehead beaded with sweat, he cast a scornful glance at the general who looked more like an office worker and was uneasily viewing the sub-machine guns trained on him. After the inevitable formalities, Armada asked Tejero to let him into the Cortes to address the ministers and deputies who had been taken hostage.

'What do you want to say to them?' asked Tejero.

'I want to suggest the formation of a government within the framework of the Constitution – an interim government, of course – where all the political forces of the country, right, left and centre will be represented. A government,' added Armada, looking away, 'over which I might preside.'

Tejero gave a bitter laugh. 'A general heading a government containing socialists and communists? Are you trying to fool me?'

For Tejero had wanted a return to pure, hardline Francoism, and nothing else. He enquired sarcastically, 'I wonder who sent you? Not General Milans del Bosch, I imagine?'

Armada gestured impatiently. 'Listen, Tejero, the army is on the point of splitting. If it does, that could mean the start of another civil war. I personally am advising you to surrender with honour and dignity.'

The word 'honour' in the mouth of a general so like a stage traitor set Tejero's back up, and when Armada offered him two DC8 aircraft to leave Getafe air base with him and his men, taking them to Argentina or Chile, Tejero exploded. No, he would not allow Armada to address his prisoners! No, he did not want those two aircraft! And no, he would not surrender!

'Go and tell whoever sent you that I will accept no government but a military government presided over by General Milans del Bosch!'

Having run out of arguments, Armada threw in the towel. The duplicitous bargain he was offering Lieutenant-Colonel Tejero had no chance of succeeding. Tejero was crazy, but far from an imbecile. He was beginning to suspect Milans of having played a double game. Since the hardliners' *coup d'état* – Tejero's – had not managed to drag the army into the insurrection, Milans was sending Armada to demand his surrender, which would allow him, Milans, to force the king's hand by suggesting a non-violent compromise.

'Get out!' Tejero's cry caused the guards surrounding him to make alarming moves, and Armada withdrew, his face even paler than when he had arrived.

Inside the Cortes, the tragi-comedy was threatening to end as pure tragedy. Several times Tejero tried in vain to get in touch by telephone again with Milans del Bosch, but on each occasion the captain-general of Valencia sent a message saying he would call himself later. Towards seven in the morning, Tejero tried to reach his superior in the hierarchy for the last time. An aide-de-camp told him that *el Señor capitán general* had gone home to bed. Now Tejero knew he was on his own, and all was definitively lost.

Better informed than he was, the hostages – one of whom had managed to conceal his transistor radio – already knew the text of Milans's last communiqué, which ended: *'Viva el Rey! Viva España!'* It was clear, therefore, that Milans had fallen back into line. Indeed, the king's telex had been a bitter blow to Milans. He knew already that he would face a court martial and he risked ending his days in prison. Moreover, Francisco Laína's threat to bring in the special operations units to storm the Cortes showed him the full gravity of the situation. As the good strategist he believed himself to be, Milans calculated that such an attack could easily leave two or three hundred victims among the attackers, the defenders and the hostages. He therefore decided to abandon Tejero, go home and get some sleep. He did so without taking the trouble to let the lieutenant-colonel know. As for Tejero himself, it took him a little longer to assess the full scale of the disaster, but he was already aware that all was lost except for honour. And he was fiercely determined to preserve that honour. His friend, Major Pardo Zancada – the only officer of the Acorazada Brunete who had joined him in the Cortes, with a few men who followed him without any real idea where they were going – advised him strongly to negotiate his surrender and that of his civil guards.

'But Milans may yet come,' objected Tejero, without conviction.

'Milans won't come to Madrid except to give himself up to justice,' replied Pardo Zancada bitterly.

Exhausted, betrayed by Milans del Bosch and Armada, abandoned by his army comrades who had refused to back him, Tejero decided to capitulate. But first he set out his conditions. They were very modest, and were accepted without too much discussion. Tejero wanted to humiliate Armada, the general whose actions hovered between felony and cowardice. He insisted that Armada himself must come to the Cortes a second time, to sign the surrender document. Tejero said he would not leave the Cortes until after the hostages were freed, and he would come out alone and in good order with his men, without journalists and photographers in the street 'to besmirch the ceremony'. The insurgents would go back to their barracks, and once there they would surrender their arms to other civil guards. Tejero personally took responsibility for the action he had led, and none of his guards must be prosecuted, 'because,' he explained, 'they followed me believing we were going to the Cortes on the king's orders, to free the government which had been taken prisoner by ETA terrorists'. 'However, your captains knew perfectly well what they were going to the Cortes for,' the negotiators pointed out. Tejero consented to the prosecution of men above the rank of lieutenant. He also asked that his friend, the frigate captain Menéndez Vives, a gentle if cranky soul who had wanted to shut himself up with him in the Cortes, should be able to surrender to the naval authorities.

This compromise was called *el pacto del capó*, 'the treaty of the bonnet', because it was signed in the street on the bonnet of a Land Rover. Initialling it in a trembling hand, Armada recognized defeat, although later, facing the military tribunal trying him for insurrection, he stuck to his denial that he had been part of the conspirators' plot. To every question the prosecution asked him about this or that meeting with this or that of his companions in misfortune, Armada replied sanctimoniously, 'I don't know; I was at Mass that morning . . . I don't remember; I was saying the rosary with my family that evening . . .'

Through that long night, Tejero in Madrid and Milans del Bosch in Valencia tried to bring Spain down to the level of a banana republic. Their failure was the failure of two men of limited vision who had not understood anything about the evolution of their country.

The freed hostages were welcomed out into the sunlit street by the ovations of a crowd of interested onlookers. Unshaven, their faces drawn, the ministers and deputies made straight for the telephones in the Hotel Palace to reassure their families. For many of them the long night of 23 February had been a night that taught them much. There were moments of drama, other moments in which human weaknesses were pitilessly exposed. The women deputies whom Tejero would willingly have allowed to go free refused to leave the Cortes, and one deputy whose plane had landed in Madrid late insisted on the guards letting him in to join his colleagues who were already Tejero's prisoners. Suárez, Carrillo and Felipe González thought their last hour had come when they heard the drunken guards shouting in the corridors, *'Los vamos a matar! Los vamos a matar!'*[1] In the small hours, when freedom was near at hand, Manuel Fraga, leader of the Right and vexed at not being shut up with the other party leaders in the Clock Room, rose abruptly from his seat, theatrically unbuttoned his shirt, and invited the guards who were watching with scornful smiles to shoot him.

Tejero and his friend Major Pardo Zancada were the last to leave the scene of their exploits. Tejero, face drawn, cheeks unshaven, uniform creased, would have liked to leave the Cortes behind his guards, keeping martial step in time with them, but most of them had already deserted the building, jumping out of the windows on the mezzanine floor.

---

[1] We're going to kill them! We're going to kill them!

Outside the palace, at the feet of the lions which guard its entrance, the pavement was littered with abandoned sub-machine guns.

It was a long night for the king too, the longest of his life. And a dangerous night as well; he was aware of a number of traps which had been set for him. While he was calling the captain-generals Don Juan Carlos realized he was walking on quicksand, and he couldn't help asking himself: how will this man react? The generals themselves, whose loyalty to the Crown was beyond question, might have fallen victim to misleading information in the mouths of their own comrades. It would be enough to say, 'The king is with us', and those few words would be interpreted according to everyone's most secret wishes. Time and again throughout that night the king asked Sabino Fernández Campo, 'Do you think this one will back us?' But they all replied, *'A sus ordenes, majestad, para lo que sea.'* It was up to the king to make it clear to them which camp he was in, and why.

One of the dangers the king feared most was going beyond his constitutional rights. As supreme commander of the armed forces, he could give the military orders, but in no circumstances could he impose his will on the commission of state secretaries and under-secretaries presided over by Francisco Laína, which in a way was assuring continuity of government. In other words, he had to be sure he never let himself perform an act of 'civil government'. He could only reign. And that was not easy, since Francisco Laína did nothing without asking his opinion. In such exceptional circumstances, where did the dividing line between reigning and governing lie? Don Juan Carlos asked himself that question many times during that interminable night.

To the king, the great revelation of that night was the extraordinary maturity of the Spanish people. They all realized that any disorder in the streets, the slightest popular demonstration, could be the ideal excuse for anyone who wanted a good reason to go over to the camp of Tejero and Milans. But the Spanish people stayed at home, glued to their radio and television sets. No one moved, and the streets of Madrid remained empty.

When Milans put out his last communiqué and ordered his tanks back to barracks, the king considered that the *coup* had failed. That was when he sent Don Felipe to bed. His lesson was over.

Everyone in La Zarzuela was dropping with fatigue. The telephone had not stopped ringing all night. Calls came in from all over the world. Pertini, Giscard d'Estaing, King Baudouin, King Hassan II, Hussein of Jordan, Queen Elizabeth and many others were calling to encourage the king and urge him to stand firm.

The Count of Barcelona, who was in Estoril, got in touch with Don Juan Carlos at about ten o'clock. He and his wife had been to the cinema to see a film called, of all things, *Los comandos del Rey*. When he heard the news that Tejero had seized the Cortes, he called La Zarzuela. In a voice shaken by emotion he told his son he had no advice to give him, since he was sure he would be able to keep the situation in hand at all times. No doubt Don Juan de Borbón was thinking of the great prestige which would accrue to the Crown if it proved possible to overcome the reactionary elements trying to drag Spain back to an age which, fortunately, was over.

'What did you do, Señor, when you heard that Tejero's hostages had been freed?'

'The same as everyone else. I took a deep breath, had a hot bath, and went to sleep for several hours. And what about you, José Luis? When did you realize it was over?'

'When Your Majesty appeared on television. Up till then I was wondering anxiously where the king was, and what he would do if he was still at liberty. I passed the longest hours of my own life between the seizure of the Cortes and your message to the nation.'

Milans del Bosch, who had gone to bed long before the king, was woken early by General Gabeiras telephoning to order him back to Madrid at once. At exactly seven that evening Milans entered the ministry of defence, where he was immediately arrested. At nine the same evening, Gabeiras summoned General Armada and relieved him of his post on the general staff.

'On the afternoon of 24 February,' Don Juan Carlos told me, 'when everyone had recovered to some extent, I received the members of the government and the principal leaders of the various political formations here at La Zarzuela. My meeting with these men and women was a very emotional one. People were all embracing each other, and many of them had eyes misty with tears. When Santiago Carrillo arrived he came over to me, took my hands between his own and said, "Your Majesty, thank you for saving our lives!" Suárez, still unaware of the true part played by General Armada, told me, "Your Majesty, I am sorry to have been wrong about Armada."

'All he knew, I realized, was that Armada had received Tejero's surrender, so I put the record straight. "No, Adolfo, you were right all along."

'As Suárez listened to me in surprise I took the opportunity to add, "We should be grateful to the armed forces, Adolfo. The vast majority of the military proved loyal to the Crown."

'I emphasized that loyalty to the Crown, because it was clear to my mind that the military had obeyed their natural commander, that is to say the king. I know that later Felipe González himself agreed that only the king could face up to sedition in the army and subdue it. He was right. If we'd been a republic ... Well, when everyone had finished congratulating everyone else, I asked for a few moments of silence to read out a very short statement on which I had been working that morning. "The Crown," I told them, "is proud to have served Spain with firmness and the profound conviction that democracy and a strict respect for constitutional principles are the expression of the will of the majority of the Spanish people. However, it should be generally realized that the king neither can nor should face incidents of such gravity again on his own responsibility." I would have liked to tell them, in simpler terms, that the role of king is not to be a fireman always ready to put out the fires which may spring up here and there. I did explain, very clearly, that those responsible for recent events must be subject to the full rigour of the law. We had to come down hard on Milans, Tejero, Armada and a few others, yes, but there must be no grudge held against the armed forces as a whole. My main preoccupation – because I am very well aware of the family feeling which prevails in the military world – was to keep the army from being rejected by Spanish society as a whole. The army had been humiliated enough; we should now pay tribute to its patriotism and the loyalty it had shown the Crown at a very difficult moment. Otherwise, we ran the risk of seeing the threat which had taken us all to the edge of the precipice rebound on us.'

Forty-eight hours later, Leopoldo Calvo Sotelo took over from Adolfo Suárez as prime minister. The investiture ceremony began with a long ovation for the king, who was absent from the semi-circle of the Cortes itself but very present in the minds of all the men and women who had spent a long night threatened by sub-machine guns. Only Blas Piñar, the histrionic representative of the extreme Francoist Right, remained seated while all around him – ministers, deputies, ushers, switchboard operators, journalists and press photographers – cheered Don Juan Carlos to the echo. In the communist tiers, headed by Carrillo, the comrades saluted the king's name by raising their fists. Many 'Juancar- lists' had become out and out monarchists since 23 February.

XI

Whenever Don Juan Carlos lights up one of his cigars in front of me I think of Stendhal's saying that a smoker of cigars is always 'a man on the point of happiness'. Relaxed, serene, the king strikes me as more open and receptive than usual this afternoon. I take my chance to ask him, 'Señor, how would you describe the queen, in a few words?'

He takes his time over replying, in remarkably solemn tones, 'The queen is a great professional.' He adds, 'A very great professional.' And choosing his words with care, he further adds, 'She has royalty in her blood.'

There is nothing surprising about that. The daughter of a king and the sister of a king, Doña Sofía has a family tree which includes two German Emperors, eight Kings of Denmark, five Kings of Sweden, seven Tsars of Russia, a King and a Queen of Norway, a Queen of England and five Kings of Greece. A pedigree to make you dizzy. But like St Francis, she knows 'there is nothing fine, good and desirable but simplicity'.

'What did the queen do during the night of 23 February?'

The gravity is still present in Don Juan Carlos's voice as he replies. 'Doña Sofía was the soul of La Zarzuela that night. Her calmness and serenity worked wonders. She looked after everything and everyone. Above all, she was at my side, her eyes always on me, encouraging me with a gesture as I spoke to the captain-generals on the telephone. I always value the queen's opinions because besides being intuitive she is a thinking woman. She is very rarely mistaken in her judgement of someone she meets for the first time. So as you will understand, I listen to her.'

'Señor, when you say Doña Sofía is a great professional, what exactly do you mean?'

'I mean she takes her job very seriously, and God knows it isn't a restful one.'

'Montaigne wrote: "The hardest vocation in the world, to my mind, is to play the king worthily." And Louis XIV, your forebear, Señor, said that "the function of the king consists principally in giving free play to common sense, which will always act naturally and easily."'

'*Los dos se quedan cortos,*[1] sighs Don Juan Carlos, melancholy.

Neither Montaigne nor the Sun King could have envisaged a Queen of Spain adopting their ideas some day and making them the golden rule of her daily life. In fact no one could carry out her difficult and demanding vocation more worthily than the queen. The Spanish people do not know much about her, but they can guess that the main purpose of her life is to serve the nation day after day, hour after hour, and the nation means the Spaniards, all of them, although with a distinct preference for those who need particular care: the young, the deprived, the sick, those approaching the end of their lives alone and deserted, those whose only school has been the street, and for whom delinquency is not a choice but the only outlet an intolerant and cruel society offers them. If the Spanish people know very little about Doña Sofía that is because of the remarkable discretion with which she conducts both her public and her private life. Yet she has won the hearts of Spaniards who are not used to seeing those in powerful positions lead a life of unpretentious simplicity, something that makes Doña Sofía a Spanish woman like any other, devoted to her husband, her children and her duty, which is often a thankless one and always arduous if not painful.

'Doña Sofía,' continues Don Juan Carlos, 'never forgets that she is the queen, but she hates authoritarianism. She believes firmly in discussion and friendly compromises. I don't think she has ever been known to use her high position in order to put someone in his place. All she has to do is adopt a very slightly chilly, distant manner. But those who work with her, you know, emphasize the cheerfulness of her character and her very

---

[1] They both fall short of the truth.

sharp sense of humour. She often bursts into contagious laughter which delights those around her. You can tell she's a woman who had a happy childhood.'

'I imagine, Señor, that being born the daughter of a reigning king gave her experience which must have been very useful when she became Queen of Spain.'

'Yes, indeed, although our monarchy here today doesn't have much in common with the Greek monarchy which Doña Sofía knew as a child. You know what struck her most when she arrived in Spain? It was discovering that people of our rank can lead an almost normal life, go to the cinema, go out to a restaurant to dine with a few friends. That just wasn't done in Athens, although heaven knows King Paul's Greece was democratic enough! But it's true that we're different in Spain. When Vaclav Havel came to visit me in Palma in Mallorca, I took him out one morning to a bar where everyone greeted me as if I were an old acquaintance. Havel couldn't get over it! What surprised him even more was seeing me pay for our drinks, even though the proprietor wanted us to be his guests. "Doing anything like this is absolutely out of the question in Prague!" the Czech president told me. Doña Sofía took some time to get accustomed to our ways too; they must have struck her as rather strange. Personally I've always felt them perfectly normal. I am the king, but I'm also a human being, and a Spaniard into the bargain, and I don't think putting yourself up on a pedestal is enough to inspire respect.'

'Did Doña Sofía soon get accustomed to Spain all the same?'

'She had some difficulty with the language at first, but she learned it quite quickly, and now I consider she speaks Spanish without any accent at all. I don't speak Greek myself, but the first time I heard people talking that language I said to myself, hallo, Spaniards! The two languages aren't really like each other, but they do have a similar kind of sound.'

'The first time I went to Athens,' I tell the king, 'I would have thought, apart from the Parthenon, I was coming ashore in Badajoz. The same heat, the same dust, the same dazzling clarity of light. I think you can fall in love with a country at first sight. My wife Syliane, who is half French and half Italian, went to a *corrida* on her arrival in Spain and saw the bullfighter Dominguín. As we left the plaza she told me, simply, "I never want to leave this country again."'

'I can well understand that.'

'Did the queen soon come to feel Spanish?'

'I think what mattered was that Doña Sofía very soon came to feel at home.'

'Your grandmother Queen Victoria Eugenia sometimes said she had often felt a stranger in Spain.'

'My grandmother was English, and the English, well ... when Doña Victoria Eugenia set foot in Spain she was entering a world which was nothing like her own. But Doña Sofía is Greek, and our two countries could easily be confused with one another, particularly when you approach them by way of the Mediterranean.'

'My mother, who was very fond of Doña Victoria Eugenia, often told me the Spanish court had always shown her a certain coolness.'

'I've heard that myself. I don't think my grandmother was always happy here.'

'I forget who it was that compared the court to a marble edifice made up of hard and very polite people.'

'Sometimes politeness doesn't make things right.'

The Spanish monarchy, endorsed by the Spanish people today, has been wise enough to end the old customs of the past. The king and queen are not surrounded by courtiers and flatterers, but by plain, efficient men and women whose principal virtue is that every morning they bring into La Zarzuela the fresh air which Miguel Maura recommended, far from the musty, unhealthy atmosphere of court cliques and coteries.

The king and queen begin their day very early. 'We're all early risers in our family,' Don Juan Carlos tells me. 'Not just because we have to be, but by inclination. For me, it's an old habit going back to my time in the military academies. In summer my father, who loves talking to his friends late into the night, is at the helm of his boat as soon as the sun rises.'

'Last August,' I said, 'at a dinner where the Count of Barcelona was present, his aide-de-camp, a delightful naval officer, told me during dessert that he was off on holiday next day. When I asked him where he was planning to go, he told me, "Anywhere, anywhere at all I can get some sleep. I haven't slept more than three or four hours a night since I've been with His Royal Highness!"'

'Yes, well, that's how we are!' Don Juan Carlos smiles. 'When our children were still at school Doña Sofía used to take them herself. She took the chance to make personal contact with the teachers educating the prince and the infantas. Nowadays Doña Sofía too gets up very early and spends the first few hours of the morning seeing the members of her secretariat in her office. They brief her on the various engagements she has that day. General Fernández Campo — it used to be Nicolás Mondéjar — gives her a detailed account of important events going on in the world, in particular anything that may concern Spain. The queen takes note of everything and acts accordingly. She's an orderly person; she doesn't like improvisation and she hates carelessness. But she doesn't spend her days shut up in her office, far from it. She's as active as I am and is always involved in all kinds of things. When we go on holiday to Mallorca in summer, she shares her passionate love of the sea with her brother King Constantine and me. As a family, we all have the sea in our blood. It's when we're on board the *Fortuna* we feel really free!'

And Don Juan Carlos adds, with a touch of melancholy in his voice, 'If I wasn't king, I feel sure I would be a sailor.'

Doña Sofía is what the Spaniards call *una mujer importante*.[1] Cultivated and extremely sensitive, she is also a convinced conservationist who will never set foot in a bullring if she is not professionally obliged to do so. However, in a country where the love of bullfighting is rooted deeply in all levels of society, this attitude of hers is sometimes controversial. Neither the Prince of the Asturias nor the infantas go to the arenas very often either. When I comment on it, Don Juan Carlos tells me, 'I'd go to the *corridas* more often myself if I had the time! Luckily my mother is there to represent the family at the *Fiesta nacional*!'

Indeed, throughout the *corridas* of the Feria de San Isidro, the Countess of Barcelona can be seen taking her place in the *palco real*[2] every afternoon, accompanied by some of her entourage.

'Not so long ago,' I told the king, 'José Carlos Arévalo, the director of *6 toros 6* told me that if the Prince of the Asturias were to appear in a *barrera*[3] at Las Ventas[4] some day, as Your Majesty does, the public of Madrid would give him a tremendous ovation.'

[1] A woman of importance.
[2] Royal box.
[3] Front seat at the bullring.
[4] The arenas of Madrid.

'I know,' agreed Don Juan Carlos, 'but there we are: if the prince doesn't go to the *corridas* very often – and I know he does go sometimes – he probably doesn't want to hurt his mother's feelings.'

Doña Sofía has a deep love of music, and has honoured some of the great musical interpreters with her friendship, among them Rostropovitch, an old friend. When he comes to Madrid Rostropovitch always plays Dvorak for the queen – from the cello concerto in B minor – at the end of his concerts.

'Is it true, Señor, that Doña Sofía has been responsible for getting the Crown to confer titles of nobility on creative artists?' I ask.

'Yes, and it was about time for Spain to recognize merit other than the kind that used to be won on the battlefield. We ought to honour artists and intellectuals as the British Crown does by giving them titles and honours.'

This was how Salvador Dalí became Marquis of Púbol a little while before his death, while the great guitarist Andrés Segovia was made Marquis of Salobreña, and Don Ramón del Valle-Inclán received the posthumous title of Marquis of Bradomín.

'However,' Don Juan Carlos continues, 'those members of Doña Sofía's entourage who are closest to her know that her chief concern, the real centre of her interest, is the *Fundación Reina Sofía*, whose founder and driving force she is. One of the purposes of this foundation is to encourage the study of "the needs of men and women in their individual reality" – in the context of their interrelation with the social community of which they are a part. It's a sincere and ambitious programme, and the queen devotes a great deal of time to it. You can't imagine what she suffers when she has to face a human problem to which no solution can be found.'

I tell myself that Doña Sofía must have suffered a good deal, for when she became queen the entire social fabric of modern Spain had yet to be constructed: aid was required for young people demoralized by a future which looked more than disquieting, for delinquents left to their own devices, for people exiled to the fringes of society, and it was needed day after day for the unemployed whose human dignity was wounded to the quick. They all needed a queen like Doña Sofía who would tackle this enormous task.

*

'Do you know Don Jacinto Benavente's[1] saying, Señor? He said having children was an illness which lasted nine months, but the convalescence took your whole life. How is your own convalescence going, Señor?'

Don Juan Carlos's face breaks into a broad smile. 'Benavente was an old bachelor who didn't know what he was talking about! Children are a blessing from heaven!' And he repeats the phrase with emphasis. 'A blessing from heaven!'

Changing position in his chair, and still smiling, he tells me, 'Having children – and you know it as well as I do – gives their parents constant anxiety, but great joy and happiness too. It's wonderful to see them growing up day by day, to try to find out their tastes and leanings so that you can understand and encourage them better. The queen and I are very fortunate parents. Our son and our two daughters are very special people in their own different ways; cheerful, straightforward and easy-going to such an extent that they sometimes have to be reminded who they are. They're also very good athletes, all three of them, and nothing could please me more. I'm convinced of the value of sports to everyone's development. Sporting activities teach you tenacity and encourage you to do better. It has been when I am engaged in sports and imposing a daily discipline on myself that I've often felt wonderfully free. Don Felipe,' continues the king proudly, 'has become an excellent sailor, like his sister the Infanta Cristina, and you've seen the Infanta Elena on horseback.

'I imagine Benavente's sally was meant to remind us it isn't always easy to understand our children. But we have to accept that they'll act like other people of their age and let them express themselves freely. Children grow up gradually before our eyes, and their attitudes to life won't always necessarily be the same as ours. However, we have to respect them. In our own case – with a son who is crown prince, and daughters who are royal princesses – it gets even more complicated, because they have to be prepared for responsibilities far beyond most people's. For instance, at an age when other boys are thinking of nothing but girls and a good time, Don Felipe was already having to travel the world representing me at the kind of ceremonies that aren't always wildly exciting.

[1] Early twentieth-century Spanish dramatist.

154

'We are very anxious to be a family whose members enjoy living together in this house where they can come and go as they please.'

'You speak of your family quite often, Señor. Perhaps we could specify exactly who the members of the royal family are.'

'That's easy enough, José Luis. The royal family consists of the king, the queen, the prince and the two infantas. I also include my parents, of course, the Count and Countess of Barcelona, and my two sisters the Infantas Doña Pilar and Doña Margarita. But not my sisters' children and husbands, who are part of the king's family but not the royal family. The same goes for my cousins. And then, as in any family, there are distant and not so distant relations: uncles, aunts, second and third cousins.'

After a brief hesitation, Don Juan Carlos added, 'And then there are other people who bear the name of Borbón, not all of them by right, José Luis.'

'Do you know what Borbóns of that kind are called in Madrid, Señor?'

'No.'

'*Los Borbones del Corte Inglés.*'[1]

'Indeed.' Not the shadow of a smile. Don Juan Carlos never jokes about those who could harm the image of the royal family from near or far. And yet there are indeed people – most of them people in 'high society' – who do make improper use of the name of Borbón. It sounds more elegant to be called Borbón than García de Lóbez, or Barucci, or Yordi, or even von Hardenberg, especially when you represent the names of international *haute couture* houses or the magic trademarks of famous perfumes at dinners and cocktail parties. I can understand that Don Juan Carlos, who himself represents Spain, does not care for such things.

Nor does the king look very kindly on certain aristocrats who like to be addressed as Highness, when apart from the members of the royal family no one in Spain may use the title of prince or princess. However, the Spaniards do not take much notice of protocol. You will often read in the press: 'Juan Carlos thinks ... Juan Carlos said ...' while you would

[1] A large department store where anything can be bought.

155

not expect to read, in an English newspaper, that 'Elizabeth had tea with her mother yesterday' when speaking of the lady who is always Her Majesty the Queen to the British people.

XII

It has been snowing over the sierra this morning, and the sky above La Zarzuela is even clearer than usual. A black wild boar trots after my car for almost a kilometre, its coat flecked with white snowflakes.

Don Juan Carlos is looking haggard. 'I've had a bad night. I must have turned over the wrong way in bed; my knee is painful.'

'Would you like us to put our conversation off till tomorrow, Señor?'

'No, no, sit down.' Attempting a smile, he asks, 'What would you like us to talk about today?'

I put my papers down on the table and switch my tape recorder on. 'Could you say, Señor, just when you felt free to take the initiative without consulting General Franco?'

It takes Don Juan Carlos some time to reply. Perhaps he thinks my question is out of order.

'It's difficult to say exactly,' he says at last. 'I took the initiative quite often, but it was one thing to act without the consent of the general and quite another to do so without consulting the opinion of the top brass of his entourage. Still, you could say I really began to shoulder my responsibilities at the time of the general's first illness.'

He thinks again before adding, 'And to fix a date, let's also say that things began to change after the assassination of Carrero Blanco.'

On 20 December 1973, the black Dodge carrying Admiral Carrero Blanco, heir apparent to the regime, was blown up on the Calle de

Claudio Coello by an extremely powerful mine. It rose in the air as if it had been picked up by a giant hand which then sent it crashing down into the courtyard of a Jesuit convent. Three corpses were pulled from it: those of the admiral, killed instantly, and of his chauffeur Pérez Mogena and the single bodyguard assigned to him for security.

'Did they ever find out who Carrero's assassins were, Señor?'

Don Juan Carlos looks at me in surprise. 'Why, ETA, of course. Didn't you know?'

'Like everyone else, I know ETA actually carried out the operation, but who was behind the Basques? Who was using ETA for their own ends?'

Don Juan Carlos gives me that glance of his which looks through you without appearing to see you. 'I don't know,' he tells me, in the tone of someone who has asked himself the same question over and over again. And he repeats, 'I don't know.'

I believe him, because if he hadn't wanted to answer my question he would simply have kept silent, as he has already done several times when my curiosity seemed to him to go beyond the proper limits.

'It was a strange crime, all the same, Señor.'

'*Y tu que lo digas.*'[1]

The first terrorists of the Txiquia Basque commando arrived in Madrid to mount surveillance on the comings and goings of the Ogre (Admiral Carrero Blanco's nickname) in December 1972. The admiral was assassinated a year later, on 20 December 1973. During the whole of that year the commando – no one ever knew exactly how many men it consisted of – changed its lodgings several times, at a period when you were not allowed to move without reporting to the local police station. When the time came a man claiming to be a sculptor hired – this was another miracle – a studio with its own basement in the Calle de Claudio Coello, down which the admiral's car drove every day. The profession of the studio's tenant would account for the sound of hammer and pickaxe when the commando started digging a tunnel some ten metres long under the road. This tunnel was duly stuffed with explosives. All this time the men of the Txiquia commando dined and drank in the local bistros and bars, and no one ever took an interest in their movements.

[1] You're telling me.

Between 19 and 20 December 1973, two terrorists, disguised as electricians, unwound two hundred metres of electric cable which would set off the explosion in the sculptor's basement. They did the job in broad daylight and watched by several bystanders, and no one asked what they were doing there. All this happened a short distance from the American embassy where Henry Kissinger spent the night before the assassination; it was supposed to be the best guarded place in Madrid. Once the assassination had been committed, the members of the Txiquia commando set off for Portugal by car. There were no road blocks, no border alerts. The terrorists could just as well have left by air, for the police were strangely absent from the airport.

'It was the perfect crime, perfectly committed.'

Don Juan Carlos nods assent. I tell him, 'Speaking of Operation Ogre one day, the secretary-general of the Communist Party told me that at the height of the Francoist period, when he sent agents into Spain after rigorous training in the Soviet and Czech schools of terrorism, the regime's political police always arrested them after a few months. It was an extremely good, efficient police force, Carrillo emphasized. "Which set me a very serious moral problem," he told me, "because I knew all the comrades I sent in were going to be captured and executed after being savagely tortured. More than once, to salve my conscience, I asked permission to go into Spain myself. But I was told that as the leader, I was too valuable to perish miserably in the slaughterhouse." Carrillo could not make out why Basques who, he said, "always looked like Basques, spoke with a Basque accent and usually wore Basque berets", were never arrested, molested or interrogated by that same very efficient Francoist police who never failed to arrest infiltrated communists, true professionals who knew all the tricks of the trade. Carrillo had the distinct impression that the ETA terrorists had been allowed to do as they liked, even given considerable assistance. That was what Carrero Blanco's widow thought too.'

The king is still looking at me, saying nothing.

'Carrillo implied that a number of people who were not strictly connected with ETA might have a good deal to gain from the disappearance from the political scene of a man who saw the only political future of Spain as the continuation of Francoism. Does that strike you as possible, Señor?'

'Everything is possible, José Luis.'

'In any case, Carlos Arias Navarro, minister of the interior and directly responsible for the admiral's security, was not summarily dismissed but made prime minister shortly afterwards. That struck Carrillo and many other Spaniards as provocative.'

'Yes. Many people asked themselves a number of questions at the time.'

'The mystery surrounding the crime thickened as time passed. When my French publisher of that period let it be known that I intended to write a book about Operation Ogre, I was summoned to the French ministry of the interior – the minister then was Michel Poniatowski – and advised, though in very pleasant terms, to drop the idea. Which I did, of course, since Paris was still worth a Mass.'

I pause before putting another question. 'Señor, who asked you to preside over the admiral's funeral?'

'No one. Franco was in no state to do it, so I took it upon myself to stand in for him. The people responsible for my security didn't all agree. Some of them said that if the ETA men had dared to attack the admiral they might try to eliminate me as well. Others did not think ETA would venture to touch the prince. I put an end to the discussion by deciding to wear my uniform and accompany the gun carriage carrying Carrero's body to the cemetery. In spite of the terrible cold, over a hundred thousand people watched in silence as the funeral procession passed through the city.'

'Were you aware of being a perfect target for any sharpshooters that day, Señor? You were walking alone behind the admiral's body, and you were the man who had been educated by Franco to continue a policy which would have been Carrero's if he had lived.'

When Don Juan Carlos becomes impatient his manner of speaking can suddenly turn very brusque. 'I've already told you, I never think of such things! The ETA people could very well have shot the admiral when he was going in or out of the church where he attended Mass every morning. They didn't. They preferred to assassinate him from a distance. These people are cowards. They don't like to risk their skins.'

I sense that the time has come to change the subject, but I have one more question to ask. The answer should clear up a number of matters in my mind.

'If Carrero had lived, Señor, could you have dismantled the actual structures of the Francoist regime as quickly as you did?'

Don Juan Carlos's expression does not change. I can only just see a tiny smile sketched at the corners of his mouth.

'I think,' he says, enunciating every word separately and slowly, 'Carrero wouldn't have agreed at all with what I had decided to do. But I don't believe he would have opposed the king's will openly.' And Don Juan Carlos's smile grows wider as he adds, 'He'd just have resigned.'

I spend a few minutes changing the batteries of my recorder. The king takes advantage of the break to make a phone call. When he puts the receiver down, I ask, 'Was Franco unable to follow the admiral's coffin because he was already seriously ill?'

'No, not at that point. It was simply the shock he suffered at the brutal murder of the admiral. However, he was strong enough to be present at the funeral service for Carrero in the church of San Francisco el Grande.'

'That was where Franco dissolved into tears as he offered his condolences to Carrero's widow.'

'Yes, and it greatly impressed all present. The general had not accustomed us to seeing him show his feelings.'

'Had he suddenly gone senile?'

'Senile? That's not a word I like. No, Franco was far from senile. He was just an old man who had let emotion overcome him when he said his final farewells to the most loyal of his faithful supporters.'

'And yet, Señor, in his end-of-the-year message in front of the television cameras some days later, he paid tribute to the admiral in terms which were strange, to say the least. He said, more or less, that a politician must be able to turn evil to advantage, and he recalled our old proverb: *No hay mal que por bien no venga.*[1] Nobody knew just what he meant by that, but tongues wagged. Was the general simply repeating a phrase he had heard from someone in his entourage, maybe even one of his own family? There were those who did not fail to deduce that certain persons close to the general saw the admiral's death as a stroke of luck rather than a misfortune. But why?'

Don Juan Carlos does not answer, and his gaze strays above my head once again. He must certainly know more than I do about the affair, and

[1] There is no evil from which good does not proceed.

his silence may indicate that the notion of 'reasons of state' is not a flight of fancy.

'Did you think it normal for Carlos Arias Navarro to be appointed prime minister so soon after the death of the man he had allegedly protected, Señor?'

'In principle Torcuato Fernández Miranda should have filled the post, as Carrero's vice-president. But Torcuato had made many enemies among the hardliners of the regime. You often arouse mistrust if you do things too well, and Torcuato had been working very cleverly. He had managed to mollify the hotheads who were demanding full powers for General Iniesta Cano, director of the *Guardia Civil*, and he had persuaded the Left, including the communists, to keep calm, since any disturbance in the streets would have been the ideal excuse for those who wanted a strong-arm policy at any price. And then, anyway, Franco had already chosen the man who was to succeed Carrero: Admiral Nieto Antúnez, an old man and a friend who was his tunny-fishing companion when he went to sea on the *Azor*.[1] But this time, perhaps because his state of health was worse than anyone knew, Franco gave way to the pressure of those closest to him: instead of Admiral Nieto Antúnez, he appointed Carlos Arias Navarro.'

'Who was to give Your Majesty considerable problems.'

'A few problems, José Luis; yes, a few.'

Carlos Arias Navarro, a small man with a hard gaze and brusque gestures, had acquired a reputation for cruelty during the civil war in his capacity as prosecutor at military tribunals, a reputation which had won him the dreadful nickname of the *Carnicerito de Malaga*.[2] He was devoted body and soul to Franco, and also to Franco's family, who regarded him as the only man besides Rodriguez de Valcárcel who could save them if the game ceased to go their way some day.

'Would you have preferred Admiral Nieto Antúnez to Carlos Arias Navarro, Señor?'

Don Juan Carlos smiles. 'I always know where I am with an admiral.'

'Was Carlos Arias intelligent?'

'He was far from being a fool, but he had no really long-term view of

---

[1] Franco's yacht.
[2] The Butcher of Malaga.

the problems of Spain. And he was *tozuda como una mula*.[1] He substituted obstinacy for force of character. I don't like denigrating people who aren't here to defend themselves, but Arias didn't have the necessary vision to face up to the radical changes the Spaniards were demanding. All the same, he realized that Francoism could not continue once Franco was gone, so he undertook various "liberal" reforms which were only for show and didn't satisfy anyone.'

'When did Franco fall really ill?'

'In July 1974, on 10 or 11 July, I don't quite remember which. He had phlebitis in his right leg. Franco was a man made to live to a hundred; he didn't smoke, didn't drink, and wasn't exactly an epicure. He lived the most regular life imaginable and spent hours in the open air, hunting, or on board the *Azor* fishing. His illness came as a great surprise to him. It was the first time in his life he'd had such a serious health problem, and it made him very depressed. He began saying: *"Esto es el principio del fin."*[2] And he must have believed it, because he told Arias to put through the decree handing over powers to the Prince of Spain as soon as possible.'

'What was your reaction on hearing that news, Señor?'

'Well, I had plenty of people around me advising me not to agree to become head of state as an interim measure. "Stay where you are and don't do anything," they said. "Content yourself with waiting." That was exactly what I myself would have liked to do – keep out of the fray – but it was too dangerous an attitude to adopt. In my heart of hearts, I knew all along that I had to accept. If I refused to become head of state when illness put the general out of action there would be a power vacuum, and other people might be tempted to fill it. No, it was too dangerous, José Luis. Having said that, I accepted with reluctance. I went to see the general in hospital and told him his illness wasn't serious enough to warrant the transfer of powers. But in fact I was wrong, because Franco suffered a violent haemorrhage that very day. His doctors were extremely pessimistic. So going against the opinion of a great number of people who wished me well, I decided to agree to be head of state. It was not the way I'd have liked things to turn out. I'd have preferred to become king in full at the right moment and have my hands left free. But when the doctors told me the general might be dying I called Arias Navarro and told him I accepted the nomination.

---

[1] Obstinate as a mule.
[2] This is the beginning of the end.

'I exercised my functions as head of state for only about fifty days,' continues Don Juan Carlos. 'Franco left hospital on 30 July and went home to the Pardo, where he stayed resting until 17 August. Then he and his family went to the Pazo de Meirás[1] to spend his convalescence there. Myself, I left Madrid for Palma in Mallorca and settled in for my summer holiday. But you know, I had a vague feeling there was something a little shady going on. I have a kind of instinct, a flair if you like, for detecting the intrigues which can sometimes weave themselves around me. One morning Nicolás Mondéjar had a telephone conversation with General Castañón de Mena, who told him the general was rapidly recovering strength. "Apparently he walks around the garden," Nicolás told me, "and he's already almost back to normal." So I told myself I'd better pay a visit to the Pazo de Meirás to see what the situation was. I got on a plane to La Coruña. Sure enough, the general was out of bed, and I thought he looked quite well. I congratulated him.

"I'm delighted to see you're better, General. You'll soon be able to take up your normal activities again, and then I can step down."

'Franco looked at me. He was sitting in a chair with a rug over his legs. "No, no, Highness, go on with your job. You're doing very well."

'I don't know why, but the compliment sounded false to my ears. I said, "General, you must understand that I'm in a very difficult position. It was all right replacing you at the head of the state while you were ill, but now that you seem to be better again the people of Spain will find it hard to understand how there can be two heads of state: the real one, you, and the one who isn't needed once you're able to exercise power again, me."

'Since he was just looking at me in silence, I became more explicit. "I'm happy to be Prince of Spain or king, but I refuse to carry out functions which are yours, General."

'Franco's only reply was to repeat, "Believe me, Highness, you're doing very well. Carry on."

'My impression that something was going on in the corridors of power was confirmed there at the Pazo de Meirás. Everyone was being too nice to me. That evening I flew back to Palma de Mallorca. Later I discovered that Cristóbal Villaverde had brought in a team of doctors of his own choice who never left the general. This team, in agreement with

[1] Franco's family estate in Galicia.

Villaverde, had decided that Franco's thrombophlebitis was almost cured, and consequently the general could soon resume his usual activities. Carmen Villaverde, the general's daughter, did not think so. She would have liked her father to take another few months off resting.'

'However,' I say, 'her husband was watching over the family's "interests", and those interests required the general to be prevented from finally handing power over to you for as long as possible. Do you think, Señor, that Villaverde thought Franco might yet remove you from the succession in favour of his son-in-law the Duke of Cadiz?'

'Villaverde wasn't the only one gambling on that possibility. With that end in view, the members of Franco's entourage were bringing very strong pressure to bear on an old man weakened by pain and illness. He had been told – and it was true – that when news of his illness was made known the Count of Barcelona had interrupted a cruise on board the *Giralda* to return to Estoril, where he had several long telephone conversations with me. They insinuated to the general that such complicity between the Count of Barcelona and the future King of Spain could endanger the very foundations of the regime I was supposed to keep going after his death.'

'Señor, did you yourself believe that Franco might oust you in favour of his grandson by marriage the Duke of Cadiz at the last minute, under pressure from his entourage?'

'You've asked me that before. No, I never believed it. Franco never went back on decisions he had made. But I was speaking of Palma: as soon as I was back in Mallorca I went to a dinner at the Duke and Duchess of Würtemberg's. When I returned to Marivent,[1] I was told that the general had phoned me. Late as it was, I returned his call. When he came on the line he said, "Highness, I just wanted to let you know I've decided to resume my powers tomorrow."

'So he was relieving me of my functions as head of state just like that! I was annoyed. "General," I said, "this is outrageous! Only a few hours ago, you were asking me to go on exercising the functions of head of state even though I was unwilling. Why didn't you tell me then that you intended to resume full powers?" And as Franco delayed replying, I went on, "Having said that, General, let me tell you that it's very good news for me. I am delighted to hear what you've just told me."

[1] The royal family's summer palace.

'Here Franco ended our conversation in his high-pitched little voice. "I am resuming my powers tomorrow. Good night, Highness."

'And that was it. That was Franco all over.'

'He gave you no further explanation later?'

'None. I remember that Giscard d'Estaing, when he heard of the situation, told me, "Highness, you should not on any account give up your prerogatives as head of state except to become king." I could only tell him, "President, we are not a republic here. Spain is a country very much *sui generis*, and I know what I have to do. I may be wrong – anyone may be wrong – but I am going to do what I feel I ought to do." And I went back to La Zarzuela. To wait.'

Franco took up the reins of power again on 2 September, which did not prevent the atmosphere from deteriorating rapidly. ETA, trying to blow up the security headquarters in the Puerta del Sol, picked the wrong building and blew up the Rolando cafeteria instead, causing the death of twelve peaceful citizens and leaving a hundred more injured. Arias Navarro, that toughest of all tough customers during the civil war, didn't know which way to turn. Liberals like Pio Cabanillas left the sinking ship of the government. Falangist generals began plotting openly. The alarmed Spaniards wondered: after Franco, what? The reply which sprang to their lips was not without its logic: the military had given Franco power, so naturally enough they would take it back after his death.

Meanwhile, 30 July saw the formation in Paris of the *Junta Democrática*, for which I had the honour of being spokesman. The *Junta* formed around a group of men of widely differing casts of mind. They included the monarchist Calvo Serer, a member of the Opus Dei, the communist Carrillo, Prince Carlos Hugo de Borbón-Parma, Professor Tierno Galván, and many others whose names mean little today. At the Congress of Suresnes in October that same year a group of practically unknown young men – Felipe González, Alfonso Guerra, Enrique Múgica – broke away from the old Socialist Party led by Rodolfo Llopis, accusing it of having lost touch with the real situation of Spain. The socialists did not contemplate the possibility of becoming part of the *Junta Democrática*, but joined Dionisio Ridruejo's social democrats and other groups on the anti-communist Left in what was called the *Plataforma de Convergencia*. The *Junta* and the *Plataforma* envisaged the post-Franco period as a democratic break with the old regime, a break which Don Juan Carlos was to manage smoothly and with great expertise.

'What was the Count of Barcelona doing at this time?'

'Tirelessly pursuing his attempts to gather the forces of opposition to the Francoist regime around the monarchy. He kept repeating that the monarchy could only be a constitutional and democratic institution. He took the utmost care not to set himself up as a political party leader. He did not believe in the statute of "political associations", which he denounced as a false liberalization of the regime, and he said so to anyone who would listen. He declared publicly in Estoril that he had never gone along with the idea of personal power, something which he thought Franco abused. When I say, as I sometimes do, that my father has played one of the most dramatic of all parts in the history of Spain, I don't feel that's any exaggeration. On the one hand, he was doing his best not to put a spoke in my wheel, and on the other he was trying to remain absolutely true to his principles. As for my nomination as Franco's successor "as king", he had stated unequivocally in his manifesto of July 1969 that the whole operation had taken place without his knowledge and without consulting the will of the people of Spain. To those who suggested that he might abdicate in my favour, he replied that he could not renounce the dynastic rights he held by the wish of his father King Alfonso XIII. However, he readily added that he was no one's rival, and although he might be described as the pretender or claimant to the throne, he was not claiming anything. Sometimes, when I try to put myself in my father's place, it sends shudders down my spine, José Luis! When the Count of Barcelona pointed out that my nomination as Franco's successor "as king" was not democratic, he was making it a question of principle, although he knew that made things no easier for me. But what else could he do? Although we both wanted to see the monarchy established again, our ways of attaining that end were very different. On 14 June 1975, my father declared in Estoril that he regarded the monarchy as a guarantee of human rights and civil liberties, but the initiative in favour of a restoration must be taken by the people of Spain when they had a chance to express themselves freely. Four or five days later Antonio Poch, the Spanish ambassador to Portugal, informed my father that access to Spanish territory was henceforward forbidden to him. And do you know, José Luis, no one in Madrid took the trouble to tell me about it!'

A wounded wild animal will react with murderous rage. In September 1975, two militant members of ETA and three members of the FRAP (the *Frente revolucionario anti-fascista patriotico*, a terrorist group of the extreme Left) were shot in Madrid, Barcelona and Burgos. Their execution was a decision taken personally by General Franco, and none of his ministers dared oppose it formally. The international outcry aroused by these executions was considerable. Spanish embassies were attacked all over Europe. The embassy in Lisbon was sacked from top to bottom. A dozen countries recalled their own ambassadors. Once again, Spain was isolated from the rest of the world.

The night before the execution of the condemned men Franco went to bed, giving orders that he was not to be woken on any account whatever. The appeals of Pope Paul VI and many other heads of state for clemency therefore remained unanswered.

'Did you intercede for the condemned men yourself, Señor?'

'Yes, without the least success. As for my father, who had appealed on their behalf too, no one even bothered to reply to him.'

'How do you explain Franco's implacable attitude in this lamentable affair, Señor?'

'I believe he thought the slightest weakness on his part – and many people see clemency as a weakness – would sap his authority and precipitate the disintegration of his regime.'

On 1 October 1975 Franco made his last public appearance. A huge crowd, duly orchestrated – there were said to be over a million persons present – thronged the Plaza de Oriente to show its loyalty to the dictator. The general appeared on one of the balconies of the royal palace and saluted the crowd with a hand shaking from the spasms of Parkinson's disease. Franco had become a little old man in sunglasses, with cheeks that looked as if they were modelled in wax. In a voice that was barely audible, despite the fact that the plaza and the nearby streets were wired for sound, the old man thanked the crowd for coming to show their support for him. As was his habit when things were going badly in the country, he spoke of a Judeo-Masonic conspiracy against

Spain, communist subversion, and leftist agents bought with gold from Moscow. He ended his speech by saying, in a voice whose shrillness he could no longer control, 'It is clear that to be a Spaniard today is to be someone of importance in the world once again!' The crowd shouted the usual slogans: *Muera el comunismo! ETA al paredón! No queremos apertura sino mano dura!*,[1] and so on. Immediately afterwards the crowd sang the *Cara al sol*, the Falangist anthem. At this the general began to weep. Standing immobile behind him and the Cardinal Archbishop of Toledo, his face showing nothing, his expression sullen, was his successor 'as king'. He did not raise his right arm in a Roman salute like everyone else surrounding Franco, even including the cardinal.

On 14 October the same year, General Franco was taken ill at home. He had severe chest pains and suffered difficulty in breathing. His personal physician, Dr Pozuelo, feared the first symptoms of a heart attack. He called in Cristóbal Villaverde, head of the cardiology unit of the hospital of La Paz and the general's son-in-law. Villaverde arranged for an electrocardiogram of his father-in-law to be taken, but insisted that it must be done at night and in the utmost secrecy, so that no news of the general's relapse should reach the outside world. He had a team of doctors picked by himself brought to the Pardo to keep permanent watch over Franco's health. Clinical materials were brought to the Pardo, also by night; Villaverde did not want his father-in-law to go back to La Paz hospital, where it would be impossible for him to conceal the course his illustrious patient's illness was taking.

On 16 October the latent crisis over the Spanish Sahara came to a head. King Hassan II was threatening to invade the territory occupied by the Spanish army, at the head of thousands of Moroccans: men, women and children armed only with the banners of the kingdom of Morocco. This was known as the Green March.

Keeping pace with the political crisis, Franco's illness became worse from day to day. He suffered cardiac difficulties, haemorrhages and gastric trouble. Pain seized upon the dictator's weakened body. *'Qué difícil es morir!'*[2] he was to tell his doctor as his death agony began. The government was panic-stricken. Arias was at a loss. Several ministers were pressing him to name Don Juan Carlos head of state again.

---

[1] Death to communism! Down with ETA! We want a strong hand, not an opening up!
[2] How difficult it is to die!

*

'Is it true, Señor, that when Carlos Arias came to suggest you should become head of state for the second time, he said, "All I ask of you, Highness, is not to insist on my doing what I can never do: ask Franco to renounce his powers for good."'

'Carlos Arias was greatly affected by the general's suffering. We all were, in fact, even though we didn't know his dreadful agonies were only just beginning. When the general first relapsed, Carlos Arias had come to see me with Alejandro Rodríguez de Valcárcel, to tell me it was appropriate to apply Article Eleven of the Organic Law again; that was the article which would make me head of state for the second time. I told them, "No, I'm not agreeing this time." That took them all aback. "You can't use me like the joker in a pack of cards," I said. "I agreed to take the general's place the first time, though I was perfectly well aware that it was – well, let's say an interim position. But this time the situation's different. The Sahara affair may explode at any moment, and I can't accept the responsibilities of head of state unless I am free to act as I would if I were king. If you want me because Franco has had a relapse from which he may yet recover, the answer is no. I will not agree to become head of state again unless the doctors caring for the general tell me that even if it lasts two or three months longer, the gravity of his illness is irreversible."'

'Did Franco know you had refused this second nomination, Señor?'

'I went to see him and told him, "General, neither of us is in any hurry. Let's wait and see how your illness goes. You may very well get better, and then you'll want to resume your powers as you have already done once. You must understand that such a contingency would put me in an impossible situation. You have named me your successor, as king, and I don't think there's any reason for me to succeed you at the moment." Franco listened without saying anything. But I think he knew very well that this time it really was the beginning of the end, as he himself had told his doctor. However, as with most sick people, it cost him something to admit it. Then, very soon afterwards, his condition became hopeless. I went to see him again, taking Doña Sofía this time. His doctors told me he had no chance of recovery; it might be possible to keep him alive for two or three more months, but his condition was incurable. So I asked Carlos Arias to come and see me, and told him he could prepare the decree making me head of state again.'

'On his sickbed, and knowing the gravity of his condition, couldn't Franco have made you King of Spain once and for all?'

'He could have asked the Cortes, yes –' Don Juan Carlos interrupts himself and says, shrugging his shoulders, 'but he didn't.'

'When King Hassan II decided to put the Green March operation into effect, did he know about Franco's state of health, Señor?'

'He must certainly have suspected something, but I don't believe he knew Franco was dying. No, I don't think it can be said that Hassan was taking advantage of the circumstances. The tension between Rabat and Madrid went a long way back. Decolonization was going on all over the world at the time, and our turn had come. The court of The Hague had already given its verdict, recognizing the right to self-determination of the peoples under Spanish rule. However, they didn't know just what to do in Madrid. The government was split between two options. One camp favoured swift entente with Morocco and the withdrawal of our troops. The other inclined towards the Algerian approach, later to be that of the Polisario guerrillas: a fight to the finish.'

'What do you think Franco would have done if he had still been in good health and at the head of the state, Señor?'

'I don't like advancing hypotheses about what someone else would have done in my place. Franco was an old Africa hand, you know. He had spent a considerable part of his brilliant army career on African soil. He knew that the Moroccans are formidable fighters, and this time they were not headed by the likes of Abd el-Krim, his old opponent, but by a very intelligent king who was both a good strategist and a clever diplomat. I'm not sure, but I think if Franco had been in my place he would have played a cautious game, but taking care not to get involved in a colonial war which would have brought general censure down on our heads.'

'What was morale in the army in Africa like at this point?'

'I'd be repeating myself if I tell you the military need to feel they are under firm command, and just then they were not. The government couldn't seem to get accustomed to the absence of Franco at the head of the state. General Gómez de Salazar, who commanded the Spanish army in the Sahara, was left more or less to his own devices. But he had understood and accepted that decolonization was inevitable. That said, Salazar was not going to tolerate any violence whatsoever against his troops. So I decided to take the matter in hand myself. I was head of state again, but on different terms this time. During the summer of 1974, all I could do was the sort of thing de Gaulle described as "inaugurating chrysanthemums". In October 1975 the situation was critical and I had to take extremely serious decisions. There had been an undeniable power vacuum in Spain since Franco fell ill. No one dared move, no one dared act or take the slightest responsibility. I therefore asked all the army chiefs of staff to come to La Zarzuela, as well as the prime minister and the foreign minister. I told them I was going to fly to El Aaiún next day. They were thunderstruck. Pedro Cortina, the foreign minister, cried, "You can't go out there!" However, I felt that even though the military men said nothing, they approved of my decision. So I said, "Listen: Franco is very near death, and I am his heir – and as such, I am in office. I am therefore going to El Aaiún to explain to Gómez de Salazar and his men what we must do and how we are to do it. We are going to withdraw from the Sahara, but in good order and with dignity. Not because we have been defeated, but because the Spanish army cannot fire on a crowd of unarmed women and children." '

'Do you really think King Hassan would have got that crowd advancing to invest the Spanish positions, Señor?'

'Well, from El Aaiún you didn't need binoculars to see a huge crowd waving green flags, just waiting for the order to advance into the mouths of our machine-guns. And I assure you, José Luis, there were more women and children than men to be seen in their front line. I was sure that if we didn't give way there'd be an appalling massacre before our very eyes. When I reached El Aaiún I spoke to the troops and explained that there was no question of abandoning our positions precipitately, but on the other hand we couldn't fire on all those unarmed people advancing towards us. Consequently, we were going to negotiate a withdrawal in perfectly honourable conditions. I thought I heard a universal sigh of great relief. I knew that the tenor of my speech would be reported in Rabat at once. When I got back to Madrid I presided over a Council of Ministers called in haste. I told Pedro Cortina, "I shall soon have a phone call from the King of Morocco telling me he's calling off the Green March." The foreign minister looked at me, bewildered.'

'You hadn't been in touch with Hassan before saying that, Señor?'

'No.'

'How did you know he was going to telephone you, then?'

'I knew he'd do that even before I left for El Aaiún. I know the Arabs.

They love a fine gesture, and their idea of the finest gesture of all is the captain putting himself at the head of his troops. So I told Pedro Cortina again, "King Hassan will call me, and he'll be calling to congratulate me. Now, gentlemen," I told the other ministers, "it is for you to tell me what I'm to say to the King of Morocco: that's your role, not mine." They were still thinking about what I ought to tell Hassan when an aide-de-camp came to tell me the King of Morocco was on the phone. When I picked up the receiver I heard his voice. "Congratulations on your gesture," he said. "Now we can hold discussions at our leisure." And King Hassan called off the Green March for good. We were accused later of retiring from El Aaiún too fast and in disorder; there's not a word of truth in that. Gómez de Salazar was a prudent, meticulous man who liked to do things properly and had an immense respect for his soldiers. Having said that, there are always flaws in such an operation when you don't have all the time you need. To my mind, the important point was that whatever happened, we had to stop that crazy march of several hundred thousand people ready to do anything to regain a territory occupied by foreign forces. So on the military level, El Aaiún was a success. On the political level, obviously things might have been done better. But it's for the politicians to occupy themselves with politics, not me.'

I sense that Don Juan Carlos wants to add something about which he feels deeply. He does so in an enigmatic manner. 'You see, José Luis, sometimes the King of Spain opens doors and no one takes the chance of following him through them.'

It is true that Don Juan Carlos often uses his personal prestige to have doors opened into all kinds of different areas, doors that were previously closed, and no one, neither businessmen nor heads of industry, can seem to take advantage of the windfall.

On 20 November 1975, at 4.20 a.m., General Franco died in terrible agony. He could have died long before, if not peacefully at least without having to bear the pointless butchery inflicted on his body. But his son-in-law Cristóbal Villaverde, with a team of doctors at his heel, fastened upon him with pitiless cruelty. His one concern was to keep Franco alive until 26 November. Why were Villaverde and the Franco tribe obsessed with that date? Because it was the day when the mandate of the president of the Cortes expired, and the president of the

Cortes was Alejandro Rodríguez de Valcárcel, a committed Francoist and the family's loyal retainer. Villaverde thought that if Franco were still alive on that date, he might renew the mandate of Valcárcel, who by his very function could prevent Don Juan Carlos from dismantling the Francoist regime and opening up the way to democracy. In his heart of hearts, Villaverde still nurtured hopes of seeing Franco go back on his first decision and nominate Don Alfonso de Borbón-Dampierre 'successor with the title of king' instead of Don Juan Carlos, which would have made his daughter Carmen the future Queen of Spain. That was the one idea in the mind of this mediocre and not very intelligent man.

'Señor, do you think Franco retained the lucidity necessary to see the intrigues going on around him until the end?'

'No, I don't think so. Franco lived the last weeks of his life in a state of semi-consciousness which prevented him from understanding anything much. I would even say that he was well below his usual capacity for the whole year preceding his death. He made considerable efforts to make it appear that he wasn't as ill as all that. He presided over the Council of Ministers – with his doctors standing ready in the next room – he received visitors and went by car from Madrid to the Pazo de Meirás, where he liked to rest during the summer months. Perhaps he didn't realize how serious his condition was himself.'

'The man's end horrified even his worst enemies. On the day Franco died, someone suggested to Felipe González opening a bottle of champagne to celebrate. Felipe refused curtly, saying, "I for one will not drink to the death of a Spaniard."'

'I'd have been astonished if he felt otherwise,' murmurs Don Juan Carlos.

'Did you know about the fears of the Franco family for what might happen to them after the general's death, Señor?'

Don Juan Carlos's face closes. 'Fears? Fears of what exactly? The Francos knew, because I'd repeated it over and over again, that my first concern when I was head of state would be to ensure, in every way I could, that no one drew up any lists of injuries inflicted by the Francoist regime. In my view, you see, it would be a very bad idea to get bogged down in revenge and personal grudges, the kind of thing which would have meant a return to the climate of the period just after the civil war. I kept on telling those around me that we needed a smooth transition without any abrupt jolts, and that meant no sudden break between the old regime and the democracy we all wanted. And I may say that in this, José Luis, I had the cooperation of people whose loyalty to Francoism was beyond doubt. Even if they didn't believe in the benefits of democracy, they were ready to work with the new power to ensure that things went smoothly. Of course there were also people of the kind who will never change and who dream of nothing but violence. But they were a minority, in a country where the majority of citizens showed exemplary good sense.'

There is another long silence. Then the king suddenly adds, 'What I am about to tell you, José Luis, is something not everyone will understand, but if you think about it ... well, I've often wondered, would the democratization of Spain have been possible at the end of the civil war?'

'Certainly not, Señor.'

'That's what I think too. I was able to do everything I have done since I was free to act because we had previously enjoyed forty years of peace ... a kind of peace which was not to everyone's liking, I agree, but all the same a peace which gave me the structures upon which I have been able to lean.'

I let the silence that falls between us again last a few moments, and then I ask Don Juan Carlos, 'What were the last words Franco spoke to you before he died, Señor?'

'The last time I actually saw him he was no longer in any state to speak. The last coherent thing he said in my presence, when he was almost in his death throes, was what I've already told you about the unity of Spain. What struck me more than his words was the force of his hands pressing mine as he told me that all he asked was that I would preserve that unity. The force of his hands and the intensity of his gaze. It was very impressive. He was obsessed by the idea of the unity of Spain. Franco was a military man, and to him, there were some things which you do not take lightly. The unity of Spain was one of them.'

XIII

'Señor, there are people all over Europe – historians, political analysts, leading industrialists – who often ask me how Spain managed to pass from being a dictatorship of forty years' standing to becoming a democracy headed by a constitutional king, without too much difficulty or agitation. The reply that springs to my lips is always the same. I tell them that here in Spain we call Don Juan Carlos *el motor del cambio*,[1] because it was he who allowed this radical transformation of Spanish society to come about, a transformation very few people thought possible. Then the second question they ask is: how did he do it? And here there are so many explanations to give that I lose track. What would your own explanation be, Señor?'

'Well ... I would begin by telling them that when I became king I had two trump cards up my sleeve. One was the incontestable support of the army. In the first few days after Franco's death the army could have made things go the way of whatever camp it chose, but it obeyed me as king. And let's be clear about this: it obeyed me because I had been nominated by Franco, and even after his death Franco's word was law in the army. Having said that, I should point out that the army's support did not lead to militaristic policies, far from it. But the point needs making, because far too many people still associate the military with a policy of *ordeno y mando*.'[2]

[1] The engine of the change.
[2] I order and command.

'What was your other trump card, Señor?'

'The wisdom of the people. The wisdom of the Spaniards lay in their ability to wait, instead of coming out on the streets, knives between their teeth, as so often in the past. This time the Spanish people said of me: We don't know this man yet, let's give him time to explain himself before we accept or reject him. Torcuato Fernández Miranda was right when he said, "It will all depend on your first speech. You must tell the Spanish people what you want to do and how you are planning to do it." I followed Torcuato's advice to the letter. In that first speech from the throne, I also made it very clear that I wanted to be "king of all the Spanish people".'

'A fateful phrase which kept your father the Count of Barcelona off the throne himself.'

'Yes, but I had made the idea my own long before.'

'How was that first speech from the throne to the Cortes written, and who wrote it?'

'I wrote the first speech from the throne to the Cortes myself; no one else did it. At that time, you will remember, José Luis, I could do and say anything. We had no Constitution yet, and I had inherited all Franco's powers, which were immense. For a whole year I was the sole master of my words and actions. I used those powers first and foremost to assure the Spanish people that in future it was for them to express their will.'

'Your father the Count of Barcelona couldn't have done all that...?'

'No. During the forty years of the Francoist regime he was insulted, humiliated and threatened, and unfortunately the campaign against him had its effect. Many people genuinely believed my father would have endangered the equilibrium brought by forty years of peace. The army wouldn't have supported him. When he first said that he wanted to be king of all the people of Spain, the victors in the civil war felt directly threatened. To them, the Count of Barcelona represented a threat they must neutralize at all costs. The army would never have given him the support they gave me.' A brief hesitation, and Don Juan Carlos adds, 'If I hadn't had the army on my side after the death of Franco, *otro gallo habría cantado en España.*'[1]

*

[1] It would have been a different story in Spain – literally, 'another cock would have crowed'.

'Some weeks ago, Señor, I met King Fouad of Egypt at a dinner – the eldest son of King Farouk, deposed by the army of Naguib and Nasser. When Farouk left Egypt his son Fouad was a small child. He was king only for a few days. Nowadays he is a pleasant, affable man living quietly in Paris. After the dinner he took me aside and asked all kinds of questions about Your Majesty. "Your king fascinates me," he said. "How did he do it?" There are a number of pretenders and ex-kings in Europe today, Señor, who ask themselves the same question. How did he do it? They all imagine the possibility of following the example of the King of Spain some day. What would you tell them, Señor?'

'I don't set up to give anyone lessons, but should the case arise, I'd tell them that above all they should take into account the difference between Spain and the former Eastern European countries. I would tell them that I myself inherited a country which had known forty years of peace, a period during which a powerful and prosperous middle class came into being: a social class which was practically non-existent at the end of the civil war, but one which very soon became the backbone of my country. I would also tell them that you can't export the example of a Spanish king to countries emerging from seventy years of communism with their economies ruined. It's a fact that there is sometimes talk in certain Eastern European countries of a possible return to the monarchy. I suspect there must be politicians in those countries who just don't know where to turn and say to themselves: suppose we recalled the king? If the king in question agreed to return to his country he'd probably be welcomed as a saviour, a hero capable of resolving all sorts of problems in a very short time, and there's the rub. In an economically bankrupt country, a country up against the wall, no one, not even a king, can do great things in a very short time. The king, unable to put a swift end to the economic misery, would be thrown out as enthusiastically as he had been welcomed back. He'd even be held responsible for many problems which already existed while he was still in exile.'

'Several of these ex-kings have lived their whole lives abroad and don't even speak their own country's language properly.'

'Which is a terrible handicap in itself. My father was right when in spite of all opposition he decided to send me to study in Madrid. Do you think I could have done what I have in Spain, José Luis, if I'd spent my entire youth in Portugal or Switzerland, or if I'd come home speaking Spanish with a French accent?'

'Obviously not.'

'I'm not very optimistic about the return of the old monarchies to Eastern European countries. I sometimes discuss it with King Simeon of Bulgaria, who came to Spain as a very small boy. He speaks Bulgarian perfectly, and keeps himself well informed about his country's problems. He has compatriots who are urging him to do what's necessary to go back to Bulgaria. But he says to himself: would I have sufficient economic means to make changes in the immediate future? No. I don't want to be King of Bulgaria just for a while; if I go back, it must be for good. And if you ask me, José Luis, King Simeon is absolutely right.'

'At the beginning of these interviews, Señor, you asked me if any monarchical feeling existed in Spain when you became king, and I said no, but people very soon became "Juancarlists". I had the impression that you didn't much like that.'

'No, José Luis, it isn't that I dislike the existence of "Juancarlism"; in fact I'm deeply flattered, but it worries me. It worries me because a man, a king, can get himself liked quickly enough. A very small thing may suffice: a gesture which catches the imagination, a word spoken at the right time, how should I know...? But a monarchy doesn't root itself in the heart of a country just like that. It takes time. And time passes so quickly. My own task is to see that the Spaniards renew their links with the monarchical tradition. That's not easy after forty years during which the monarchy was so often denigrated. Three or four generations of Spaniards have heard more bad than good said of us. I have to show the people of Spain that the monarchy can be useful to their country. Personally I don't want to say anything about "Juancarlism" in relation to the monarchy. God willing, I shall continue to work for the Spanish people to accept that the man they call just "Juan Carlos" embodies an institution, and it is the institution that counts. At present I'm doing my best to see that my son, the Prince of the Asturias, follows the advice General Franco gave me: "Highness, let the Spanish people get to know you." And I hope Don Felipe will be loved by the Spanish people as it appears that I am. That's all I ask.'

'Can a king's ability to meet another king or make private contact with him ease relations between two countries?'

'What kings are you thinking of?'

'Your Majesty and King Fahd of Arabia, for instance.'

'Yes, I see. My relations with King Fahd of Saudi Arabia are certainly easier than those I might have with some African dictator. Yes, I get on very well with King Fahd, and have done ever since we were both crown princes. I remember when Franco was still alive there was an oil crisis which affected us quite badly – I forget exactly what year this was. Barrera de Irimo, then finance minister, came to see me and said, "Highness, Spain's oil stocks are very low just now. I was wondering if Your Highness, in view of your personal relations with Prince Fahd, couldn't explain that a speedy shipment of oil would get us out of our difficulty. If we take such a step government to government, the whole affair could take several months, whereas ..." Barrera didn't finish his sentence, but I understood that he was going to say "things could be arranged more quickly between princes". And he was right. So I sent an emissary to Prince Fahd, who replied at once. "Tell my brother Prince Juan Carlos that we will send him all the oil Spain needs." Soon afterwards we received from Saudi Arabia the oil we needed to see us through the crisis.'

'In spite of that friendship, I believe the Arabs reacted rather poorly to the stance Spain adopted towards Israel.'

'That's true, and indeed it's another example of what a king can do to defuse a situation. Obviously the Spanish government couldn't take the Arab attitude into account when our entente with Israel became more and more positive. But I myself could. As a personal friend of many Arab leaders I was able to intervene behind the scenes. I told my Arab brothers: look, this is not a question of betraying a friendship, still less of ignoring our fraternal bonds. You can ask a lot of me, but you can't insist that a democratic state like Spain should not have diplomatic and commercial relations with other democratic states, including Israel. They accepted my point of view – reluctantly, it is true. They might not have reacted in the same way to explanations from a republican president. The Emir of Kuwait, Sheikh Sayeed – a remarkable character! – and even sometimes King Fahd have been in touch with me, asking for more assistance in resolving the problems of the Middle East. And I have always told them: the Spanish government and I myself are ready to help you as far as we can, but you will have to ask us jointly, not separately and one by one.'

'They never will.'

'Our Arab friends have a great regard for Spain. In a way, Spain is their paradise lost. It was they who wanted the peace conference held here in Madrid, and that was the first time in thirty years they'd agreed to meet to discuss their problems.'

'So the fact that Spain has a king as head of state has eased our relations with the Arab world a good deal?'

'So far as the monarchical states are concerned, yes, certainly.'

'Do you think, Señor, that you have these privileged contacts with King Fahd and the emirs because they regard you as "one of us"?'

'It's an idea to be taken into consideration,' smiles Don Juan Carlos. 'But you know, in spite of the friendship uniting us and the Saudis – they prefer the word "fraternity" themselves – our relations aren't always easy. Islam is a closed world to those who don't take the trouble to adjust to its puritanism, its code of honour and its very strict religious observance. Then again, the Saudis don't like speaking languages other than their own, so one is rarely alone with them. There's always an interpreter present. Actually I think many of them use the interpreter because it gives them time to think twice between the question you ask them in English – a language they nearly all understand – and their reply. For instance, King Fahd understands English very well but speaks it with some difficulty. Sometimes, when he and I are together, he sends his interpreter away and we both speak English. But in principle, when he talks to a foreigner he always has his interpreter beside him. It keeps the person he is talking to from being too informal, which would be a grave breach of the very strict protocol which regulates his life. The King of Arabia must not have relations of too personal a nature with a foreigner.'

'Except the King of Spain.'

'Spain isn't altogether a foreign country to King Fahd, and he calls me his "brother". He is fond of me, and feels a friendship for me which I heartily reciprocate.'

'The Arabs have a very different concept of time from ours, too.'

'Almost all the Arab princes I know have spent quite a long period in the desert, their true home. And out in the desert the idea of time evades logic. The Arab disdain for time sometimes exasperates us impatient Europeans.'

'You know, Señor, some years ago I went to Riyadh to interview King Faisal. I hadn't been given a date or a time for the meeting, I was simply told to come, which was surprising in itself. After a week spent sitting by the telephone in my hotel bedroom I lost patience and told all concerned I was going back to Paris. I had the impression they thought I'd suddenly gone mad. They simply could not understand my attitude. One of the diplomats asked me, "What's the matter? Aren't you comfortable here? It's the best hotel in town, and you are the king's guest!"'

'So you left without seeing Faisal?'

'No, he did receive me, ten days or so later. A remarkable character who asked me, among other things, if I had just arrived.'

'That Arab concept of time, one we can't accept, has lost contracts for a good many Europeans who get infuriated by all the waiting about,' says Don Juan Carlos. 'But those who have waited patiently have sometimes done the deal of their lives.'

'How do the Arab monarchs react when you talk to them about democracy, Señor?'

'They don't react at all. I think they simply do not understand. The equality of mankind is not an idea which has any place on their scale of values. It's not that they reject the idea of democracy out of hand. They don't know what it means, still less how it works. For instance, when the Spanish press says something rather critical of Morocco and its king, as it does on occasion, King Hassan will ring me up and ask, genuinely hurt, "How can you let your newspapers say such things about my country and me? When are you going to put a stop to it?" I explain, patiently, that they are not "my" newspapers, and I personally have no power at all to forbid the Spanish press to express its opinions freely – because, I tell him, this is a democracy! But I get the impression that although he is a very intelligent and very experienced man, Hassan just cannot understand me. Sometimes I wonder if he even believes me. Such misunderstandings distress me because I know King Hassan loves Spain, and after all, we're neighbours and ought not to be at odds. There's nothing but the Straits dividing us.'

'And democracy.'

'Yes, and democracy. But in spite of this occasional lack of understanding, the links between Spain and the Maghreb are very, very strong.'

'As strong as those linking us to Latin America?'

'Oh, well, our links with Latin America are a family matter!'

'*La Madre Patria*,[1] Señor?'

---

[1] The mother country.

'It's not an expression I ever use there. When I speak to them of Spain I always say *vuestra patria hermana*,[1] but they themselves, the Latin Americans, do often speak of the mother country. You know, José Luis, I think that our links with Latin America go far beyond trite sayings, commonplaces and clichés. When I went to Colombia for the first time the president received me with the words: "We have been waiting four hundred years for a visit from the King of Spain."'

'A fine rhetorical flourish, Señor.'

'No, rather more than that. When the President of Colombia said that he meant a great deal else too. As I drove down the streets of Bogotá in an open car, children trotted all along the motorcade shouting, "*Ha vuelto nuestro Rey! Ha vuelto nuestro Rey!*"[2] When I go to Latin America I know I'm really welcome. The respect they show me isn't mere protocol; it springs from a deeper, more sincere feeling. All the South American heads of state were present at the peace conference in Guadalajara in Mexico. Whenever one of them rose to speak he first addressed our host, Carlos Salinas de Gortari: "*Señor Presidente...*" Then, immediately afterwards, he would turn to me: "Your Majesty..." And a few seconds later he addressed the other heads of state: "My dear comrades, my dear friends ..." It gave me gooseflesh every time. They all showed me a respect and affection that no one had obliged them to show. However, I could see that to them, beginning with President Salinas who always placed me on his right, the King of Spain was not just a head of state like any other; in their eyes I was someone particular, someone special. A Spaniard.'

'Although after 1936 Mexico wasn't always kindly disposed towards Spain.'

'Not Mexico, José Luis: certain Mexican governments. But I have never felt the slightest animosity from the people themselves. Besides, you must remember, in 1936 Mexico welcomed Spanish exiles with open arms. It was partly to remind people of that generosity shown by the Mexicans that I was anxious, when I first visited the country, to meet the widow of Manuel Azaña, a very prominent Spanish republican exile, and receive her personally at our embassy.'

'A handsome gesture on your part, Señor.'

---

[1] Your sister country.
[2] Our king is back!

'I merely wanted to remind our hosts that in Spain today all men are equal, whatever their ideology. I told Señora Azaña, "Your husband and you yourself, Señora, are as much part of the history of Spain as I am."'

'During the celebrations of the quincentenary of the discovery of America, there was a great deal of talk about the extortion and genocide committed by the Spanish conquistadores. Even here in Spain there are people trying to revive the old murky legends, which strike me as being very tenacious of life.'

'That's inevitable. But there's a good deal of dishonesty and exaggeration in these attacks on us.'

'Carlos Fuentes, one of the great Mexican writers of today, has written an article –'

'I've read it.'

' – in which he says: *hay que dejarse de tonterias y de genocidios*,[1] and says that Spain has left the Mexicans a legacy of the greatest of its treasures: the Spanish language.'

'I think we gave them something else very important too, José Luis: our blood. Unlike the Anglo-Saxons, the Spaniards mingled their blood with that of the inhabitants of all the Latin American countries.'

I can feel that Don Juan Carlos is rather tired. We have been talking for hours. But I can't help asking him one last question.

'Señor, did you have any contact with Fidel Castro in Guadalajara?'

'Yes, of course. A very pleasant man, very amiable. But it was very superficial contact. We both knew we couldn't talk about anything really serious.'

Don Juan Carlos pushes back his chair, rises and gives me his hand. 'Come a little later tomorrow afternoon, would you? I am receiving Pilar Miró to congratulate her on the award she won in Berlin.'

---

[1] Let us stop talking about stupidity and genocide.

XIV

'Señor, many people are rather surprised by the lack of protocol surrounding the King of Spain, whereas in Franco's time...'

Don Juan Carlos interrupts me with a wave of the hand. 'In Franco's time no distinction was drawn between the head of state and the private man. General Franco never at any moment considered himself a private man. Personally I am very anxious to enjoy privacy when I'm free of the constraints of my job.'

'All the same, Señor, you can't just—'

Don Juan Carlos interrupts again. 'I know, I know. I can't just say, "José Luis, let's go and have a Scotch in the bar on the corner," because it would cause panic in the ranks of the security men. But all the same, I do draw a distinction between the head of state and the King of Spain when, as the latter, I go to dine at Lucio's with Doña Sofia and a few friends. I don't draw that distinction solely for my own pleasure. I do it chiefly out of respect for the people of Spain.'

'How do you mean, Señor?'

'It's simple enough. When General Franco went to Madrid even on unofficial business, he still left the Pardo at the centre of a motorcade of eight cars preceded by outriders on motorbikes going full speed ahead. The streets along which this procession was to pass had been closed to traffic well in advance, causing huge traffic jams in Madrid. One day when I was still Prince of Spain I was stuck at the wheel of my own car because the general and his retinue were about to pass on their way I can't remember where. I saw the looks on the faces of the other drivers around me, and I could guess what they were thinking with no trouble at all. I told myself: when I am King of Spain all this will have to change. If I'm going somewhere as head of state today I travel in the official Rolls, with an escort and all the rest of the paraphernalia. But if I want to go somewhere as a private person I take the wheel of my car and drive off like anyone else – well, not exactly like anyone else, alas, because I'm always under the watchful eye of the security men. But I do stop at the red lights, and no one gets stuck in a traffic jam because the King of Spain is going to visit his tailor. What it all amounts to is that if I want the respect due to my position as head of state, I ought also, as a private person, to respect my fellow citizens' liberty of movement.'

'One day I was in London,' I tell Don Juan Carlos, 'and my taxi was waiting at a red light when the driver told me, "Look over to your right, sir." The tone of pleased respect in his voice surprised me. So I looked to my right and saw an ancient black Rolls Royce with the Queen Mother in the back, chatting away to the woman with her while they waited for the lights to change.'

'That strikes me as perfectly natural. It's really a question of good manners. You should trouble people as little as possible. There's no reason why they shouldn't get to work on time or get home when they want to, just because some official person, even the king, is on business of some kind which does not concern them at all.'

'It can't always be easy.'

'Oh yes, it is, it's simply a question of organization and punctuality. I don't want to bring up the old cliché about punctuality being the politeness of kings, but as far as I'm concerned it's quite true. If you are waiting somewhere for the king at twelve-fifteen, then the king ought to be there at twelve-fifteen, not twelve twenty-five or twelve-thirty. I do all I can to make the people who organize my movements accept that idea.'

'It's not the most obvious of ideas, Señor, in a country where punctuality isn't always regarded as a virtue. If you're invited to dinner at ten in the evening in Madrid, and you arrive at the appointed hour, the mistress of the house will very likely still be in her bath.'

'Yes, perhaps. But unpunctuality is not acceptable in official life. I was amazed, José Luis, by the punctuality of the Japanese. In Japan you're told, "The emperor will arrive at three minutes past eleven," and the emperor does arrive at three minutes past eleven. It's all a question of coordination.'

'Isn't it also something to do with a country's characteristic way of life – the lack of importance accorded to some things here?'

'You may be right, but personally I still don't want any citizen wishing me in hell because he's been stuck in his car for hours waiting for me to pass.' Don Juan Carlos pauses, and goes on in the same tone, 'All this is more important than it may seem. If the king systematically complicates people's lives, they may well end up disliking him. That's why I am so anxious for the Spaniards to see the distinction between the head of state, himself a prisoner of the constraints of his position, and the king, a human being doing his best not to cause his fellow citizens too much trouble. When they see me in the middle of a traffic jam too they may say to themselves: well, at least he isn't taking advantage of his position to make life easier for himself.'

'The people of Madrid don't often see a cabinet minister, for instance, stuck in a traffic jam, Señor. Ministers are more frequently seen crossing the city at speed, preceded by police cars with sirens deafening the passers by. It annoys people. They don't think the ministers have anything so very urgent to do anyway.'

Don Juan Carlos listens without offering the slightest comment. I take my chance to go on.

'Not so long ago in Paris, Mitterrand was asked on television about the huge traffic jams caused by certain strikes, and he said in a disillusioned tone, "These things happen, you know. We have to suffer in silence. I spend quite a bit of time in traffic jams myself, like everyone else.' The people of Paris, who have never seen President Mitterrand stuck at the wheel of his car, were outraged by these remarks. Next day the opinion polls – as you know, Señor, the French adore opinion polls about anything and everything – the polls showed that Mitterrand's popularity had dropped several points.'

'Well, people know I don't lie to them,' said Don Juan Carlos, 'since on more than one occasion they've seen me snarled up in the same way as themselves. In the Scandinavian countries – where the monarchies have courts keeping jealous watch over the monarchs' activities – no one is surprised to see the king out shopping with an aide-de-camp or a friend. I've been out on foot myself with the late King Olaf of Norway and Prince Harald, now king, as if walking round town were the most natural thing in the world. The Scandinavians are very civilized people.'

'Did you know, Señor, that under the German occupation the Jews of Denmark were forced to wear yellow stars sewn to the lapels of their jackets?'

'As they did everywhere in occupied Europe.'

'Yes, well: in Denmark, King Christian emerged from the palace for his daily ride one morning with a yellow star on his uniform tunic.'

'What a fine gesture! That's the way a king can identify with his people at a single stroke. Gestures like that ought to be made more often, to show that a man in power isn't a soulless puppet but a human being with feelings like any other: joys, frustrations and griefs.'

'The mother of the Queen of the Netherlands, Princess Juliana, used to take her children to school by bicycle, and the present Queen Beatrix goes walking round the cities on her birthday. Don't you think that's taking informality a little too far?'

'I'd say simplicity is typical of the Dutch, and as for cycling, that's probably their way of suggesting we all forget our cars from time to time. I'm against pollution myself!'

'Yes, Señor, but your liking for driving your own car or riding through Madrid on your motorbike –'

'Oh, back in the old days, José Luis, back in the old days,' murmurs Don Juan Carlos, suddenly melancholy.

' – or dining in restaurants in town with the queen and going to visit friends never looks as if it was done to impress.'

'Well, no, and the reason is that everything I do *me sale de dentro*.'[1]

---

[1] Comes from within.

XV

This afternoon Don Juan Carlos can get about without his crutches. I feel he is ready to go into action again.

'Señor, we've almost finished this series of interviews, and we haven't yet broached a subject which strikes me as important.'

'What's that?'

'Your speeches from the throne. More precisely, the messages delivered by the king at Christmas and the *Pascua Militar*.[1] Some people await these speeches with trepidation, knowing the king may tackle subjects they'd rather not see brought out into the open.'

'All I ever do is say out loud what the great majority of Spaniards are saying under their breath, and it's natural enough that not everyone will be happy with that. But if we're discussing my speeches I might as well explain something about the Spanish monarchy today. It's not entirely like other monarchies. There are still people not sure whether it was actually *instaurada*, established, or *restaurada*, restored. To some people it was "established" because I was Franco's designated successor. To others, it was fully "restored" on the day my father the Count of Barcelona stepped down in my favour. Anyway, an impresario, a farmer, a grandee of Spain and a workman certainly aren't all going to have the same idea of the monarchy. But I think that when the king speaks, when he delivers his message at Christmas or the *Pascua Militar*, the monarchy

---

[1] Military Easter.

does mean the same thing to everyone. And when the king addresses the people of Spain he does it with complete liberty. In the United Kingdom, Queen Elizabeth reads a speech from the throne written by the prime minister and his colleagues. Myself, I say what I myself have written, and I write it without help from anyone. And I think people know it by now; they know that what the king says is what the king thinks.'

'Do you mean, Señor, that the government doesn't know what you are going to say to the people?'

'The prime minister knows what I'm going to say – it wouldn't be very loyal of me to keep it from him – but he doesn't know in what terms I shall express myself. My speech is the outcome of a pact between the prime minister and myself. I tell him, "This is what I am planning to say to the people of Spain; what do you think?" Usually he agrees with me about the content. We sometimes discuss a shade of meaning, a word which might be better put in or left out. What matters – and this is a luxury I allow myself – is for me to be able to tell the Spanish people what they expect me to tell them. I have to put it all very clearly, so that everyone will understand. In fact it is this clarity which sometimes upsets people who'd rather certain things remained in the dark.'

'Are your Christmas and Easter messages written long in advance?'

'Well, all sorts of things can happen at the last moment, things I couldn't possibly leave out.'

'I've always been surprised, Señor, by – well, let's call it the internal "architecture" of your speeches.'

'I try to make sure there is no gap between my speech and reality. I want everyone listening to be able to believe that my words are addressed to him or her personally. So as the speech will be heard by the impresario, the farmer, the grandee of Spain and the workman we spoke of just now all alike, it's important for it to be clear, precise, well composed and constructed. In fact I want my speech – but you're right, I do prefer the word "message" – to be a faithful reflection of my character.'

'In any case, Señor, you give the impression of always being very judiciously advised. How many people are involved in the actual construction of your speeches? How many people could tell you: no, don't say that – or on the other hand could ask you to emphasize this or that subject?'

'The basic theme of my messages is always my own. I discuss it here in the palace with my closest colleagues. Then, depending on the subject I'm going to discuss, I take advice from lawyers, sociologists, sometimes from the foreign ministry, even the army.'

'But no one else does the actual job of writing your speeches?'

'No; there are no speech-writers in Spain as there are in the United States or England.'

'In France, I've been told, General de Gaulle, who had the reputation of writing with the elegance of a Chateaubriand, had actually engaged a graduate in the French language to help him, and that was how Georges Pompidou became one of his team.'

'Here in Spain I put the finishing touches to my speeches myself.'

'Well, Señor, I can say without flattery that I think for someone who is not a writer by profession, you construct your speeches very well, particularly when you are speaking to the military.'

'It's just logic and common sense. But the fact is, I can often spend an hour trying to get a sentence exactly as I'd like it. It isn't easy to write well, José Luis.'

'How right you are, Señor!'

And for a few seconds we are accomplices. Then the telephone on the desk rings. Don Juan Carlos picks up the receiver and I hear him speaking in English. I take advantage of this pause to look through my notes. When Don Juan Carlos hangs up, I ask, 'In what way does the king intervene in political affairs?'

'He doesn't.'

Judging by the tone of this reply, I am supposed to stop there. But I persist. 'Surely the king has to give his opinion when he's asked for it, though?'

'Indeed. But I am very sparing indeed with my opinions.'

'Why is that, Señor?'

'Well, suppose, for instance, that a minister comes and asks me, "What do you think I ought to do about this or that, Majesty?" And again, suppose I tell him, "If I were you, Minister, this is what I'd do..." then the minister might go off and say, "The king said we ought to do this, that or the other." Moreover, José Luis, if I really had told the minister what he ought to do, I'd be encroaching on territory that isn't mine.'

'So, Señor?'

'So I reply – and I've done it quite often – "Why have you come to ask me this? It falls within your own department's province. If your department doesn't know what to do about it, how should I know?" I can't allow myself to "govern", José Luis, even behind the scenes. That's not my role. Having said that, if I can be useful to the government I am always there. But it has to be the government who approaches me, not the other way round.'

'You don't intervene in foreign policy either, Señor?'

'No.' And after a short silence, Don Juan Carlos continues, 'I do sometimes put the weight of my prestige in the scales. I don't like boasting, but it is true that the prestige of the Crown is considerable. From time to time an Arab head of state telephones to ask me, "Would you please tell the King of Morocco this or that?" It happened several times during the Gulf War. Messages like, "Tell Kuwait that we are very close to them."'

'So you do in a way have considerable concealed power, Señor?'

'Let's say I have a certain influence. But I make very careful use of it, because the boundaries of my territory are dangerously fuzzy here and there. And as you know, the powers of the King of Spain are very limited.'

The telephone rings again. This time Don Juan Carlos talks about boats for several minutes.

'Was it an advantage to the Crown when the Left came to power?'

'At least it demonstrated to people that the monarchy is above all ideologies.'

'I have always felt, Señor, that the monarchy should not be the monopoly of the Right. Do you remember that shortly after the *coup d'état* of 23 February, I wrote you a letter telling you I intended to join the Socialist Party?'

'I remember that very well.'

'I did it because I found it difficult to remain politically neutral after the *coup d'état*. Up till then I had prided myself on being a kind of liberal sceptic, but now the moment had come to take sides clearly. I was not, and I still am not, a true socialist, but I felt the Socialist Party was the only one which could make Spain a modern state open to European trends in general, and in the context of a monarchy which, for the first time in history, would be the monarchy of all the people of Spain. Later, when Felipe González was already head of Your Majesty's first socialist government, I told him I'd asked you in writing for permission to join his party.'

Don Juan Carlos raises an amused eyebrow. 'But José Luis, you never asked permission at all!'

'Yes, I did, Señor, because if Your Majesty had written back saying you didn't look kindly on my attitude I'd have abstained from joining the Socialist Party.

'Anyway, Felipe asked me, rather intrigued, "But why did you write to the king?"

' "Because not so long ago grandees of Spain always did inform the king of their major decisions," I told him.

' "Was it an actual obligation?" asked Felipe.

' "No, an old tradition rooted in the courtesy we owed our natural sovereign."

' "And what did the king reply?"

' "Well, I received a letter from General Fernández Campo, who was secretary-general of the king's household at the time, telling me that His Majesty had taken note of my letter."

'As you know, Señor, in Spanish "to take note" can mean more than one thing, and this reply made me quite anxious. As Felipe suggested himself, "That could mean that they've put you on a black list." '

Don Juan Carlos laughs heartily at this. 'How else could I have replied, José Luis? It wasn't for me to approve or disapprove of your decision. But perhaps "taking note" isn't the ideal formula for replying to letters like yours.' His smile widening, Don Juan Carlos concludes, 'You know that I don't like to inspire anxiety in those I esteem.'

My conversations with His Majesty Don Juan Carlos I de Borbón y Borbón, King of Spain, came to an end as the sun sank in hazy light among the branches of the cork oaks which surround La Zarzuela. In the course of my professional life, I have talked over the years to many of the men and women who make the world go round. I have got to know some exceptional people, listened to what they had to say and admired them. Some of them have become my friends, others are only memories more or less dear to me. But none has aroused in me the emotion I felt in taking leave of the King of Spain at the door of that room where we spent so many hours, one talking, the other listening.